The Great **BIG** Book of Super-Fun Math Activities

Compiled by Jean Liccione

S C H O L A S T I C
PROFESSIONAL **B**OOKS

New York • Toronto • London • Auckland • Sydney
Mexico City • New Delhi • Hong Kong

The activities in this book are adapted from Scholastic's *Math Power* magazine

Edited by Jean Liccione

Cover design by Jaime Lucero

Cover illustrations by Alfred Schrier

Interior illustrations by Teresa Anderko, Michael Moran, Chris Murphy, Manuel Rivera, and Alfred Schrier

Interior design by Ellen Matlach Hassell for Boultinghouse & Boultinghouse, Inc.

ISBN 0-439-07755-9

Contents

Introduction

Get ready for THE GREAT BIG BOOK OF SUPER-FUN MATH ACTIVITIES!

Do you need an idea for homework assignments? With *The Great Big Book of Super-Fun Math Activities*, invite students to participate in activities such as Fraction Carnival, Wise Buys, or How to Measure a Monster.

Do you need additional active learning ideas for those bright early finishers in math class? Use *The Great Big Book of Super-Fun Math Activities*. Challenge students' critical thinking in ways they will enjoy, with games such as Diving for Decimals, Mining for Multiplication, and Place-Value Pumpkin.

Do you want to challenge students' problem-solving abilities? That's easy when you use *The Great Big Book of Super-Fun Math Activities*. You'll have plenty of pages to encourage reasoning and logical thinking, such as Picky Penguin Pens, Throw Around Some Statistics, and Logic Rules the Jungle.

In This Idea-Packed Volume...

You'll find over 300 pages filled with great ideas for reinforcing the important concepts you teach. You'll find opportunities for application and problem-solving practice highlighted in the National Council of Teachers of Mathematics (NCTM) Curriculum Standards.

Just check the table of contents for the math strand you want students to practice or apply, and you're set to provide student-oriented games and activities that reinforce number sense, geometry, fractions, computation, statistics, and lots more.

With most activities you'll also find ideas for extensions and suggested answers. Many activities have curriculum connections too—to science, social studies, language arts, art, and music! All these activities represent adaptations of successful activities first published in Scholastic's *Math Power* magazine.

Assessing Students' Work

In many of the activities included in this book, students record answers to problems or write to explain their thinking. You can review their responses to assess their understanding of a concept.

By observing individuals as they work with manipulatives and/or paper and pencil, you will also identify those students who understand a particular concept and those who are having difficulty. Student presentations, projects, teacher observation, oral discussion—all of these methods are legitimate forms of assessment and add to the information obtained through more formal assessments such as focused written tasks and tests.

Use the Individual or Group Scoring Rubrics on page 302 to record your observations of student performance and their level of engagement with the task or activity at hand. Periodically, invite students to complete the Self-Evaluation Form on page 303 after they complete an activity to see how they gauge their own understanding.

The Content Standards of the National Council of Teachers of Mathematics

In line with the recommendations of the NCTM (National Council of Teachers of Mathematics), the activities and games in this book all focus on several overarching "themes" of the standards: Problem Solving, Communication, Reasoning, Connections, and Patterns and Relationships.

▶ **Problem Solving** Students should learn to solve problems and to pose problems of their own. They should also be afforded opportunities to use a variety of problem-solving strategies, such as guess-and-check, working backward, solving a simpler problem, or making a list.

▶ **Communication** Students need to talk about and write about mathematical ideas. They should be encouraged to describe procedures and explain their thinking.

▶ **Reasoning** Students grow mathematically as they come to understand that mathematics is not simply a collection of rules or procedures, but a logical system that makes sense.

▶ **Connections** Students should be encouraged to make connections within and among mathematical ideas and between mathematics and other areas of the curriculum. Connecting models, symbols, and ideas is key to understanding mathematics.

▶ **Patterns and Relationships** Students should recognize, describe, extend, and create patterns. They should understand the logic behind mathematical patterns and be able to describe the visual or numerical relationships.

The standards include additional strands, which are also addressed in the strands of the contents of this book:

▶ **Number Sense and Numeration**

▶ **Geometry and Spatial Sense**

▶ **Estimation**

▶ **Measurement** (including concepts of time and money)

▶ **Whole-Number Operations and Computation**

▶ **Fractions and Decimals**

▶ **Statistics and Probability**

You'll discover that as students work with the games and activities included in this book, they will become more confident and competent mathematicians.

Next Up—Numbers!

Using numbers in everyday life

Making a list

LANGUAGE ARTS CONNECTION: Writing in math

Aim

Students study a picture and list the ways they see numbers being used at a baseball game.

Before the Activity

Copy and distribute pages 8–9. As a warm-up to this activity, have students find some of the numbers in your classroom. Ask students to describe how the numbers are being used.

During the Activity

Students can do this activity individually or in groups. Students' descriptions of the ways numbers are used will vary. For example, one student might say that seat numbers help you find your seat, while another will say that seat numbers tell how many seats are in the stadium. Both are correct. After students have found all the numbers, help them to understand how numbers can be used in more than one way. Have students work in groups and compare their descriptions of how the numbers in the picture are used.

After the Activity

Ask: *How did you keep track of the numbers you found as you made your list?*

Extension

Have students write a story about the baseball game. Students should include some of the numbers they see in the picture. Then challenge students to write a word problem that is based on the information in their story. Students can then exchange problems with classmates and try to solve each others' word problems.

ANSWERS

Answers will vary. Students' lists may include: ticket prices, numbers on players' uniforms, numbers on scoreboard, section numbers, money, time, and temperature.

BRAIN POWER: Answers will vary. Other kinds of math in the picture might include: shapes of baseball diamond, bases, bats, ball, and pennants.

Next Up—Numbers!

Numbers have hit a home run at this baseball game!
How? Numbers help count, measure, and organize.
Make a list of all the numbers you see. Then tell how
each of those numbers is being used. For example:

Prices for snacks—
tell you how much the food costs.
Numbers on seats—help you find your seat.

Trim off this strip and attach to page 9.

Attach to page 8 here.

BRAIN POWER
What other kinds of math can you find in this picture?

The Amazing Hundred Chart

Finding number patterns

Exploring place value

Aim

Students use a hundred chart and counters to explore number patterns.

Before the Activity

Copy and distribute pages 11–12. You may want to laminate the hundred charts for durability.

During the Activity

Encourage students to write descriptions of the patterns they find as they work through this activity. It may also be helpful to have students compare their descriptions. Because patterns are often perceived in more than one way, students can gain alternative perspectives by working together.

After the Activity

Have students suppose they were looking at a hundred chart with some counters on its numbers. Then ask students: *Do you think you can tell just by looking at the chart whether a rule was used to put the counters in place or whether they were put in place randomly? Why do you think so?*

Extension

Have students put two or more hundred charts together (matching the bottoms and the tops) to show all the numbers up to 200, 300, 400, and so on. Then have students use the combined charts and the rules from the activity to extend some of the patterns they made. Students should explore if and how the patterns change with larger numbers. You may need to remind students that each chart stands for numbers in the hundreds, so they will have to add extra digits onto each number on the additional charts.

ANSWERS

Patterns will vary. Be sure students can identify a pattern to verify that counters are not placed randomly.

The Amazing Hundred Chart

When you count by 2's, every other number is covered. Neat!

And they're all even numbers!

You Need:
50 or more colored counters small enough to fit on the spaces on the chart, or small pieces of paper cut to fit the spaces

⟩BRAIN POWER⟨
Make a pattern on the chart and try to find a rule to describe it.

What's so amazing about the Amazing Hundred Chart? It's filled with hidden patterns! To find a pattern, just follow a rule. For example, try following this rule:

▶ Count by 2's and put a counter on all the numbers you land on.

Do you see a pattern? What is it?

Here are some more rules. Try them out and find the patterns! Describe each pattern.

▶ Put counters on all the numbers with a 1 in the ones place.

▶ Cover all the numbers that end in 5 or 0.

▶ Count by 3's. Put a counter on each number you land on.

▶ Count by 4's and cover the numbers with counters of the same color. Leave those counters on the board, and count by 6's using a different color. Put two counters on the same space if you need to.

▶ The digits in the number 16 can be added together like this: $1 + 6 = 7$. Cover all the numbers that add up to 7.

▶ Put counters on the numbers that equal 2 when you subtract the smaller digit from the larger. For example, 42 and 24 will both equal 2. Can you find others?

Now make up your own rules and have a friend find the patterns.

The Great Big Book of Super-Fun Math Activities Scholastic Professional Books

1	2	3	4	5	6	7	8	9	10
11	12	13	14	15	16	17	18	19	20
21	22	23	24	25	26	27	28	29	30
31	32	33	34	35	36	37	38	39	40
41	42	43	44	45	46	47	48	49	50
51	52	53	54	55	56	57	58	59	60
61	62	63	64	65	66	67	68	69	70
71	72	73	74	75	76	77	78	79	80
81	82	83	84	85	86	87	88	89	90
91	92	93	94	95	96	97	98	99	100

The Great Big Book of Super-Fun Math Activities Scholastic Professional Books

Numbers in the News

Understanding numerical information

Reading and writing whole numbers

SOCIAL STUDIES CONNECTION: Current events

REAL-LIFE CONNECTION: Reading the newspaper

Aim
Students make charts of numbers clipped from a newspaper and explain how those numbers are being used in context.

Before the Activity
Copy and distribute page 14. Review reading and writing numbers to the tens, hundreds, and thousands place (and higher according to numbers studied by your class).

During the Activity
Help students read the numbers from their news articles as they place them on their charts.

After the Activity
Invite students to discuss the kinds of numbers they found in their newspaper articles. Then help students categorize the numbers according to type or purpose: for example, numbers that show time, monetary amounts, addresses, attendance records, sports scores, etc.

Extension 1
Send students' finished number charts to the editor of your local newspaper along with a note explaining the lesson. You might also invite the editor for a visit, or arrange a class field trip to the newspaper office.

Extension 2
Copy and distribute Newspaper Math on page 15 to extend students' awareness of how numbers are used in the newspaper and in daily life.

Extension 3
Two great resources for classroom newspaper activities are *Newspaper Fun Activities for Young Children* by Bobby S. Goldstein and Gabriel F. Goldstein (Cameron, WV: William Gladden Foundation, 1994) and *Newspapers* by B. Balcziak (Vero Beach, FL: Rourke Publishing Group, 1989).

Numbers in the News

From the cover to the comics, a newspaper is full of numbers. You can count on it!

Read all about what? Math, of course! Take a look at your local newspaper. In it, you'll find numbers that tell when, where, how big, how many, and much more! Organize the numbers you see by making a chart.

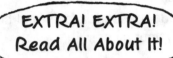

You Need:

your local newspaper
scissors
tape
paper or cardboard

What to Do:

1. Scan a page of your newspaper for numbers. (Don't forget numbers written in words!) Circle about 20 numbers.

2. Decide how each one is being used in the news article. If you need help, check out the examples.

3. Cut out each article that has a number or numbers. Then create a chart on a large piece of paper or cardboard. Tape your example in the first column. In the next two columns, record the page and headline of the story where you found the example. In the last column, write the type of number your example describes. Use all of your numbers to finish your chart.

EXAMPLES: Newspaper Numbers Tell...

A person's age
The score of a game
An amount
An address
A time
A temperature
A date
A unit of measurement
An estimate
A price
and more!

My Example	Page	Story Headline	Type of Number
1:30	A1	Main Street Is Site of Accident	A time
three	A1	Main Street Is Site of Accident	An amount
2501	A1	Be Wise! (ad)	An address

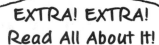

NUMBER SENSE AND PLACE VALUE

Newspaper Math

EXTRA! EXTRA! Read All About It!

What to Do:

Use a newspaper to find the numbers listed below. Cut out your answers from the newspaper and tape them in the box with each question.

1. From the weather report, find the temperature in two cities.

2. Pick three items advertised for sale.

3. Find two different times that the same movie is playing.

4. From the TV listings, pick three programs that you would like to watch. Include the channels that those programs will be on.

5. Choose two numbers from an article of your choice.

Add-'ems Family Place Values

✎ **Identifying place value**

✎ **LITERATURE CONNECTION:**
Reading a play

🎣 Aim

Students read a play that is based on a humorous movie and TV show about the Addams Family.

Before the Activity

Copy and distribute page 17.

During the Activity

Students may enjoy acting out this play. Assign three students the parts of Tuesday, Bugsley, and Cling, or have the class work in groups of two or three and let each group perform the play. This play is a great addition to any Parents' Night function your school holds.

After the class is finished reading or performing the play, move on to a discussion of place value. Ask: *Why did Bugsley think that there were only 15 bugs in the fish tank?*

Extension 1

Copy and distribute Place-Value Puzzler on page 18. Students will solve a riddle as they learn more about place value.

Extension 2

Look in a newspaper for numbers in headlines and advertisements. Cut out the numbers and hand them out to your class. Then play a place-value game by asking questions such as: *Who has a number that shows a 5 in the tens place? Who has a number that includes three hundreds?*

🗝 ANSWERS

1. There are 6 ones in 136.

2. There is 1 ten in 314.

3. There are 8 hundreds in 874.

4. There are 2 tens in 1,529.

5. 4,960

PLACE VALUE PUZZLER: The answer to the secret riddle is A SECRET.

Add-'ems Family Place Values

Meet the Add-'ems Family! Nobody's "bugged" by place value in this wacky family!

CHARACTERS

Tuesday Add-'ems, A teenage girl
Bugsley Add-'ems, Tuesday's little brother
Cling, A walking hand

The scene: Tuesday and Bugsley are in Tuesday's bedroom. Bugsley is looking at a fish tank full of creepy bugs.

Bugsley: Tuesday, can I bring your bug collection to school tomorrow?

Tuesday: Why? Mom already made us worm sandwiches for tomorrow's lunch.

Bugsley: No, not for lunch. I want to bring your collection for show-and-tell.

Tuesday: Bugsley, you know what happened when you brought my iguana, Itch, into class...

Bugsley: He scared everybody! I guess you could call it show-and-yell!

Tuesday: Well, if you take good care of my bugs, I guess it's OK.

Bugsley: *(looking into a glass tank filled with bugs)* Just how many bugs are in here?

Tuesday: I keep track of the number of bugs on this piece of paper. *(She holds up a sheet of paper that says "429" on it.)*

Bugsley: Hmmm...so you have 15 bugs, because 4 plus 2 plus 9 equals 15.

Tuesday: That's not how to read a number, Bugsley! You need to use the place value. Cling and I will "show" and "tell" you how to do it.

Cling: The last number on the right tells you how many ones are in a number. There are 9 ones in 429.

The next number to the left tells you how many tens are in a number. There are 2 tens in 429. Two tens equal 20.

The next number to the left tells you how many hundreds are in a number. There are 4 hundreds in 429.

Bugsley: I think I get it. In 429, there are 4 hundreds, 2 tens, and 9 ones. That makes four hundred and twenty-nine. You know what, Tuesday?

Tuesday: What?

Bugsley: I can always "count" on you!

What to Do:

Use place value to answer the questions.

1. How many ones are in 136? _____

2. How many tens are in 314? _____

3. How many hundreds are in 874? _____

4. How many tens are in 1,529? _____

5. How would you write a number that has four thousands, nine hundreds, six tens, and no ones?

_____

The Great Big Book of Super-Fun Math Activities   Scholastic Professional Books

Place-Value Puzzler

**What is too much fun for one, enough for two,
and means nothing to three?**

Find the answer to this riddle by using place value! Take a look at each
number below. One digit in each number is underlined. Circle the word in
each line that tells the place value of the underlined number. Write the letters
next to each correct answer in the blanks below. The first one is done for you.

A.	1<u>5</u>,209	**a** thousands	**i** hundreds
B.	4,7<u>2</u>9	**n** hundreds	**s** tens
C.	<u>4</u>25	**e** hundreds	**o** tens
D.	7,6<u>1</u>8	**c** tens	**g** ones
E.	1,<u>1</u>12	**p** thousands	**r** hundreds
F.	8,63<u>6</u>	**a** hundreds	**e** ones
G.	2<u>2</u>2	**t** tens	**m** ones

a
___ ___ ___ ___ ___ ___ ___
A   B   C   D   E   F   G

A Valuable Abacus

✎ **Understanding place value to thousands**

✎ **LITERATURE CONNECTION: Reading a story**

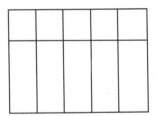

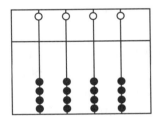

🔑 **ANSWERS**

Here are the numbers shown on June's abacus:

Heads of lettuce: 19
Boxes of cereal: 48
Apples: 186
Peanuts: 1,253

✎ Aim

Students learn to use an abacus as they read a math story.

Before the Activity

Students can make their own abacus with a cardboard box top, such as a shoe box top, string, and round oat cereal such as Cheerios. Help them cut and tie four lengths of string vertically and one horizontally, as shown at right.

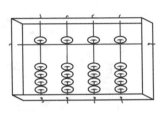

Be sure students string 5 oat rings before they tie both ends of the vertical strings, and then move one to the top before they tie the horizontal string in place.

Copy and distribute pages 20–21.

During the Activity

Students should follow along with the story to practice counting with an abacus. They can use the abacus they made before the activity, or they can use paper and counters to represent an abacus. For a paper abacus, each student will need a large sheet of paper and 20 counters, 16 of one color and 4 of another. Have them draw 4 vertical lines and 1 horizontal line on the paper, as shown at left. Ask each student to arrange the counters on the paper as shown.

Each student is now ready to match his or her abacus to June's throughout the story, helping her count the different types of food in the store.

After the Activity

Give students other numbers, in the ones, tens, hundreds, and thousands, and have them represent each number using their cardboard or paper abacus. If they work in pairs, each student can represent the given number and then check each others' work.

Extension

Students may enjoy performing this story in play form. Choose students to play the narrator, June, and Mai-Lin.

A Valuable Abacus

In this tale, a young girl learns to count with an abacus. Read the story and you can help her!

O nce upon a time, there was a girl named June. She lived with her grandmother, Mai-Lin, who was from China. Mai-Lin owned a market. People came from near and far to buy her fruits and vegetables. Mai-Lin worked hard to make sure the store always had enough food.

June worked at the store, too. June loved being with her grandmother. June was smart and quickly learned how to do things.

One day, June was very sad. "What's wrong?" her grandmother asked.

"My calculator broke and I don't know what to do," June answered. "I need to count all the food in the store. Now I can't count any of it."

June's grandmother smiled. "Don't worry. I will show you how to count with my abacus. You can count everything in this store with it." Then she added: "People have used the abacus for thousands of years. Many people in China, Japan, India, and Russia still use an abacus today."

June frowned, but her grandmother knew June would master the abacus quickly. She pointed to the abacus. "Each row of beads stands

for the different digits in a number—from ones all they way up to thousands," she said.

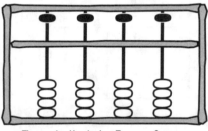

Thousands Hundreds Tens Ones

Then June's grandmother pointed to the beads. "Each bead at the bottom of the abacus stands for 1 unit. Each bead at the top of the abacus stands for 5 units."

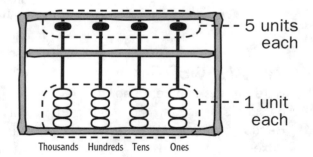

5 units each

1 unit each

Thousands Hundreds Tens Ones

She moved some of the beads toward the middle of the abacus so it looked like this:

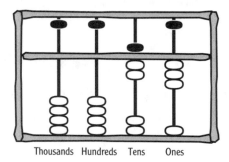

Thousands Hundreds Tens Ones

"To make a number higher than 0, you move the beads to the middle," she said. "This shows the number 73 because I moved 7 tens and 3 ones to the middle."

Soon June was counting on the abacus all by herself. She was ready to count the food in the store. First she counted heads of lettuce. The abacus looked like this:

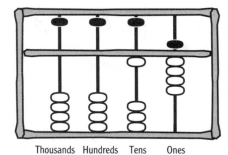

Thousands Hundreds Tens Ones

How many heads of lettuce did June count?

_____

Next, June counted boxes of cereal, and the abacus looked like this:

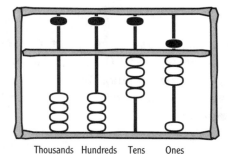

Thousands Hundreds Tens Ones

How many boxes of cereal did June count?

_____

Then June counted apples, and the abacus looked like this:

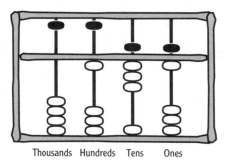

Thousands Hundreds Tens Ones

How many apples did June count?

_____

Finally, June counted the peanuts in the store. There were lots of peanuts, and when she was done, the abacus looked like this:

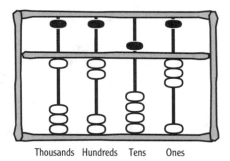

Thousands Hundreds Tens Ones

How many peanuts did June count?

_____

June was proud of her new skill. Her grandmother hugged her because she had learned so quickly. From that day on, June always kept an abacus handy. And, with or without her calculator, she always knew how much food was in the store.

Collect a Million

- Using a model

- Conceptualizing large numbers

- Estimating large numbers

- Estimating length

- Working with powers of 10

Aim

Students use small objects to conceptualize one million and to estimate lengths.

Before the Activity

Copy and distribute page 23. Help students choose and collect the items they will need to complete this activity. You may want to have members of other classes or people in your community contribute to your students' collections.

During the Activity

Ask: *If the students in the story can collect 50,000 pop tops every year, in how many years will they complete their collection of one million?* (19 years)

For Steps 3 through 6, have students multiply 100, 1,000, 10,000, and 100,000 by 10 to help them understand why these numbers are used in the activity. In Step 6, students may be better able to visualize the length of one million objects if they rename centimeters as meters. If necessary, show them a meterstick and explain that there are 100 centimeters in one meter.

After the Activity

Ask: *Once you knew the length of a million items, how did you use that information to help you think about where you would store one million items?*

If you would like students actually to collect one million objects, have them think about the best kinds of things to collect, based on where they will store their collection.

Extension

Have students work together to find out how much $1,000,000 is. Students can work in small groups assigned to find each of the following: What you can buy with $1,000,000; how long it takes to earn $1,000,000 at a few common teenagers' wages; how big a book would have one million words. Groups can then present their findings to the class.

ANSWERS

1–6. Answers will vary.

BRAIN POWER: Answers will vary depending on the size of the items collected.

Collect a Million

You Need:
at least 100 of an item
you want to collect
(like stamps, buttons,
stickers, cards)
metric ruler

Yyou hear the word "million" a lot. Close to one million people live in the city of Detroit. Americans eat about one million hot dogs every half hour. But what does one million of something look like? Collecting a million can help you find out.

In one fourth grade, students started collecting the tabs from soda cans. At the end of each week, they counted the week's total and added that number to their old total. Each week, to find out how many more tabs they needed to get to one million, they subtracted the new total from one million.

If you and your classmates want to find out what a million looks like, start your own million collection. (Before you pick the item to collect, it's a good idea to estimate how much room it will take up.)

> **⚡ BRAIN POWER ⚡**
> If you collected a million of your item, where would you keep them?

What to Do:

1. Take a guess: How long would a row of a million of your items be? _____

2. Work with your classmates. Take 100 of your items and line them up in a row. How many centimeters long is your row? _____

3. Multiply that total by 10. How many centimeters is that? _____ That's how long your row would be for **1,000** items.

4. Multiply your last total by 10. How many centimeters is that? _____ That's how long your row would be for **10,000** items.

5. Multiply your last total by 10. How many centimeters is that? _____ That's how long your row would be for **100,000** items.

6. Multiply your last total by 10. How many centimeters is that? _____ That's how long your row would be for **1,000,000** items! (If you like, divide your answer by 100 to find the length in meters.) How close was your original guess?

Place-Value Pumpkin

- Using place value to thousands

- Additing and subtracting whole numbers

Aim

Students work with place value and computation as they play a board game.

Before the Activity

Copy and distribute pages 25–26. You may want to laminate the game board for durability.

During the Activity

Students can use a calculator, paper and pencil, or mental math to keep score. For any calculation method, suggest that students say the score earned for each turn aloud before they add it to their running total. Make sure all players agree on each new score before it is added to the old score.

After the Activity

Ask students: *If you wanted your final score to be in the millions, how could you change the rules of the game to make this possible?*

Extension

Students can play a challenging decimal game by renaming the spaces on the board "ones," "tenths," "hundredths," and "thousandths." For example, if a player spins 3 and lands on hundredths, the score for the spin would be three hundredths, or .03.

Place-Value Pumpkin

'Round and 'round the pumpkin you go!
Place value helps to make your score grow!

You Need:
pencils and paper
playing pieces
paper clip

Object:
To reach the center of the pumpkin
with the most points.

Number of Players: 2 players or 2 teams

To Play:

- Decide who will go first. Each player begins on START.

- Take turns spinning. Move ahead the number of spaces shown on the spinner.

- When you land on a space, read what it says. If it says ONES, TENS, HUNDREDS, or THOUSANDS, use that word and the number you spun to make your score.

- Keep adding your scores as you go around the board. If you lose points during the game, subtract them.

- The game ends when each player or team reaches or passes END. The player or team with more points wins.

I spun a 2 and landed on a HUNDREDS place. That's 200 points. I add that to the score I already have.

Spin the paper clip around the pencil.

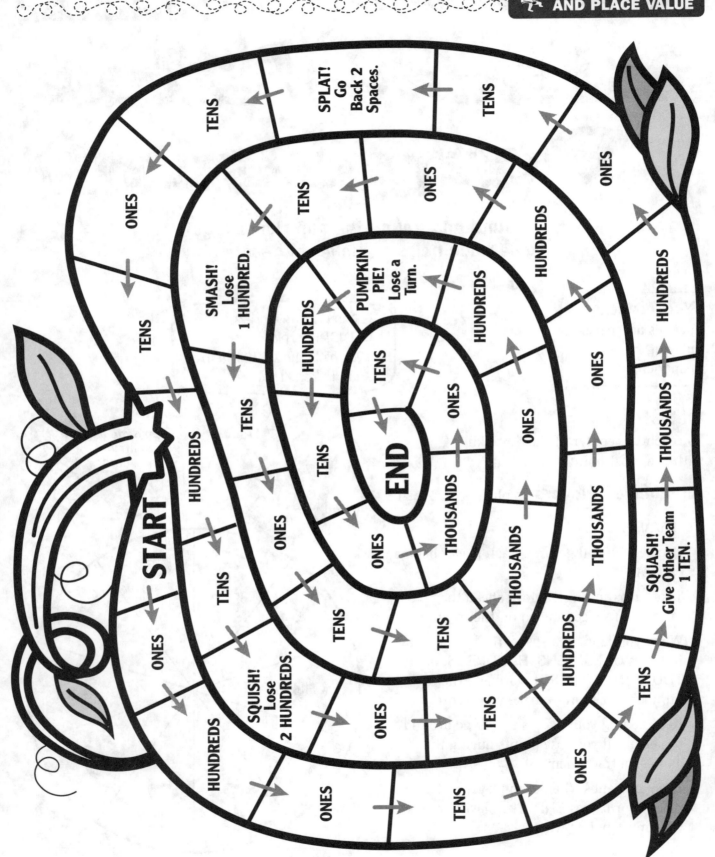

Spin Four—Whose Number Is More?

 **Place value to thousands**

🖉 Aim

Students explore place value and probability as they play a spinner game.

Before the Activity

Remind students that numerals can take differing values depending on where they appear in a number. For example, build understanding that 7 in the ones place is 7, 7 in the tens place is 70, 7 in the hundreds place is 700, and so on.

You may also need to review that to compare numbers, students must compare the digits in each place, from left to right. If necessary, have students practice that skill before they play the game.

Copy and distribute page 28.

No fair peeking at the other player's paper!

⌐ ANSWERS

BRAIN POWER: Answers will vary. One strategy: Place the greater digits in the thousands and hundreds places. Encourage students to think about the chances of spinning the greater digits (for example, 8 and 9).

Spin Four—Whose Number Is More?

You Need:
pencils
paper
a paper clip

Object:
To make a higher four-digit number than the other player.

Number of Players: 2

To Play:

▶ Each player draws four blanks on a paper, like this:

$$\_\,\_\_\_$$

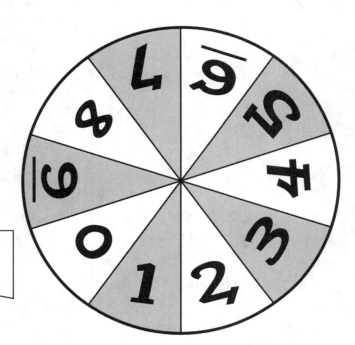

▶ Make a spinner using a pencil, a paper clip, and the number wheel.

▶ Players take turns spinning. Both players write the digit the spinner lands on in any of their unfilled blanks. (No fair peeking at the other player's paper!) Once a digit is written, it can't be erased or moved.

▶ A round ends after four spins. The player who makes the higher number wins the round and gets 1 point. (If the players have the same number, they both get a point.)

▶ The first player to get 5 points wins the game.

Spin the paper clip around the pencil.

SAMPLE ROUND

The digits spun were 3, 2, 7, and 5.

LaTosha
7,532

Kevin
5,732

⇒ BRAIN POWER ⇐
Did you find different ways to play? List the best strategies.

LaTosha wins the round because 7,532 is greater than 5,732.

Moosebumps: The Curse of the Rounding Hound

Rounding whole numbers to the nearest ten or hundred

LITERATURE CONNECTION: Reading a story

Aim

This spoof of the popular Goosebumps book series shows students how to round whole numbers to the tens and hundreds places.

Before the Activity

Copy and distribute pages 30–31. Review rounding with students. Drawing a number line on the board may help students to conceptualize the idea of rounding. As an example, write *40* on the left side of a number line and *50* on the right side. Introduce the idea of rounding up or rounding down. Write the number *43* in the proper place on the number line. Tell the class you want to round 43 to the nearest ten. Ask: *On the number line, is 43 closer to 40 or to 50?* (It is closer to 40. So 43 rounded to the nearest ten is 40.)

During the Activity

Have volunteers read different paragraphs in the story, or select two students to read the parts of Marty Moose and the Rounding Hound for the rest of the class.

Extension

Ask students who have read any of R. L. Stine's Goosebumps stories to explain them to the class. As a cross-curricular activity, have students write their own Moosebumps stories. The heroes should use math to escape strange or scary situations.

ANSWERS

1. right

2. 730

3. 460

4. 40

5. 100

6. 900

BRAIN POWER: Answers will vary. Some things we might not need to know the exact number of could include crowd sizes, long distances, weight of a large object, time needed to do a task.

MOOSEBUMPS: The Curse of the Rounding Hound

By R. L. Swine

In this moose-terious tale, you'll see there's nothing scary about rounding numbers!

I'm Marty Moose, the mailmoose in Mooston, Texas. I was walking down the street one day, delivering the mail. All of a sudden, I couldn't move! I looked down at my feet and realized they had turned into giant circles!

Just then, I heard a loud growl behind me. I spun around and saw a big, drooling dog with glowing eyes and razor-sharp teeth.

"I am the Rounding Hound," growled the dog. "I made your feet round. I can make anything round!"

"I never saw a talking dog before," I said.

"I never saw a talking moose before," replied the hound. "I am going to turn you into one huge circle! There is only one way to stop me: Show me that you also have rounding powers."

I wasn't nervous anymore. "No problem," I told the hound. "I'll show you how to round numbers. For example, here's how you round a number to the **nearest ten**."

"I'm not ready to set you loose, moose,"

Rounding to the Nearest Ten

✔ Find the number in the tens place. You may want to put a circle around it.

✔ Now look to the right, at the number in the ones place.

• If it is 5 or greater than 5, add 1 to the number in the tens place.

• If it is less than 5, leave the number in the tens place alone.

✔ Finally, turn the number in the ones place into a zero.

So... 3⑦2 becomes 370

3⑦8 becomes 380

barked the hound. "What if someone asks me to round a number to the **nearest hundred**?"

"Simple!" I said. "Find the hundreds place. You can circle that number to help you remember where it is."

"Now it's just like rounding to the nearest ten. But instead of looking at the ones place, you look at the number in the tens place. And be sure to turn the numbers in the ones AND tens places into zeros."

I looked down at my feet. They were normal

Rounding to the Nearest Hundred

✔ Start with the number in the hundreds place. You may want to put a circle around it.

✔ Now look to the right, at the number in the tens place. See if it is 5 or greater, or less than 5.

Examples:

③84 becomes 400
(the 8 in the tens place is greater than 5)

③28 becomes 300
(the 2 in the tens place is less than 5)

again! The Rounding Hound had released me from his spell. "Thanks for the math lesson," said the hound. "I'll see you a-round!"

What to Do:

Uh-oh! The Rounding Hound is coming to your town! Keep him happy by answering these questions.

1. You're rounding a number to the nearest ten. The ones place is to the   left | right   of the tens place. (Circle your answer.)

2. Round 729 to the nearest ten.

_____

3. Round 464 to the nearest ten.

_____

4. Round 37 to the nearest ten.

_____

5. Round 116 to the nearest hundred.

_____

6. Round 853 to the nearest hundred.

_____

⋟ BRAIN POWER ⋞

We use rounding when we want to know about how many there are of something. (Instead of saying, "I have 57 pieces of candy," you might say, "I have about 60 pieces of candy.") When are some times when you might not need to know the exact number of something?

NUMBER SENSE AND PLACE VALUE

Rounding at the Square Dance

 Place value to thousands

 Rounding to the nearest ten, hundred, thousand

Aim

Students round numbers to the nearest ten, hundred, or thousand as they play a board game with a square dance theme.

Before the Activity

Copy and distribute pages 33–34. You may want to laminate the game board for durability. Have a number cube available for each group playing the game.

Lead a class discussion about rounding numbers. Ask: *When might it be helpful to use a round number?* Review rounding to the nearest ten, hundred, or thousand.

During the Activity

Remind students that the number showing when they roll the number cube determines how each number on the board will be rounded.

Extension

Here is another rounding game your students will enjoy. Supply each player with two number cubes. Each player takes a turn rolling the cubes. After each roll, the player creates a two-digit number with the cubes and rounds that number to the nearest 10. Players record the rounded number and add each rounded result as they go. The first to reach 200 points wins.

NUMBER SENSE AND PLACE VALUE

Rounding at the Square Dance

Swing your partner, do-si-do.
Round these numbers high and low!

You Need:
playing piece for each player
number cube numbered 1 to 6

Object:
Be the first player to finish the square dance.

Number of Players: 2 players or 2 teams

To Play:

▶ Decide who will go first. Each player begins on START.

▶ Take turns rolling the number cube.

- If it shows a 1 or a 2, move your piece that number of spaces. Round the number you land on to the nearest ten.

- If it shows a 3 or a 4, move your piece that number of spaces. Round the number you land on to the nearest hundred.

- If it shows a 5 or a 6, move your piece that number of spaces. Round the number you land on to the nearest thousand.

▶ Players should check that each number is rounded correctly. The game cannot continue until players agree on an answer.

▶ If you don't land on a number, do what the space tells you to do.

▶ The game ends when the first player or team lands on or passes DANCE OVER.

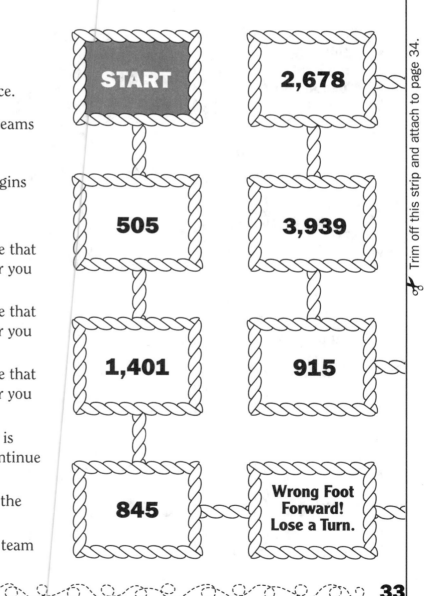

START

2,678

505

3,939

1,401

915

845

Wrong Foot Forward! Lose a Turn.

Trim off this strip and attach to page 34.

NUMBER SENSE AND PLACE VALUE

Attach to page 33 here.

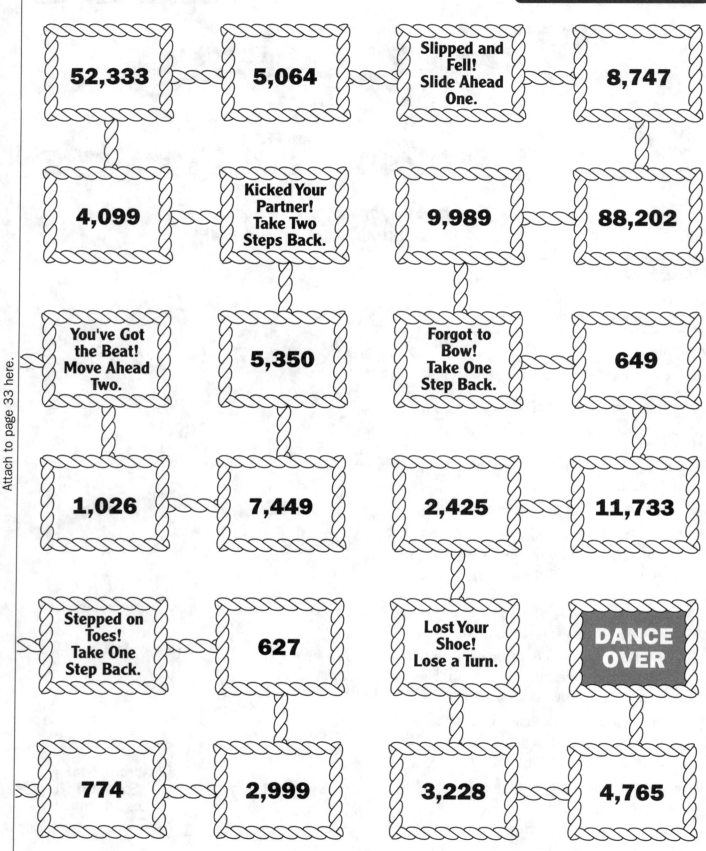

52,333

5,064

Slipped and Fell! Slide Ahead One.

8,747

4,099

Kicked Your Partner! Take Two Steps Back.

9,989

88,202

You've Got the Beat! Move Ahead Two.

5,350

Forgot to Bow! Take One Step Back.

649

1,026

7,449

2,425

11,733

Stepped on Toes! Take One Step Back.

627

Lost Your Shoe! Lose a Turn.

DANCE OVER

774

2,999

3,228

4,765

34

Roman Numerals from Planet VIX

 Using Roman numerals

 Understanding place value

LITERATURE CONNECTION:
Reading a story

✎ ANSWERS

1. III = 3

2. VII = 7

3. XIV = 14

4. XXV = 25

5. XXI = 21

6. XXIX = 29

7. XVI = 16

8. XXXI = 31

BRAIN POWER: Here are some places where you can often find Roman numerals: on clocks and watches; dates on older buildings; the volume numbers of a set of encyclopedia; the date at the end of the credits on a television program or a movie; the copyright date of a book; the chapter numbers of a book.

✎ Aim

Students learn about Roman numerals as they read a cartoon story.

Before the Activity

Copy and distribute pages 36–37.

During the Activity

Class members can read the story aloud or act out the different parts. Write the values of the Roman numerals on the board for easy reference.

Extension

Celebrate a whole day in honor of the Romans. Look up their many mathematical contributions in an encyclopedia and discuss them during the day. Make sure to write all numbers in Roman numerals! A resource you might use is the book *Roman Numerals* by David A. Adler (New York, NY: HarperCollins Children's Books, 1977).

Name _____

Roman Numerals from Planet VIX

These aliens know that Roman numerals are out of this world!

Greetings, people of Earth! I am Rom, from Planet VIX. We visited your planet 2,000 years ago and fell in love with your Roman numerals.

What are Roman numerals, you ask? They're a system of numbers invented by some of your Earthlings in Europe about 2,500 years ago.

Roman numerals were popular on Earth until the 1500s. Although it was easy to add and subtract with Roman numerals, it was tough to do other kinds of math. So people started using Arabic numerals, the kind you still use today.

We are visiting you Earthlings again to remind you how great Roman numerals are!

I is the Roman numeral for 1.

V is the Roman numeral for 5.

X is the Roman numeral for 10.

1 My friends team up to form any number! Read Roman numerals from left to right, adding the numbers as you go. If I-Man stands to the right of V-Woman, they make the number 6. That's because in Roman numerals, V (5) plus I (1) equals VI (6).

We equal **6**!

2 I-Man can be pretty tricky, though. If he is to the left of V-Woman, they make the number 4.

Now we equal **4**!

3 And if I-Man stands to the left of X-Guy, they make the number 9.

We equal **9**!

4 Sometimes you'll see two or three I-Men or X-Guys standing next to each other. That way, they can make even more Roman numerals!

We equal **20**!

We equal **3**!

> **⇒BRAIN POWER⇐**
> Where are some places you've seen Roman numerals?

What to Do:

Read the Roman numerals below. Remember to read from left to right. Watch out for I-Man standing to the left of V-Woman or X-Guy. For each Roman numeral, write the Arabic numeral in the blank.

1. I I I = _____

2. V I I = _____

3. X I V = _____

4. X X V = _____

5. X X I = _____

6. X X I X = _____

7. X V I = _____

8. X X X I = _____

Count Like a Computer!

 Whole number addition

 **Number sense**

TECHNOLOGY CONNECTION: Understanding computers

Aim

Students learn to count in the binary code used by computers.

Before the Activity

Copy and distribute page 39. After students read the information about bits and bytes, you might ask eight students to stand up as "bits" and model the number 70. Help the other students in the class add the numbers above the bits that are "on." Write a number sentence on the chalkboard to show students which numbers to add. (70 is shown when the bits for 64 + 4 + 2 are on.) Then have the eight students model another byte and have the rest of the class find which number the byte stands for. Remind students that 1's represent numbers that are on and 0's represent numbers that are off.

Ask students what they notice about the numbers over each bit in the illustration of the number 70 on page 39. (Students should note that each number is half as large as the number to its left.)

After the Activity

Ask students: *If you looked at a byte, how could you tell if the number it stood for was greater than 5? Greater than 10? Greater than 100?*

Extension

Have students list the bytes that stand for the numbers from 1 to 15 and then look for counting patterns in their lists.

ANSWERS

    7 = 00000111
  100 = 01100100
   35 = 00100011
  205 = 11001101
   24 = 00011000
  108 = 01101100
    0 = 00000000
  255 = 11111111

Name _____

Count Like a Computer!

You Need:
calculator (if you have one)

What would a computer say if you asked it, "How are you?" Not much. After all, computers don't have brains or feelings the way we do. But they sure seem to know a lot!

How does a computer "think"? With bits. A bit is a tiny switch inside the computer that can turn on and off. To show that the bit is on, we write "1." When the bit is off, we write "0."

A byte is a combination of eight bits. Each byte stands for a different number. For example, the byte 10111110 stands for 190. The byte 01000110 stands for the number 70.

The bits that stand for 64, 4, and 2 are "on." Those three numbers add up to 70.

I get it. The **1**'s tell you which numbers to add. You don't count the **0**'s.

What to Do:

▶ Make 8 small squares of paper, the same size as the empty signs the 8 kids in the picture at the bottom of the page are holding. Draw a **1** on one side of each paper and a **0** on the other side.

▶ The eight bits in a byte always stand for the same numbers in the same order. The numbers are: 128 64 32 16 8 4 2 1

▶ To show a number like a computer, you show combinations of cards with 1 or 0. When the 1 shows, the number is "on." When the 0 shows, the number is "off." The kids below show how your byte would look for the number 70.

128 64 32 16 8 4 2 1

0 1 0 0 0 1 1 0

▶ Now use the empty squares and your little paper squares to count like a computer! You can make any number from 0 to 255 using a combination of eight 1's and 0's.

How would you show these numbers with 1's and 0's?

7 _____   100 _____   35 _____   205 _____

24 _____   108 _____   0 _____   255 _____

Prime Time

- Identifying prime numbers
- Understanding factors

Aim

Students find prime numbers by arranging small squares into rectangular grids.

Before the Activity

Copy and distribute page 41.

During the Activity

Point out to students that a rectangle arranged left to right and one arranged top to bottom is the same rectangle. For example, a rectangle with 1 square down and 4 squares across is the same rectangle as one with 4 squares down and 1 across. If you placed them on top of one another, you could see they are the same size.

In addition, remind students that a square is a kind of rectangle—so they will find several numbers for which they can build both a long rectangle and a square rectangle.

Extension

This activity can lead to an introduction or review of area and perimeter. By counting sides of the all the squares that make up a rectangle, students can find the rectangle's perimeter. By multiplying the number of squares across by the number of squares down, students can find a rectangle's area. Remind students that area is expressed in square units. For example, the area of a 2-by-3 rectangle is 6 square units.

ANSWERS

The prime numbers between 2 and 20 are 2, 3, 5, 7, 11, 13, 17, and 19.

Prime Time

You Need:
scissors

Factors are numbers that you multiply together to equal another number. For example, 1 x 6 equals 6. And 2 x 3 also equals 6. So 1, 2, 3, and 6 are all factors of 6.

You can use squares to build some special numbers called **prime numbers**. A prime number has only 2 factors—itself and 1. You can find out if a number is prime by making rectangles. If you can make only 1 rectangle from a number, that means it's prime. Start with the number 2. Take 2 squares. You can build only 1 rectangle:

Squares DOWN = 1
Squares ACROSS = 2
$2 \times 1 = 2$

Since you can build only 1 rectangle, the only factors of the number 2 are 2 and 1. That means 2 is a prime number. Number 3, as you see, is the same way—only 1 rectangle:

Squares DOWN = 1
Squares ACROSS = 3
$3 \times 1 = 3$

So 3 is a prime number, too. Now try using 4 squares. You can make a rectangle like this:

Squares DOWN = 1
Squares ACROSS = 4
$4 \times 1 = 4$

But you can also make a rectangle like this:

Squares DOWN = 2
Squares ACROSS = 2
$2 \times 2 = 4$

Now you know all the factors of 4: 1, 2, and 4. Since there are more factors than 1 and the number itself, 4 is not a prime number.

Now try some more building!

What to Do:

▶ Cut out the 20 squares below. Build rectangles for each number from 5 to 20.

▶ Try to make as many different rectangles as possible for each number. If you can only make 1 rectangle (a straight line of squares), the number is prime.

▶ List the prime numbers between 2 and 20.

_____

The Great Big Book of Super-Fun Math Activities Scholastic Professional Books

 **GEOMETRY**

Picky Penguin Pens

 Forming squares and triangles

 Identifying patterns and relationships

Aim
Students look for and identify patterns while developing an understanding of the concept of functions.

Before the Activity
Copy and distribute pages 43–44. Ask: *How many wheels are there on a tricycle?* Make a table with the heading "T" for the number of tricycles and "W" for the number of wheels. Write the number 1 under "T," and draw three wheels under "W." Extend the chart to seven tricycles, drawing sets of wheels on the board to represent each answer. Ask if anyone can identify a pattern in the chart.

During the Activity
Challenge students to form the greatest number of pens with each given number of toothpicks. Remind them that pens can be squares or triangles; have students examine their drawings to see which shape is more efficient in terms of fewest toothpicks (sides) and greatest number of pens able to be formed.

Extension
Students can learn more about penguins in the books *Penguin: A Season in the Life of the Adelie Penguins* by Lloyd Spencer Davis (New York, NY: Henry Holt, 1994), and *Little Penguin* by Patrick Benson (New York, NY: Putnam and Grosset, 1994).

ANSWERS

Students' "pens" will vary. Check that each arrangement contains the correct number of toothpicks specified on the chart.

BRAIN POWER: Answers will vary. Students might work backward, building 1, 2, 3, 4, etc., pens with the fewest number of toothpicks in order to identify one possible pattern.

Picky Penguin Pens

Pen up some picky penguins with geometry!

Hi, I'm Penny, and I'm glad you stopped by! I'm having trouble with my picky pet penguins. They're so picky about who they live with that I've decided to build each one a pen of its own. I'm not sure how many walls I'll need to build. But I know that I want to use the fewest walls possible. Can you help me with this "pet"-icular problem?

You Need:
toothpicks

What to Do:

- Give Penny a helping hand. Use toothpicks to design the penguins' pens. One toothpick will stand for each wall. The pens can be shaped like squares or triangles.

- Then complete the chart to show what each pen looks like and how many walls it has. The first three are done for you.

> **⇒ BRAIN POWER ⇐**
> Can you find a pattern?
> How are the number of sides and
> the number of pens related?

If I use this many toothpicks...	I can make this many pens.	This is what they will look like.	If I use this many toothpicks...	I can make this many pens.	This is what they will look like.
3	1	△	9		
4	1	▢	12		
5	2	◿	16		
6			19		
7			24		

Shape Up!

✏ **Identifying two-dimensional and three-dimensional shapes**

✏ **Using a model**

✒ Aim

Students open and flatten three-dimensional containers in order to study the relationship between three-dimensional and two-dimensional shapes.

Before the Activity

Have students collect containers that can be easily cut open. Prepare the containers beforehand or in front of the class yourself, if you do not want students to use scissors. Try to cut the shapes open along a seam, in order to preserve the greatest number of two-dimensional shapes. Once students' boxes are prepared, copy and distribute pages 46–47.

During the Activity

Students might find it difficult to grasp the abstract concept of dimension. It may be helpful to describe three-dimensional shapes in terms of the space they take up or the objects they resemble. Use a sheet of paper to represent a two-dimensional shape. Demonstrate that two-dimensional shapes take up space on a flat surface but have no sides.

Cut open at least one container in front of the class to show how it changes from three dimensions to two.

After the Activity

Have the class draw pictures of their shapes, whole and flattened. Then exhibit the drawings in the classroom.

🔑 ANSWERS

Milk carton: rectangles, triangles

Oatmeal box: rectangle, circle

Ice cream carton: closed curve, circle

Soup mix box: rectangles

Shape Up!

Walk into your kitchen and you'll find three-dimensional (3-D) shapes all around. But did you know that many 3-D shapes are made from two-dimensional (2-D) shapes?

3-D shapes have height, length and width.
2-D shapes are flat.

Watch what happens when a cereal box is cut open:

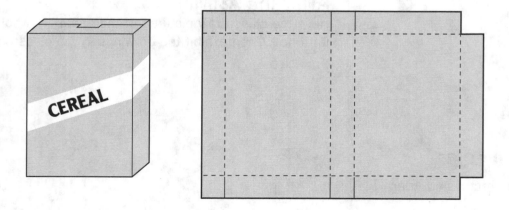

CEREAL

That 3-D cereal box is really made up of lots of 2-D squares and rectangles!

You Need:
empty boxes and containers
scissors

Look at the chart showing other 3-D shapes that have been cut open. Next to each one, list the 2-D shapes you see.

3-D Shape	2-D Shapes	2-D Shapes I See
Milk		
Oatmeal		
Oatmeal		
Soup Mix		

Now it's your turn! Cut apart your 3-D containers. Then draw the 2-D shapes you see. How many can you name?

 **GEOMETRY**

Shapes and Shadows

✏️ **Understanding properties of three-dimensional shapes**

✒️ Aim

Students use light and three-dimensional objects to learn about properties of three-dimensional shapes.

Before the Activity

Collect three-dimensional objects that can be used to complete this activity. Some appropriate objects include erasers, pens, pencils, books, rulers, food boxes, fruit, or toys. Display the shapes and review their names with students. Also, experiment with several light sources to find which will make the best shadows. You may want to use a table lamp, a flashlight, or the sun.

Copy and distribute page 49.

During the Activity

If students are having difficulty avoiding tracing the shadows cast by their hands, suggest that they use larger shapes.

To help students answer Question 6, display a collection of the objects students traced. Students can try to match each object with its traced shadow shape.

After the Activity

Ask students: *Why is it possible for the shapes' shadows to look so different from the actual shapes? How can you make a shadow look a lot like the actual shape?*

🔑 ANSWERS

BRAIN POWER: a sphere

Name _____

Shapes and Shadows

 square   **cube**

What's the difference between a square and a cube? A square is a **two-dimensional** shape. It's flat. And you can see all the sides of a square at the same time.

A cube is a **three-dimensional**, or **3-D**, shape. It's not flat. You can hold a cube in your hands. But you can't see all the sides of the cube at once.

Turn a cube around in your hands. As you turn the cube, you can see how it looks at different angles. Sometimes it looks like this.

Sometimes it looks like this.

And sometimes it even looks like this!

You Need:
three-dimensional objects
lamp or other light source
crayons and paper

What to Do:
Tracing the shadows of 3-D shapes will help you see the different ways they can look. Here's how:

1. Make sure that your lamp is far enough or close enough to your shapes to make a shadow. Place a sheet of paper on a flat surface in the lamp's light.

2. Have a partner hold one of the 3-D shapes under the lamp, so that it makes a shadow on your paper.

3. Ask your partner to turn the shape under the lamp until you see a shadow that you want to draw. Then have your partner hold the shape still.

4. Trace the shape's shadow on the paper. Don't trace your partner's hand!

5. Repeat Steps 3 and 4 to make a design on your paper. Trace the same shape in different positions.

6. When you are finished, put your designs up on the bulletin board. Try to guess which shapes your friends used to make their designs. Then let them guess yours.

> **BRAIN POWER**
> Can you find a 3-D shape whose shadow always looks the same?

Space Shapes

📝 **Using a model to explore polygons**

📝 **Spatial relations**

🔑 **ANSWERS**
See shapes below.

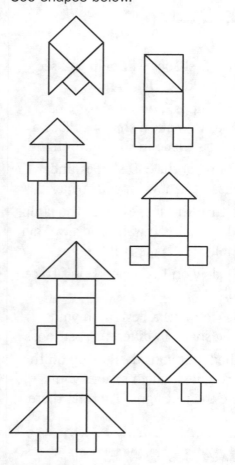

BRAIN POWER: Answers will vary.

🏹 **Aim**
Students fold paper and cut out regular polygons. They then combine them to form pictured shapes.

Before the Activity
Copy and distribute pages 51–52. Review the properties of triangles, squares, and rectangles with students. Have them describe the number of sides and angles in each shape and identify the right angles.

Students can use a rectangular piece of paper of any size to complete this activity. However, paper that is other than 8½ inches by 11 inches may produce space shapes with different proportions from those shown.

During the Activity
Students can do this activity individually or in groups of three or four. If they work in groups, suggest that each group member try to make a different shape. It may also be helpful for each group member to demonstrate, one piece at a time, how to build his or her shape.

Extension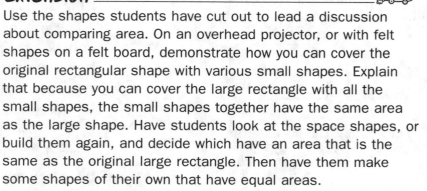
Use the shapes students have cut out to lead a discussion about comparing area. On an overhead projector, or with felt shapes on a felt board, demonstrate how you can cover the original rectangular shape with various small shapes. Explain that because you can cover the large rectangle with all the small shapes, the small shapes together have the same area as the large shape. Have students look at the space shapes, or build them again, and decide which have an area that is the same as the original large rectangle. Then have them make some shapes of their own that have equal areas.

Space Shapes

See the spaceships on these pages? We call them space <u>shapes</u>. That's because they're made from triangles, squares, and rectangles. You can make space shapes, too. First follow these steps to make your own pattern.

You Need:
$8\frac{1}{2}$-inch by 11-inch sheet of paper
scissors

1. Fold the paper in half, like this:

2. Fold only one top corner down until it touches the other side. Cut the paper **below** the triangle, like this:

Fold
Cut

3. Unfold both pieces. Cut both pieces down the middle fold. Set aside one square and one rectangle.

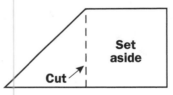
Cut **Set aside** **Cut** **Set aside**

4. You should have one square and one rectangle left. Cut the square along the fold into two triangles. Fold the rectangle in half. Cut along the fold.

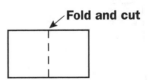
Cut **Fold and cut**

5. You should now have these six pieces:

⋙ BRAIN POWER ⋘
What other shapes can you make with the pieces?

The Great Big Book of Super-Fun Math Activities Scholastic Professional Books

Use the pieces to make the seven space shapes on this pages.
(You won't need to use all of the pieces for some designs.)

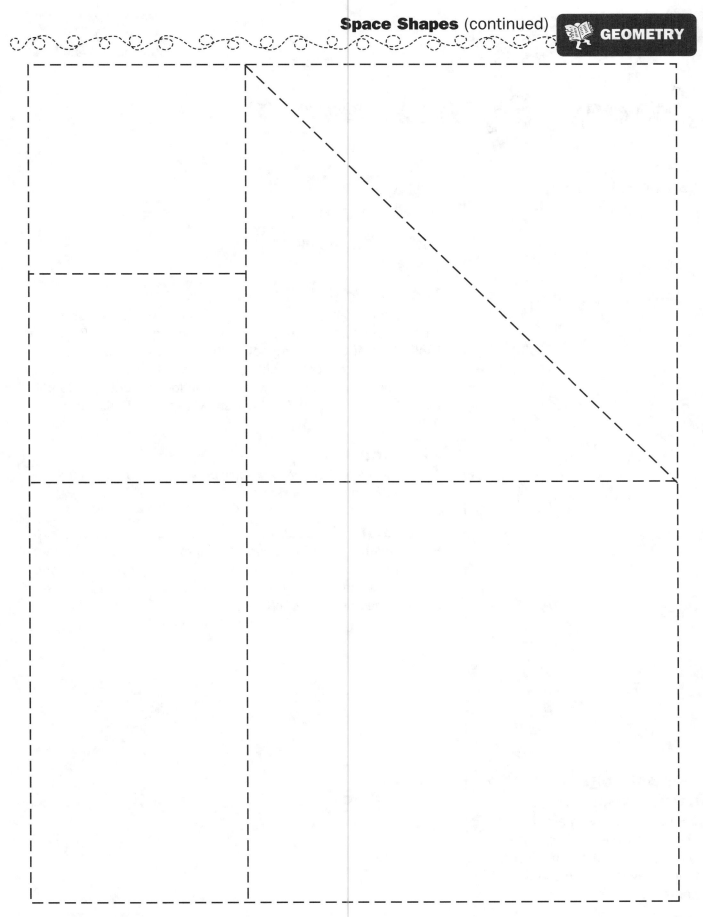

Snow Symmetry

Exploring symmetry

Aim
Students make paper snowflakes to learn about symmetry.

Before the Activity
Copy and distribute page 55.

During the Activity
As students read the directions and look at the pictures, be sure they understand that a line of symmetry is like a fold. Explain that if they fold something that is symmetrical along its line of symmetry, its two sides will match up exactly.

As they make their snowflakes, caution students not to cut too much off of the fold or their snowflakes will easily fall apart.

After the Activity
Ask: *How many lines of symmetry do you think a snowflake can have? Why do you think so?*

Extension
Have students draw four animals, plants, places, or things that have at least one line of symmetry. Then challenge students to draw things that have more than one line of symmetry. Display the drawings on a bulletin board.

ANSWERS
BRAIN POWER: Yes. The number of lines of symmetry in snowflakes that students make will depend on the number of times they fold the piece of paper.

Snow Symmetry

It's a fact: no two snowflakes are exactly alike. And here's another fact: snowflakes that you can make have lines of **symmetry** (SIM-uh-tree). That means that if you draw a line down the middle of a snowflake, the parts of the snowflake on each side of the line will look exactly alike.

Lots of things have lines of symmetry. Look around you. Can you find any?

Not everything has a line of symmetry!

Some things, like snowflakes, have more than one line of symmetry.

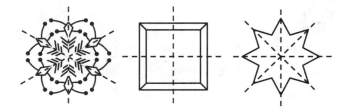

You might not be able to find a real snowflake right now. But you can make your own—as long as you have paper, scissors, and symmetry!

You Need:
scissors
paper

What to Do:

1. Fold a sheet of paper in half, like this:

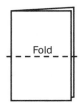

2. Cut pieces off of your paper any way you like. But don't cut too much off the fold!

3. Unfold the paper and look at it. Presto! It's a snowflake—with one line of symmetry.

4. Fold a new sheet of paper in half, then in half again, like this:

Fold

5. Cut out pieces like you did in Step 2. Unfold the paper. This time, your snowflake will have two lines of symmetry. Can you find them?

Don't stop at one snowflake—make a whole symmetry snowstorm!

> **⇒ BRAIN POWER ⇐**
> Can you make a snowflake that
> has four lines of symmetry?

The Great Big Book of Super-Fun Math Activities Scholastic Professional Books

Create a Castle

Understanding transformations: flips, slides, and turns

Spatial relations

Aim
Students flip, slide, and turn polygons to color a castle.

Before the Activity
Copy and distribute pages 57–58. Have students cut out the 5 castle flip bricks on the bottom of page 58. Then ask students to experiment to find ways they can lay each brick on the castle. Be sure students understand that they can flip and turn the bricks. Also encourage students to experiment with placing the bricks next to each other on the castle.

During the Activity
As students play their first few games, ask them to describe their thinking as they color in the shapes on the castle. Once students have played the game several times, encourage them to play without placing the flip bricks on the board. Give students several copies of the castle, so they can play several games.

Extension
Have students use graph paper to design their own castles or other shapes to use as game boards. They can test the designs by playing on the boards. After they have tested several designs, discuss what they found. Did all the game boards work? Were some boards better suited to the game than others? What traits, if any, did the best game boards share?

Create a Castle

You Need:
Castle Flip bricks
scissors
paper clip
crayon

Object:
To color more of the castle than the other player.

Number of Players: 2

To Play:

▶ Cut out the Castle Flip bricks.

▶ Make a spinner using a pencil, a paper clip, and the shape wheel. (See the picture near the wheel.)

▶ Each player chooses half the castle and plays only on that half.

▶ Decide who will go first.

▶ Each turn, spin to see what shape to color on the castle. Use Castle Flip bricks to find ways the shape fits on the castle. Remember—you can flip the shape you spin...or turn it!

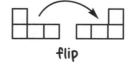
flip

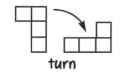
turn

▶ When you can't color a shape that you spin, you're out of the game. The game is over when both players are out.

▶ The player who colors more of the castle wins.

▶ Ready to play again? Ask your teacher for another game board.

Trim off this strip and attach to page 58.

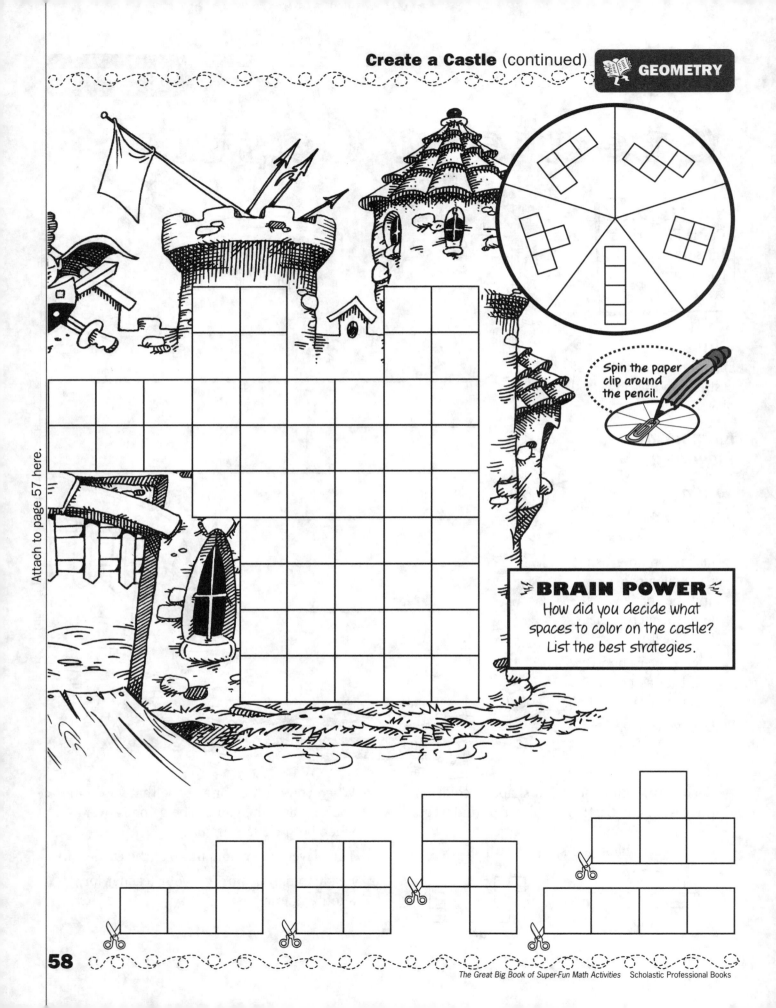

Spin the paper clip around the pencil.

Attach to page 57 here.

> **BRAIN POWER**
> How did you decide what spaces to color on the castle? List the best strategies.

 **GEOMETRY**

A Secret Garden Takes Shape

✎ **Identifying congruent shapes**

✎ **LITERATURE CONNECTION: Reading a story**

✐ Aim
Students match congruent shapes by rearranging triangular pieces to find a picture of a secret garden.

Before the Activity
Copy and distribute pages 60–61. To create a sturdier set of manipulatives, you may want to laminate the page with the triangle shapes before students cut out the puzzle pieces.

Extension 1
Read aloud Frances Hodgson Burnett's classic story *The Secret Garden* to your class. Students may also enjoy watching the video of the story.

Extension 2
Marilyn Burns's *Math and Literature* (Sausalito, CA: Math Solutions Publications, 1992) contains many ideas for incorporating children's books into math class.

🔑 ANSWERS
Here is the finished puzzle:

A Secret Garden Takes Shape

In the book *The Secret Garden* by Frances Hodgson Burnett, a robin helps a girl named Mary find the key to a hidden garden. In this version of the story, Mary finds that geometry is the "key" to unlocking a garden puzzle.

It's a beautiful spring day. Mary is following the song of the little robin. She finds herself standing in the middle of a puzzle of triangle-shaped pieces. Mary looks down at the confusing sight. "This is no place to play," she thinks. Just as Mary is about to leave, the robin speaks. "Stay and play and you will not be sorry. If you can find the right pattern, you will make the garden of your dreams."

Mary looks closely at the puzzle. There are three figures in each piece. She arranges some of the pieces so that the figures that are the same size and shape lie next to each other. The robin chirps, "Very good, Mary! Now you know that the key to unlocking this puzzle is by matching congruent figures!"

"What are congruent figures?" Mary asks.

"Why, they are geometric figures that are exactly the same size and shape," the robin tells her. "When all of the congruent figures are touching, your secret garden will appear. Good luck!"

What to Do:

▶ Cut out the puzzle pieces.

▶ Arrange the pieces so that the congruent figures face each other. (Some of the figures will not have a match.)

▶ When you are done, you will find just what a splendid garden you and Mary have made!

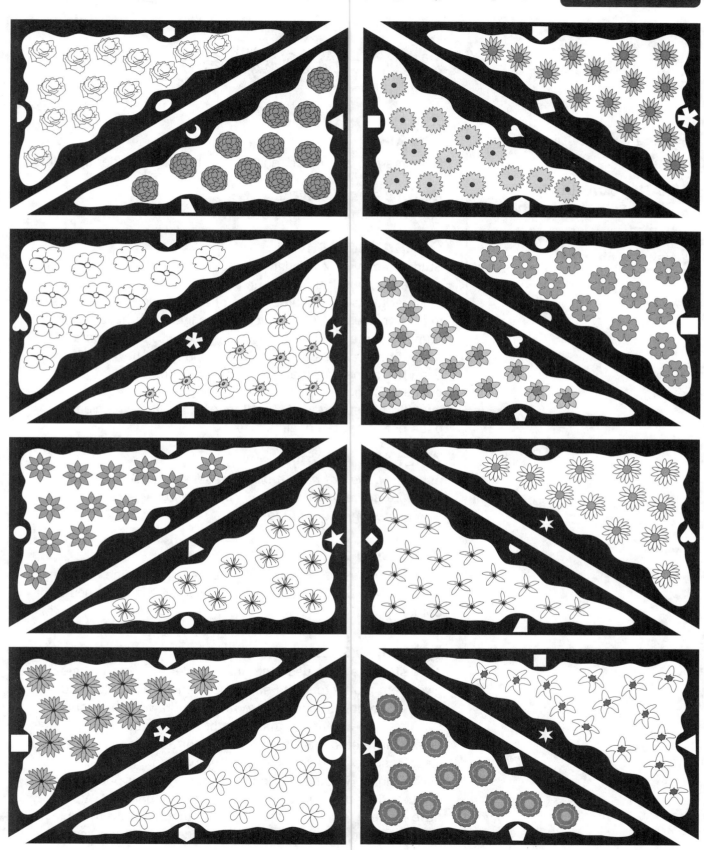

What's Your Angle?

✎ **Using a model to classify angles**

✎ **MATH VOCABULARY: Right, acute, and obtuse angles**

✎ **Using a chart**

✐ Aim
Students find and model angles with the Angle Finder diagram.

Before the Activity
Copy and distribute pages 63–64.

During the Activity
Students can work through this activity individually or in groups of three or four. If they work in groups, be sure each group member looks for all three types of angles. On stairs, tables, or in other places, students might find angles that have slightly rounded corners. Have students bend their pipe cleaners to match these angles as well as they can. Then have them re-bend the corners of their pipe cleaners to make them more pointed. Encourage students to use pipe cleaners of different lengths to test and verify that the length of the pipe cleaner does not affect the angle's size.

After the Activity
Ask: *If you did not have a pipe cleaner and an Angle Finder, what are some other ways you could decide whether an angle was acute, right, or obtuse?*

Extension 1
Copy and distribute page 65. Students can examine each angle in the letters MATH and determine whether it is right, acute, or obtuse.

Extension 2
After students have used the Angle Finder to classify angles, give them protractors and show them where 90° is located. Show them how to use the protractor to draw and measure a 90° angle and point out that all right angles measure 90°. Finally, have students use the protractor as an angle finder to classify some angles modeled with pipe cleaners. Students should notice whether angles are acute, right, or obtuse, and whether their measures are greater or less than 90°. After they have made a few comparisons, have students write to explain what acute angles have in common and what obtuse angles have in common.

What's Your Angle?

> An **acute** angle is narrower than a right angle.

> A **right** angle looks like the corner of a square or rectangle.

> An **obtuse** angle is wider than a right angle.

Don't look now, but you may be sitting on an angle! An angle is formed where two lines meet at a point. The place where the back of your chair meets the seat of your chair makes an angle. Are you wearing jeans? The corners of your back pockets form angles. Are your arms or legs bent? They make angles, too!

There are three types of angles—**right, acute,** and **obtuse.**

RIGHT   ACUTE   OBTUSE

You can find angles just about anywhere! They're in the edges of a table, the letters of the alphabet, the hands of a clock.

Hunt for some angles in your classroom. Then follow the directions to find out what kind of angle each one is.

You Need:

pipe cleaner

What to Do:

1. Use the pipe cleaner to match the angles in your classroom. When you find an angle, bend the pipe cleaner to match it.

2. Hold the bent pipe cleaner up to the Angle Finder. It will tell you which kind of angle you've found. (It doesn't matter how long or short your pipe cleaner is— the angle will be the same.)

3. As you find each type of angle, list it on the Angle Chart. (We listed a few to get you started.) Then straighten out the pipe cleaner and start again.

Here's how to use the angle finder.

ANGLE FINDER

RIGHT

ACUTE

OBTUSE

Place the left side of your angle along this side.

Put the corner of your pipe cleaner on the dot.

Angle Chart

RIGHT	ACUTE	OBTUSE
Corner of my notebook	Space between my fingers	Clock hands at 10:30

Angles from A to Z

Angles are hiding everywhere—even in the words you're reading now. When two straight lines meet, they make an angle. There are three kinds of angles:

- The corner of a square or rectangle makes a **right angle.**

- Angles that are **smaller** than right angles are called **acute angles.**

- Angles that are **larger** than right angles are called **obtuse angles.**

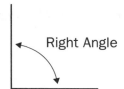
Right Angle

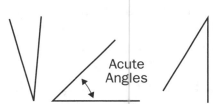
Acute Angles

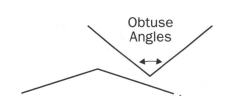
Obtuse Angles

Take a look at the letters below. Circle each angle you see in the letters.
Tell whether it is right, acute, or obtuse.

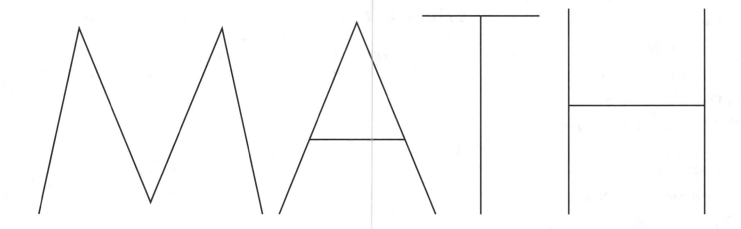

The Great Big Book of Super-Fun Math Activities Scholastic Professional Books

 **GEOMETRY**

Coordinate Carnival

✎ **Using coordinate graphing**

✎ **Following directions**

✎ **SOCIAL STUDIES CONNECTION: Map reading**

🔑 ANSWERS

Here is the order in which Rowena visited the attractions, starting at the Lost and Found:

First: Blubber Burgers

Second: Bobsled Blast Off

Third: Six Story Ski Jump

Fourth: Rinky Dink Ice Rink

Fifth: Cave of the Abominable Snowman

Sixth: Garden of Ice

Seventh: Hot Chocolate stand

Where's Rowena's lost puppy? She's behind the Hot Chocolate stand, fast asleep!

⟜ Aim

Students follow coordinates to locate a lost puppy on the grounds of a winter carnival.

Before the Activity

Copy and distribute pages 67–68. Review the information in How to Follow Coordinates with the class. Stress that following the order of the two numbers in each pair is very important. The first number tells how far to move horizontally across the grid from zero. The second number tells how far to move vertically up the grid from zero.

During the Activity

If students follow two coordinates and find themselves in a location that is a blank space, they may have followed the coordinates in the wrong order. Ask them to retrace their routes until they land on an attraction.

Extension 1

Let class members extend their coordinate-reading skills to real maps. Using a map from a road atlas or world atlas, give students a list of coordinates and ask them to find the towns or countries they describe, or name locations on the maps and ask students to tell you their coordinates.

Extension 2

Have students draw their own maps with coordinates and write about an imaginary journey to that city, country, or world. (Don't forget that other planets and solar systems need maps, too!)

Coordinate Carnival

There Rowena was, having lots of fun at the winter carnival. She was carefully keeping an eye on her pet puppy, Bowser. (She's full of mischief!) But then she turned around, and Bowser was gone!

Luckily the carnival grounds are marked in coordinates. Coordinates are pairs of numbers that describe a certain point on a grid. And Rowena will need them to find her pet puppy.

Read about using coordinates. Then meet Rowena at the Lost and Found. Help her follow the carnival workers' clues to find her lost puppy. Where did Bowser go...

...first? _____

...second? _____

...third? _____

...fourth? _____

...fifth? _____

...sixth? _____

...seventh? _____

Where's the puppy? _____

How to Follow Coordinates:

Coordinates are pairs of numbers, like 1 and 4. They are written inside parentheses, like this: (1,4). Say you want to go to the coordinates (3,2). Start at 0 on the coordinate grid. The first number in the coordinate tells you how many spaces to go across the grid. The second number tells you how many spaces to go up. So (3,2) tells you to across 3, then up 2. You should see a snowman.

Trim off this strip and attach to page 68.

Constellation Coordinates

 **Using coordinate graphing**

SCIENCE CONNECTION: Astronomy

ANSWERS

Here are the plotted stars and their conventional connections. Accept any method of connection, as long as the points are located correctly.

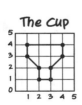

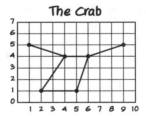

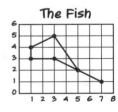

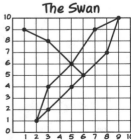

Aim

Students graph coordinates to plot the stars in four constellations.

Before the Activity

Copy and distribute pages 70–71.

During the Activity

Make sure that students are graphing the coordinates in the correct order (across, then up). Encourage them to connect their stars in any way they wish. Students may also want to include heads, eyes, and other details for each of the animal constellations in order to make the pictures complete.

Extension 1

Tell students that Native American, Chinese, Indian, and Egyptian people all saw different pictures in some of the same constellations and gave them different names. Have students suppose that they were the first people to notice the constellations they graphed in the activity. Ask students to invent a different animal, person, or object for each constellation and draw pictures that show what they see in each one.

Extension 2

Make up blank grids, numbered across the bottom and left side, for the class. Have each student draw his or her own constellation and list its coordinates on a separate piece of paper. Then ask each student to give the list to a classmate to graph and challenge the classmate to find the hidden picture.

 **GEOMETRY**

Constellation Coordinates

What do you see when you look at the night sky? The same stars people have looked at for thousands of years! There are millions of stars. But some groups of stars seem to form pictures in the sky. Those groups are called **constellations** (KON-stuh-LAY-shuns).

One constellation looks like this:

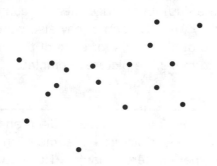

Long ago, people in Greece and Rome imagined that those stars were connected, like this:

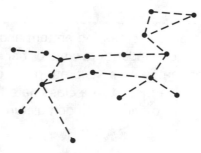

They called the constellation "The Big Dog." They named other constellations after people, animals, and objects. Today, we find many constellations by looking for the shapes the ancient Greeks and Romans found. You can use math to see some of them.

What to Do:

▶ Under each grid is the name of a constellation. Each pair of numbers under the name stands for one star in that constellation. The numbers are called **coordinates**.

▶ The first number in each pair tells you how many numbers to go across from left to right on the grid. The second number tells you how many numbers to go up. The first pair of coordinates under The Crab, (1,5), tells you to go across 1, then up 5. We put a point on the grid to represent that star for you.

▶ Make a point on the grid for each pair of coordinates. After you find each star using the coordinates, draw a point on the grid and cross off those coordinates. When you finish, connect the points to make a picture of the constellation.

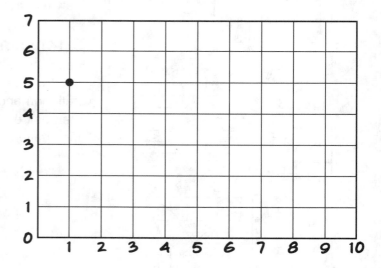

The Crab
(1,5) (4,4) (9,5) (5,1) (6,4) (2,1)

 **GEOMETRY**

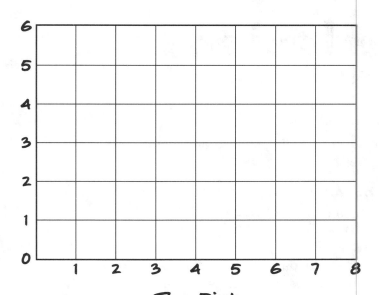

The Fish

(1,3) (3,3) (5,2) (7,1) (3,5) (1,4)

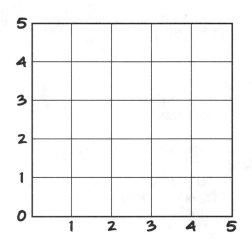

The Cup

(1,4) (1,3) (4,4) (2,2)
(2,1) (3,1) (3,2) (4,3)

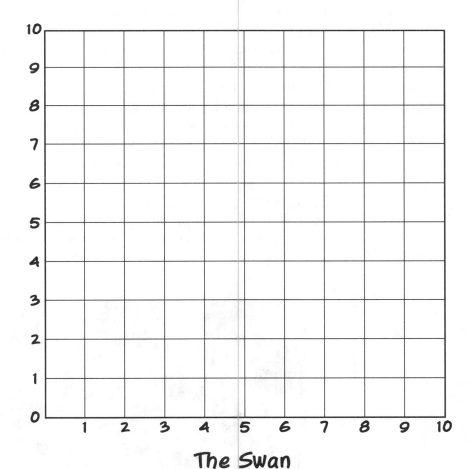

The Swan

(3,4) (3,8) (9,10) (6,5) (1,9) (5,6) (8,7) (5,4) (7,9) (3,2) (2,1)

Terrific Tessellations

- **Understanding tessellations**
- **Exploring area**
- **CURRICULUM CONNECTION: Art**

Aim

Students create tessellating shapes and then trace their shapes to cover a piece of paper.

Before the Activity

Copy and distribute pages 73–74.

During the Activity

When making tessellations, students can cut more than one simple shape from sides A and C, as long as they correctly slide the shapes to the opposite side of the square.

After the Activity

Ask students: *Where have you seen tessellating shapes? How were they used? Do you think your tessellations could be used in the same way? Why or why not?*

Extension 1

Have students trace some regular polygons or use pattern blocks to find out which tessellate and which do not. Then have students cut and paste shapes from one of the tessellating polygons to make their own tessellations.

Extension 2

Show students some of the works of the artist M. C. Escher. Invite them to discuss the art, then encourage them to try their own "Escher" tessellations.

Terrific Tessellations

What do math and art have in common?
Everything—if you're making tessellations!

A **tessellation** (tess-uh-LAY-shun) is a design made of shapes that fit together like puzzle pieces. People use tessellations to decorate walls and floors, and even works of art.

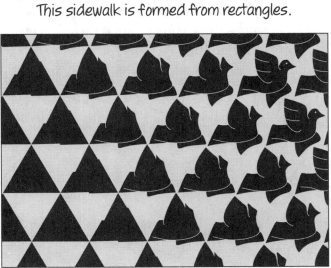

This sidewalk is formed from rectangles.

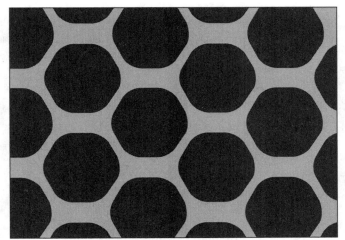

Hexagons form this beehive.

Here is a tessellation made from more than one shape.

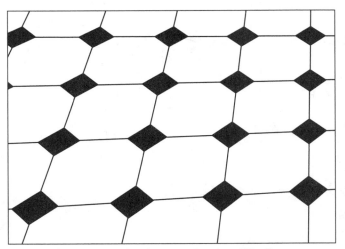

Squares and octagons form a tile floor.

You Need:
heavy paper
scissors
tape
crayons

What to Do:

Here's how you can make your own tessellation.

1. Start with a simple shape like a square. (Cut your shape from the heavy paper). Cut a piece out of side A . . .

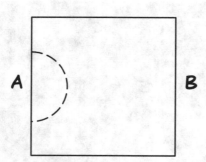

2. . . . and slide it over to side B. Make sure it lines up evenly with the cut out side, or your tessellation won't work. Tape it in place on side B.

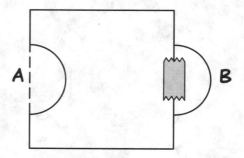

3. If you like, do the same thing with sides C and D. Now you have a new shape.

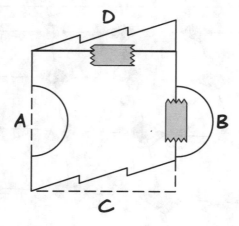

4. Trace your new shape on paper. Then slide the shape so it fits together with the one you just traced. Trace it again. Keep on sliding and tracing until your page is filled. Decorate your tessellation.

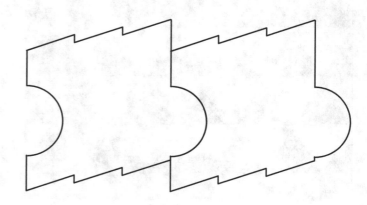

Plan a Party Play

Estimating quantity

Whole-number multiplication

ANSWERS

Estimates and strategies will vary. A range of estimates and a possible strategy is given for each item. Ask students to justify their answers.

1. 25–45 cans. Most of the 25 guests will want one can and some guests will want more than one.
2. 25–45 slices
3. 4–6 bags of chips. 1 bag should serve about 5 people, so at least 5 bags would be needed.
4. 25–40 sandwiches. Each guest can have at least 1 sandwich and some can have 2.
5. 50 or more plates. Each guest may use at least 2 plates.
6. 50 cupcakes. Each guest will have 2 cupcakes.

When to Estimate
1. Exact Answer 2. Estimate
3. Exact Answer 4. Estimate
5. Estimate 6. Exact Answer
7. Estimate 8. Exact Answer

How Would You Estimate...
Answers will vary. Ask students to explain their estimation method in their writing.

Aim
Students read a play about estimation. They use estimation to plan what to buy for a party of their own.

Before the Activity
Copy and distribute page 76.

During the Activity
Suggest that students write a number sentence to show how Sleeve estimated the amount of cheese Moldo needed to buy. Point out that although Moldo's guests might eat a little less or a little more cheese than Sleeve estimated, 40 pieces is a good estimate.

After the Activity
Ask: *What estimation strategy would you use to make sure there was definitely enough of any item for all of your guests?*

Extension 1
Have students work in groups to compare and discuss their answers to the activity. Then have group members decide which estimation strategies, among all those the group used, they preferred. After they have decided, bring the class together and have each group present their favorite strategies for one or two items on the list.

Extension 2
Copy and distribute the follow-up estimation activity sheet on page 77. Have students complete the activities and then discuss their answers.

Extension 3
As an extension for When to Estimate, ask students to think of situations for each question that would require an estimate and an exact answer.

Name _____

Plan a Party Play

Characters

Sleeve Circle, a teenage boy
Adora, Sleeve's neighbor
Moldo, the kids' friend
Carl, Adora's father, a police officer

The scene: Sleeve and Adora are behind the counter at Big Sal's Cheese-O-Rama. Moldo enters the store.

Sleeve: I can't believe it! I'm surrounded by cheese! And I'm working beside my darling Adora! It must be a dream. Pinch me, Adora.

Adora: No thanks, Sleeve. Why don't we help our customer?

Sleeve: No sweat, my pet. How can we help our customer?

Moldo: I need some cheese for my party. I think I need 4,000 pieces. Or maybe 12 pieces. Or 300. I just can't figure it out.

Sleeve: Never fear, Moldo. I think our old friend estimation can help you.

Moldo: How? Does she work here too?

Adora: No, Moldo. Estimation is the kind of math to use when you're not looking for an exact answer. For example, you don't need to know the exact amount of cheese for the party. You need a good guess. And that's an estimate.

Sleeve: How many guests did you invite, Moldo?

Moldo: Ten.

Adora: And about how many pieces of cheese do you think each guest will eat?

Moldo: About four, I guess.

Sleeve: Okay. Since each person will eat about four pieces of cheese, we'll multiply 10 times four. So you'll need 40 pieces. See? It's cheesy–uh, easy!

Moldo: But what if somebody can't come? Or someone's allergic to cheese?

Sleeve: Calm down, Moldster. Your estimate isn't exact. But it gives you a pretty good idea.

Adora: Right! If you estimate, you won't get way too much cheese—or way too little. *(Carl enters the store.)*

Adora: Dad, what are you doing here?

Carl: There's a cheese bandit in the area, and I'm trying to catch him.

Sleeve: No problemo, big guy. If we see him, we'll call 1-800-KITTENS. *(Sleeve practices the chop. He knocks over a giant cheese display. Cheese flies everywhere.)*

What to Do:

You're having a party. You've invited 10 adults and 15 kids. Use estimation to decide how much of each item to buy. On another piece of paper, write about how you figured each estimate.

1. Cans of soda _____

2. Slices of pizza _____

3. Bags of chips _____

4. Peanut butter and
   jelly sandwiches _____

5. Plates _____

6. Cupcakes _____

Name _____

When to Estimate

Estimation is a great way to solve many problems.
But some problems need an exact answer. How can you decide?

Read each question below. Think about what kind of answer you need.
Then circle Estimate or Exact Answer.

1. How much sugar do you need to make cookies?   **Estimate**   **Exact Answer**

2. How much money could your school play earn?   **Estimate**   **Exact Answer**

3. How many plates will you need to serve dinner?   **Estimate**   **Exact Answer**

4. How much money will three new tapes cost?   **Estimate**   **Exact Answer**

5. How long will it take to get to the airport?   **Estimate**   **Exact Answer**

6. How much money is in a bank account?   **Estimate**   **Exact Answer**

7. How long would it take you to run a mile?   **Estimate**   **Exact Answer**

8. How many kids are in your class?   **Estimate**   **Exact Answer**

How Would You Estimate...

On another sheet of paper, write about how you would estimate each of these.

...the height of a tree?

...how long it would take to walk from Miami to Seattle?

...how much water you use in a year?

...the number of gumballs in a gumball machine?

...the number of students in your school?

...how much one million pennies would weigh?

Busy as Beavers with Estimation

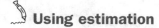 **Using estimation**

Aim

Students learn how to use estimation strategies and multiplication to keep track of the beaver population.

Before the Activity

Copy and distribute page 79. Talk with students about the reasons a wildlife worker would use estimation to count animals. Ask: *Why might it be difficult to get an exact count of the beavers in a particular area?* Also discuss why the state might want to know the number of beavers living there. (Overpopulation or underpopulation could cause damage to the environment, food chain.)

After the Activity

This article mentions that Gordon and his crew estimated that there were about 81,000 beavers in New York State in 1995. Ask students to figure out about how many beaver lodges that might be. (16,200 lodges)

Extension 1

Students can practice their estimation skills by estimating how many students are in your school. Start with an estimate of about how many students are in a classroom. Determine how many classrooms are in your school and multiply the two figures. After students have come up with an estimate, find out the actual number and see how close they were!

Extension 2

If students would like more information on beavers, we recommend *Busy Beavers* by M. Barbara Brownell (Washington, DC: National Geographic Society, 1988) and *The Beaver* by Margaret Lane (New York: Dial Books, 1982).

ANSWERS

1. 3 lodges × 5 beavers = 15 estimated number of beavers

2. 100 beavers

3a. 6 lodges × 5 beavers = 30 estimated number of beavers.

b. 8 lodges × 5 beavers = 40 estimated number of beavers

c. 70 beavers

4. 7 lodges

BRAIN POWER: Answers will vary. One method would be to multiply the estimated number of people living in each home by the number of houses or apartments on the street.

Name _____

Busy as Beavers with Estimation

Use estimation to count our furry friends!

Does your teacher keep you as busy as a beaver? Well, if you worked for the New York State Department of Fish and Wildlife, part of your job might be to count the beaver population in the state. In 1995, wildlife conservationist Gordon Batcheller and his crew counted more than 81,000 beavers in New York! Can you imagine counting all of those fuzzy little heads one by one? Neither could Gordon. That's why he made an estimate. An estimate is a number close to the number you're looking for. It's like making a really good guess.

To make a good estimate of the number of beavers in the state, Gordon went up in an airplane and took pictures of the beavers' homes, called lodges. Gordon estimated that 5 beavers live in each lodge he counted.

> ### Estimating Beavers
> number of lodges × 5 beavers = estimated number of beavers

Now it's your turn to count critters! Find some beaver estimates in these problems!

What to Do:
Use the information in the box to answer the questions.

1. One day, while flying over a lake in New York, you count 3 beaver lodges. Fill in the blanks:

   _____ lodges × _____ beavers =

   _____ estimated number of beavers

2. Now you find the beavers' favorite stream. You count 20 lodges! What is the estimated number of beavers living in the stream?

   _____

3. You fly over a pond and a stream. In the pond, you count 6 lodges. In the stream, you count 8 lodges. Fill in the blanks:

   a. POND: _____ lodges × _____ beavers =

   _____ estimated number of beavers

   b. STREAM: _____ lodges × _____ beavers =

   _____ estimated number of beavers

   c. What is the total estimated number of beavers in the pond and the stream?

   _____

4. If Gordon estimated that 35 beavers live in one river, how many lodges did he count in that river?

   _____

....
⇒ BRAIN POWER ⇐
How many people would you estimate live in each home in your neighborhood? Using this number, how would you estimate the number of people living on your street? Try out your method.
....

Oh! Let's Estimate!

✎ **Using an estimation strategy: start with a known quantity**

🗝 ANSWERS

These are two estimates that we felt were reasonable.

There are 250 oat rings in an 8-ounce cup and 15 cups in a 10-ounce box, for a total of about 250 × 15, or 3,750 oat rings in a 10-ounce box.

There are about 15 oat rings in 1 gram. Since our box holds 283 grams of oat rings, there are about 15 × 283, or 4,245 in the box.

Averaging the estimates, there are about 4,000 oat rings in a 10-ounce box.

BRAIN POWER:

1. Answers will vary. One way is to measure how far a small part of the box stretches and to estimate how many of those small parts are in the whole box.

2. Answers will vary. One way would be to weigh the contents of a smaller sample, such as 100 oat rings, and then use the weight of the entire box. Using a proportion:

$$\frac{100}{\text{Weight of 100}} = \frac{x}{\text{Weight of entire box}}$$

🖋 Aim

Students develop estimation skills as they estimate the number of oat rings in a box of Cheerios.

Before the Activity

Copy and distribute page 81. Do this activity with the whole class or have students work in groups of three or four. Begin by telling students that in this activity they will be estimating about how many oat rings will fit in a small container and using what they learn to estimate the number of oat rings in a whole box.

During the Activity

Throughout the activity, students are asked to revise their estimates. Each time they do so, encourage them to discuss their reasoning.

Students' estimates will vary according to the sizes of the cup and box of Cheerios, and the estimation methods they use. How close their final estimates come to the actual number of oat rings is less important than whether they are able to improve their estimates from the beginning of the activity to the end. A good way to assess students' work is to see whether their estimates become more reasonable as the activity progresses.

After the Activity

Ask: *How did placing 50 and 100 Cheerios next to your cup help you to make a better estimate of the number of Cheerios in your cup? How does having a good idea of how many Cheerios are in a cup help you to estimate the number of Cheerios in a box?*

Oh! Let's Estimate!

Did you ever wonder how many oat rings are in a box of Cheerios? Counting a whole box of Cheerios would take a long time. Instead, estimate. You'll find out about how many are in a box. And you won't waste oodles of hours counting little Os.

> **You Need:**
> box of Cheerios (or counters or beans)
> clear plastic cup
> very large jar, big enough to hold all the Cheerios

First Look at a Small Part

1. About how many Cheerios will fit in your cup?

Guess: _____

2. Fill the cup with Cheerios. Look at it carefully. About how many Cheerios do you think are in the cup?

Estimate: _____

Explain: Did you change your first guess? Why or why not?

_____

_____

3. Count out 50 Cheerios from the box. Put them in a pile next to the cup. (Decide what you're going to do with the broken ones. Don't eat them!)

• Are there more or fewer than 50 Cheerios in the cup? A lot more or only a few more?

_____

• Now how many Cheerios do you think are in the cup?

New estimate: _____

Explain: How did you decide on your new estimate?

_____

_____

4. Count out 100 Cheerios. Put them next to the cup. Now how many Cheerios do you think are in the cup?

New estimate: _____

Now Get the Box of Cheerios

Pour all the Cheerios into the large jar. About how many cupfuls of Cheerios are in the box?

Estimate: _____

Use your earlier estimates to find out about how many Cheerios are in the box.

Estimate for all the Cheerios in the box: _____

> ### ⋟ BRAIN POWER ⋞
> 1. How far would the Cheerios stretch in a line? How could you find out? Try it!
> 2. What else could you do to find out about how many Cheerios are in the box?

Do the Spaghetti Stretch

- **Estimating length**

- **Whole number addition and subtraction**

- **LANGUAGE ARTS CONNECTION: Writing in math**

ANSWERS

4. Answers will vary. Sample answers: length of one piece + length of one piece + length of one piece (and so on) = length of a bunch, or, length of one piece × number of pieces in bunch = length of bunch.

5. Answers will vary. Students could count the groups of bunches that are the same size as their bunch, or find how many bunches are in half of the box and multiply that number by 2.

6. Answers will vary. Sample equations: length of bunch × number of bunches in box = total length of spaghetti. Or, length of one piece × number of pieces in bunch × number of bunches in box = total length.

BRAIN POWER: Answers will vary. Students could cook several pieces of spaghetti and compare their lengths to uncooked pieces.

Aim

Students develop estimation skills as they find the length of all the pieces in an entire box of spaghetti.

Before the Activity

Copy and distribute page 83. To help students think about the length of the distance they will be measuring, lead a class discussion about the tools used to measure length. Then ask students if it would be practical to use any of those tools to measure the length of the spaghetti. Discuss the benefits of estimating the length of the spaghetti versus measuring each piece (saves time, not necessary to get an exact number).

During the Activity

Students can complete this activity individually or in groups of three or four. If they work in small groups, have them discuss each question before they answer it. This will be particularly helpful for Question 3, in which the choice of the piece measured will affect the final estimate. Group members may be able to arrive at an agreement that the piece they measure should be of an average length.

Students can measure their spaghetti pieces to the nearest whole, half, or quarter inch or centimeter. Because they will need to compute with these units, you may want to review how to add and/or multiply with fractions or decimals.

For Questions 4 and 6, it may be necessary to review the meaning of the word *equation*. Tell students that they should use words to write a math sentence that tells how to find the answers. Have students rename their final estimates from smaller units (inches/centimeters) to larger units (feet or yards/meters).

After the Activity

Once students have made an estimate, they can show (using a yardstick or paces) how far their box of spaghetti could stretch (down the hall, to the next classroom, outside).

Name _____

Do the Spaghetti Stretch

How far can you go with a box of spaghetti? Estimate!

It's spaghetti day in the lunchroom again. Spaghetti is fun to eat. But did you ever wonder how far all that spaghetti would stretch if it was in one long line? Where would it end up? Perhaps it would stretch to the principal's office. Maybe it would make a line to the ball field. It might even stretch all the way around your school!

It would take a long time to line up and measure all that spaghetti. And what a mess! There must be a better way . . .

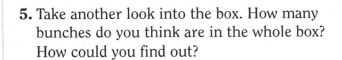

You Need:
16-oz (453-g) box of uncooked spaghetti
ruler

What to Do:

1. Look into your box of spaghetti. Then look at your ruler. Take a guess—how many feet or meters do you think all of the spaghetti would stretch?

   My guess: _____

2. Here's one way to estimate the distance. Grab a small bunch of spaghetti pieces out of the box. How many pieces are in the bunch?

   _____

3. Measure one spaghetti piece with your ruler. How long is it?

   _____

4. Write an equation that would help you figure out how far your bunch would stretch. Then solve the equation.

   _____

   _____

5. Take another look into the box. How many bunches do you think are in the whole box? How could you find out?

   _____

   _____

6. Write an equation that would help you figure out how far all the spaghetti pieces in the box would stretch. Solve the equation, and write your estimate below. Then compare it to your guess.

   My estimate: _____

   How far would your spaghetti stretch?

   _____

7. On a separate piece of paper, write a story about estimating spaghetti. What will the story's title be?

   _____

> **BRAIN POWER**
> Would your estimate change if the spaghetti were cooked? How?

How Do You Measure Up?

Understanding measurement

LANGUAGE ARTS CONNECTION: Writing in math

Aim
Students measure height, length, and distance using nonstandard units of measurement.

Before the Activity
Copy and distribute page 85. Review standard units of measurement. Have students name some tools that are used to measure length, height, and distance. (ruler, yardstick, meterstick, tape measure)

During the Activity
As students work through the steps of the activity, help them to understand why it can be difficult to measure short distances with long units. Have them measure a pencil with a hop or with a shoelace and then try to explain how long the pencil is. (Some students may use fractions: $\frac{1}{2}$ of a shoelace. Others might say "part of a shoelace" or "less than one hop.") Explain that while they can use long units to measure short distances, shorter units will give answers that are easier to work with.

After the Activity
Ask students which units were easy to work with. Encourage them to tell why. Then ask: *Suppose you wanted to tell someone exactly how long to draw a line. What unit would you use to tell them. Why?*

Extension

Discuss with students the need for standardized units of measurement, based on the activity. The long-ago units mentioned in Brain Power became common units, but the original system was not very successful because people come in different sizes. A "five-foot" length of rope could be a different length for each person who measured it. Eventually, each unit was standardized, so a "foot" became the same length for everyone who used it.

 **ANSWERS**

Answers will vary.

BRAIN POWER: Answers will vary.

How Do You Measure Up?

You can't believe it. You've just kicked your soccer ball farther than ever before. You can't wait to tell your friends how far it went. But hold on—you don't have anything to measure with. Or do you?

Search your pockets, look around. A stick of chewing gum, a shoelace, even a cartwheel can all be units of measurement. A unit of measurement helps you answer questions like, "How tall?" "How far?" "How heavy?"

Use something you have to measure with. Then you can tell your friends that you kicked the ball 30 shoelaces or 10 cartwheels.

What to Do:

1. Measure someone's height. Pick a unit you could use. (Don't use a ruler!)

   My unit: _____

2. Measure a friend's height with your unit.

   How many units tall is your friend? _____

3. Can you use your unit to measure the length of a pencil? Or do you need to use a new unit? Measure the pencil.

   What was your unit? _____

   How many units long is the pencil? _____

4. Use one of your units or pick a new unit to measure the distance across your classroom.

   What was your unit? _____

   How many units across is the classroom?

   _____

⇝ BRAIN POWER ⇜

1. What else you could measure with each of your units?

2. Some of the units we measure with today came from everyday life.

   • An **inch** came from the width of a person's thumb.

   • A **foot** came from the length of a person's foot.

   • A **yard** was the distance from the nose to the longest fingertip on one outstretched arm.

   • A **mile** was the length of 2,000 of a soldier's steps.

3. What problems might those original units have caused? Why do you think rulers with standard measurements are used today?

Wild West Measurement Roundup!

Estimating height, distance, weight, time

LANGUAGE ARTS CONNECTION: Research skills

ANSWERS

1. blue whale; 200,000 to 500,000 pounds or 100,000 to 250,000 kilograms
2. about 1 mile; 5,280 feet or 1610 meters
3. Candlestick Park, built in 1960; 400 feet at centerfield
4. Possible answers: paper clip, rubber band, stamps, candy
5. 2:00 P.M. in New York; 7:00 P.M. in London; 4:00 A.M. the next day in Tokyo
6. A ten-gallon hat holds about one gallon. Some experts say the name comes from the Spanish word for braid, *galón*. (Some ten-gallon hats were decorated with a braid.) It may have been named to poke fun at the hat's large size.
7. Divide the height of the Space Needle, 605 feet, by the total height of your class.
8. 8 to 14 days. It's about 800 miles from Dallas to Cheyenne. Students should support their estimates.
9. Bar graphs should reflect correct class information.
10. A fathom is 6 feet long; a rod is $16\frac{1}{2}$ feet long; a furlong is 660 feet long.

Aim

Students research measurement history and solve measurement problems as they participate in a scavenger hunt with a Western theme.

Before the Activity

Copy and distribute page 87.

During the Activity

Students can work independently, in groups, or as a whole class to answer the questions. Some resources students might use are: an almanac, an atlas, record books, the encyclopedia, and the dictionary. It may also be helpful to consult an expert or other adult. Encourage students to list all sources used to answer each question.

Wild West Measurement Roundup!

Howdy, pardner! We know you love contests. That's why we're sending you to round up some wild and woolly measurement facts! Read through the steps carefully. Then try to find all the items. Maybe everyone in your class can work together to lasso the information.* Then challenge another class to join the measurement roundup.

What to Find:

1. What is the world's heaviest living critter? (That's an animal, in Texas talk.) How much does it weigh, in pounds and in kilograms?

_____

2. How deep is the Grand Canyon, at the deepest point, in feet and in meters?

_____

3. Which is California's oldest major league ballpark? How far would a player have to hit a ball into center field to get a home run at that park?

_____

_____

4. Rustle up three different items that each weigh about one gram. What did you find?

_____

_____

5. You live in Denver, Colorado. It's noon, and you're eating some lunch grub. What time is it for the cowpokes in New York, New York; London, England; and Tokyo, Japan?

_____

6. Can a ten-gallon hat really hold ten gallons? Why does it have that name?

_____

_____

7. What is the total height of all the kids in your class? About how many classes like yours would it take to reach the top of the Space Needle in Seattle, Washington?

_____

8. Estimate how long it would take you to walk from Dallas, Texas, to Cheyenne, Wyoming.

_____

9. On another page, create a bar graph showing how many months each member of your class has been alive.

10. Back in the old days, a cowboy or cowgirl might have used these units of measurement. Tell how many feet are in each one:

fathom _____

rod _____

furlong _____

*Be sure to list the sources (newspaper, encyclopedia, an expert, and so on) that helped you answer each question.

Zoning In on Baseball

✎ **Measuring height and length**

✏ **Aim**

Students find and measure each other's strike zones and answer questions.

Before the Activity

Copy and distribute pages 89–90.

During the Activity

To help students answer Question 2, have them measure each other's strike zones in crouched and standing positions.

After the Activity

Ask students: *How would you change the strike zone to make it easier to pitch or bat? How would you change it to make it harder?*

Extension

Here is an interesting real-life story involving the strike zone, which you may want to tell your class. We found it in the book *Baseball's Strangest Moments* by Robert Obojski (New York: Sterling Publishing Co., 1988).

> In August 1951, last-place team the St. Louis Browns were playing the Detroit Tigers. In an effort to liven up the game, Browns manager Zack Taylor sent in a new pinch hitter named Eddie Gaedel. Gaedel's height: 3 foot 7. Needless to say, Tigers pitcher Bob Cain found it difficult to strike him out!
>
> After being pitched four straight balls, Gaedel walked to first base, where he was replaced by a regular team member.
>
> The next day, the American League outlawed any such tricks for future games.

🔑 **ANSWERS**

1. Answers will vary depending on students' heights.

2. The strike zone shortens when you crouch and lengthens when you stand.

3. Answers will vary. Students may say they would rather pitch to the bigger strike zone of a taller person.

Zoning In on Baseball

The pitcher throws the baseball. Should you swing at the pitch? If the ball is in your strike zone, swing away!

Your strike zone is an area next to your body. A ball thrown there could turn into a home run. But if the ball is in your strike zone and you don't swing, you might hear the umpire say, "Strike three—you're out!"

How can you (or an umpire) tell whether a ball is in your strike zone? Your strike zone is an invisible rectangle reaching from your underarms to your knees, and across home plate. If a baseball passes through that rectangle, it's in your strike zone.

Every strike zone is shaped like a rectangle. But the strike zone's size depends on your size! Check the pictures to see why.

The strike zone starts at your underarms and goes to your knees. Every strike zone is 17 inches wide. Why? That's the width of home plate!

You Need:

yardstick or tape measure
17-inch square sheet of
    paper to be "home plate"

What to Do:

▶ First find your strike zone. Put "home plate" on the floor. Bend over it a little and pretend you're about to swing at a pitch. Use a yardstick or a plastic bat if you like.

▶ Have a friend measure the distance from your underarms to your knees while you're in your batting position. That measurement is the height of your strike zone. The width is 17 inches.

▶ Switch places with your friend and measure his or her strike zone.

Now answer these questions.

1. Is the height of your strike zone the same as or different from your friend's?

_____

2. What happens to your strike zone when you crouch lower? What happens to it when you stand up?

_____

_____

_____

3. If you were a pitcher, would you rather pitch to a tall person or a short person? Why?

_____

_____

_____

_____

On the Wagon Trail

 Estimating distance and time

SOCIAL STUDIES CONNECTIONS:
History/pioneer life
Reading a map

ANSWERS

Note: The answers should be estimates. Use the following answers only as a guide. Allow students to present different answers, and encourage them to justify their answers.

1. It would take about 133 days to travel the Oregon Trail at 15 miles a day.

2. It would take about 83 days to reach Los Angeles traveling about 12 miles a day.

3. Your family will reach Santa Fe in about 31 days. The man on horseback will reach Santa Fe in about 22 days, nine days sooner than your family.

4. Note that the Mormon and California Trails overlap for about 50 miles, making their combined length between 1,900 and 2,000 miles. At 16 miles a day, the trip would take about 122 days. You would reach Sacramento around July 1.

Aim

Students discover different ways to estimate distance and time while reading about the American pioneer era.

Before the Activity

Discuss the hardships and challenges faced by the pioneers. Have students talk about what it might have been like to be a family traveling by wagon across the American West in the 1800s. Ask: *In what ways might your life have been different from your life now? In what ways might it have been the same?*

Copy and distribute pages 92–93. Point out that this activity will focus on estimation. Ask students to think about why estimation would have been so important to the pioneers while they were traveling. You may want to explain that the pioneers faced a difficult trip west, braving rough roads, hunger, disease, and inclement weather. A family's estimate of how many days or months the journey would take, or how much food the wagon could carry, could literally be a life-or-death matter. (It should be noted that many pioneer families began their trips in the spring, in order to reach their destination before winter.)

During the Activity

If students are not comfortable with division yet, ask them to find different ways to answer Question 1. These could include ideas such as drawing a picture to represent groups of 15 days, counting by 15 to 2,000, etc. Then suggest that they use the most successful method to work on the other questions. Remind students that once they have arrived at an estimate, they may want to add some extra time to allow for the difficulties mentioned above.

Extension _____

For more information about pioneer life: *Patty Reed's Doll: The Story of the Donner Party* by Rachel K. Laurgaard (Fairfield, CA: Tomato Enterprises, 1989; 707-426-3970), and the Little House series by Laura Ingalls Wilder. If your school uses Macintosh computers, try out the software program "The Oregon Trail" (MECC).

On the Wagon Trail

You're traveling with your parents on a long, dusty road. You're tired and hungry. You ask, "Are we there yet?" Mom says, "We'll be there in about a month, dear."

A month! Why is this trip taking so long? Because the year is 1850 and your family is crossing America in a covered wagon. You're looking for land and a new life.

Wagon travel was hard. If your ox got sick or tired, you waited for it to get better. If it rained, you got soaked. If you came to a river, Dad drove the wagon through the water—and you swam across.

Today we can drive a car hundreds of miles in a single day. In pioneer days, people were lucky if they traveled 15 miles in a day in their wagon!

How long did those trips west take? Use the map and estimation to find out!

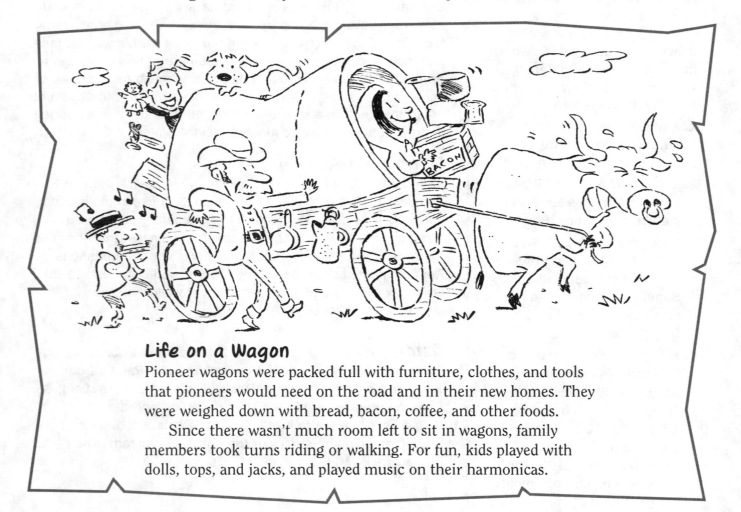

Life on a Wagon

Pioneer wagons were packed full with furniture, clothes, and tools that pioneers would need on the road and in their new homes. They were weighed down with bread, bacon, coffee, and other foods.

Since there wasn't much room left to sit in wagons, family members took turns riding or walking. For fun, kids played with dolls, tops, and jacks, and played music on their harmonicas.

ESTIMATION AND MEASUREMENT

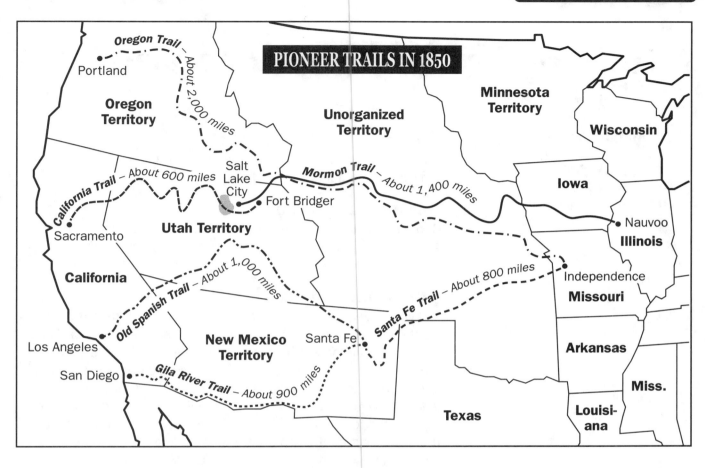

What to Do:

The map shows some of the pioneer trails in 1850. Imagine that you're a pioneer traveling by wagon. Use the map and estimation to answer each question.

1. About how many days would it take to travel the whole Oregon Trail, going about 15 miles a day?

_____

2. You're starting out in Santa Fe on the Old Spanish Trail. Crack! A wagon wheel breaks. You repair it as best you can. Your wagon can now travel only about 12 miles a day. About how long will it take you to reach Los Angeles?

_____

3. Your family is halfway through the Santa Fe Trail, traveling about 13 miles a day. A man on a horse catches up with you. He's going about 18 miles a day. Estimate how much sooner he'll reach Santa Fe than your family will.

_____

4. It's March 1, and your family is in Nauvoo, Illinois. You hope to travel 16 miles a day. On about what date will you reach Sacramento, California, using the Morman and California trails?

_____

Mushing with Measurement

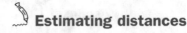 **Estimating distances**

SOCIAL STUDIES CONNECTION: Reading a map

Aim

Students use a map of the annual Alaskan Iditarod race to plan their own race schedule.

Before the Activity

Copy and distribute pages 95–96. Choose a student to locate Alaska on a map or globe and point out some of the main cities along the race route.

During the Activity

To give students a better idea of the scale of the race route, locate your hometown on a large map or in an atlas. Then find a city or a landmark that is about 100 miles away and another that is about 1,000 miles away. Use the cities or landmarks as benchmarks to help students imagine how long the race is. (Using New York as an example: "Imagine we were driving sled dogs in the Iditarod race. Every day we would travel a distance that's as long as it is from here to Philadelphia. By the end of the race, we would be as far as Disney World!")

Encourage students to round the distances on the map to estimate their travel distances. Remind them that they should not go more than 100 miles without making a stop.

After the Activity

Ask students to explain their race plans and to justify their planned rest stops.

Extension _____

Read aloud from the book *Stone Fox* by John Reynolds Gardiner (New York: Harper & Row, 1980).

ANSWERS

Answers will vary. Check that there are not more than 100 miles between rest stops.

Mushing with Measurement

Welcome to Alaska, home of the Iditarod (eye-DIT-ah-rod) Trail Sled Dog Race. In this race, people called "mushers" compete on sleds pulled by 16 dogs.

The Iditarod racers travel more than 1,000 miles across ice and snow. The record for finishing the race is 10 days and 13 hours. Some racers take almost three weeks to finish!

All of the hard work makes mushers and their dogs very hungry and tired. But putting lots of food on a sled makes it too heavy to pull. So each musher sends food ahead to checkpoints along the race route. When the mushers and dogs reach those places, they can stop to eat and rest. Where are the best places to stop during the race? That's for a musher to decide. But keeping his or her dogs well fed and rested is important. After all, a dogsled won't go anywhere if its dogs are dog tired!

What to Do:

You're just in time to enter the Iditarod. Get ready...get set...to plan your race schedule! Use the map to decide where you and your dogs will stop to eat and rest. Then fill out the Race Plan. Here are some tips and rules to follow:

- Your dogs cannot travel more than 100 miles without making a food and rest stop.
- The best place to eat and rest is at a checkpoint.
- You and your dogs can stop as often as you need to during the race.

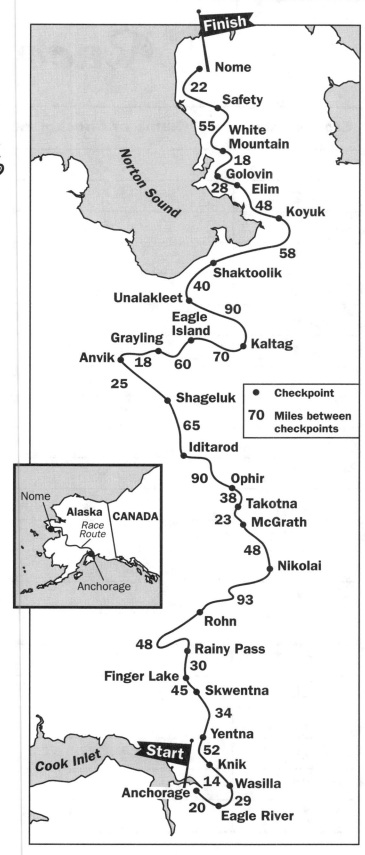

Finish
Nome
22
Safety
55 White Mountain
18
Golovin
28 Elim
48 Koyuk
58
Shaktoolik
Norton Sound
40
Unalakleet
Eagle Island 90
Grayling
Anvik 18 60 70 Kaltag
25
Shageluk
65
Iditarod
90 Ophir
38 Takotna
23 McGrath
48
Nikolai
93
Rohn
48 Rainy Pass
30
Finger Lake
45 Skwentna
34
Yentna
Start 52
Knik
Cook Inlet 14 Wasilla
Anchorage 29
20 Eagle River

• Checkpoint
70 Miles between checkpoints

Nome
Alaska CANADA
Race Route
Anchorage

Race Plan

Stop Number	Name of Checkpoint	Miles from Last Checkpoint	Total Miles
1			
2			
3			
4			
5			
6			
7			
8			
9			
10			
11			
12			
13			
14			
15			
16			
17			
18			
19			
20			
21			
22			

The Great Big Book of Super-Fun Math Activities Scholastic Professional Books

How to Measure a Monster

Estimating lengths

Aim

Students use units of measure based on their arm spans to estimate the lengths of some very long creatures.

Before the Activity

To prepare students for measuring their arm spans, have them review finding the number of feet in a yard, or, if they will be using metric measures for this activity, the number of centimeters in a meter. Students should also find the number of feet (or cm) in half a yard (meter), and the number of inches in half a foot. Copy and distribute pages 98–99.

During the Activity

This activity is best completed as a whole class or with students working in groups of three or four.

Because some of the lengths in this activity will exceed the length of any wall or diagonal in your classroom, students may have to work in hallways, a gymnasium, or outside. Showing the lengths of some of the creatures may require more students than are available in your class. Encourage students to devise ways of addressing this problem. (One way is for students to place a piece of tape on the floor or on the wall at the beginning of a series of arm spans. They can then "recycle" themselves through the line of arm spans.)

Students should first decide how they will keep track of finding the length of the combined arm spans. Students may elect one person as an "adder" of arm spans or they may work as a group to add the arm spans.

After the Activity

Ask students: *How would you change this activity if you wanted to show the exact length of the creatures?*

Extension

Have students use their own arm spans, foot lengths, hand widths, or finger lengths to measure the lengths of ten objects or creatures of their choice. Students should use one unit of measure for each object and describe why they chose that unit of measure.

How to Measure a Monster

You Need:
yardstick, meterstick, or tape measure

A Komodo dragon is one creature you wouldn't want to meet at a Halloween party. These lizards are the largest reptiles in the world. They can grow as long as 10 feet (3 meters)! But how long is that? It isn't easy to find a real Komodo dragon, or a 10-foot ruler. So get some friends together and try measuring with something you always have with you— yourselves!

Spread your arms as wide as you can. Have a friend measure the distance from your longest fingertip on one hand to the longest fingertip on the other hand. That measurement is called your arm span. How long is your arm span? (Round to the nearest foot or meter.)

Now that you and your friends have found your arm spans, you can show how long a Komodo dragon is. Line up next to each other so that your fingertips touch. How many arm spans do you need to show about 10 feet?

That's as big as a Komodo dragon!

What to Do:
Use arm spans to show how long these other real-life "monsters" are.

Giant Squid

Your arm span is about 4½ feet.

And your arm span is about 4 feet.

The Great Big Book of Super-Fun Math Activities Scholastic Professional Books

Trim off this strip and attach to page 99.

Komodo Dragon

> **≥BRAIN POWER≤**
> Look up other information about animals in books at the library or on the Internet. Write information about the size of the animals you find. Then use arm spans to show how long they are.

Bootlace Worm

1. Giant spider crabs live in the waters off Japan. A giant spider crab's body is about a foot wide. But its claw span can be as long as 20 feet!

2. A giant spider crab would feel like a shrimp next to a giant squid. The longest one ever measured was 55 feet (17 meters) long. Giant squids have the largest eyes of any animal. They're 15 inches (38 centimeters) wide!

3. Blue whales are the heaviest animals on Earth—and they're pretty long, too! They can grow to be 110 feet (34 meters) long. Even a baby blue whale is born about 23 feet (7 meters) long.

4. What's the world's longest creature? It's the bootlace worm. These undersea worms can reach 180 feet (55 meters) in length!

Attach to page 98 here.

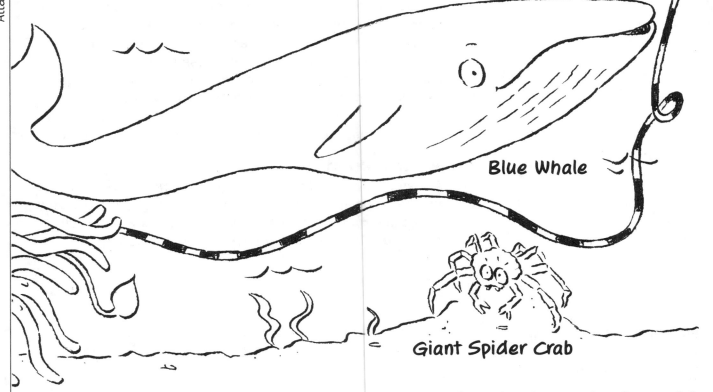

Blue Whale

Giant Spider Crab

Vacation Estimation

Using an estimation strategy: Taking a sample

Number sense

Aim

Students develop estimation skills and number sense as they estimate the number of penguins shown in a picture.

Before the Activity

Collect rectangular objects such as playing cards, baseball cards, or index cards that students can trace as boxes on their pictures. Copy and distribute page 101.

During the Activity

Students can work individually or in groups of three or four. Before students begin, have them guess how many penguins are in the whole picture. Write a range of guesses on the board. When students finish the steps of the activity, have them compare their estimates to their guesses. Stress that an estimate is still a guess, but an educated one.

Suggest that students draw boxes that are smaller than $\frac{1}{4}$ of the whole picture. If they work in groups, have each member draw a different-sized box.

Encourage the class to talk together when figuring out how many boxes they can fit on the picture. Suggest that they try different methods. Some students, for example, might try to draw rows and columns of boxes across the picture. Others might try to stagger boxes like bricks over it. For any chosen method, a remainder of the picture will probably be in a place that cannot be covered by a whole box. Students will need to figure out how to box and count these remaining penguins.

After the Activity

Ask students: *Why did you multiply the number of boxes by the number of penguins to come up with an estimate? Why is your final answer an estimate and not an exact answer? Do you think you could make your estimate more accurate? How?*

ANSWERS

Estimates and answers will vary. The range we estimated is from 250 to 300 penguins.

Vacation Estimation

Counting the penguins on the beach seems as hard as counting grains of sand. But why sweat it—when you can estimate?

What to Do:

▶ Draw a box on the picture. Count as many penguins in the box as you can.

Number of penguins in the box = About _____

▶ Next, figure out how many boxes of the same size could fit on the page to cover the entire picture.

Number of boxes = _____

▶ Now multiply the number of boxes on the picture by the number of penguins in the first box. That number will be your estimate.

Number of boxes x Number of penguins in first box = _____

My estimate = About _____ penguins in all

> **⇒ BRAIN POWER ⇐**
> Can you think of another way to estimate the number of penguins in the picture?

Sizing Up Reptiles

✐ **Measuring to the nearest half inch**

✐ **Completing a table**

Aim

Students measure the length of pictured reptiles and record their work in a table.

Before the Activity

Review how to align the end of a ruler with the object to be measured. Copy and distribute pages 103–104.

During the Activity

If necessary, help students find the half-inch marks on their rulers. Encourage students to label those points and show them how.

Extension

Discuss with students how they could create a Record Box to show the growth of a baby reptile over 3 weeks. (One way would be to add 3 columns to the right of the box and label the columns Week 1, Week 2, and Week 3.)

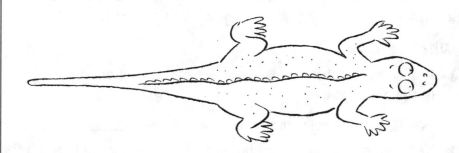

ANSWERS

Water Dragon—6 inches
Sidewinder—7 inches
Pygmy Rattlesnake—$6\frac{1}{2}$ inches
Basilisk Lizard—5 inches
Hog-Nosed Snake—$7\frac{1}{2}$ inches
Banded Gecko—$3\frac{1}{2}$ inches

Name _____

Sizing Up Reptiles

Rita Ruler calls herself the Measurement Marvel. Rita works at the zoo. She is in charge of the reptile nursery. Part of her job is to measure the baby lizards, turtles, crocodiles, and snakes growing up there.

What do the measurements tell her? If a reptile is too small, it can mean the animal is sick. Its cage might be too hot or too cold. Or another animal might be eating its food.

Rita keeps a record of the reptiles she measures. That way, she and the other zoo workers can learn more about the animals.

What to Do:

Help Rita measure some reptiles.

- Cut out the reptile ruler.
- Measure each reptile from head to tail.
- Write each reptile's measurement in the Record Box.

Now Try This:

If you and your classmates have pets, measure them and make your own Class Record Box.

Record Box

Reptile	Length
Water Dragon	
Sidewinder	
Pygmy Rattlesnake	
Basilisk Lizard	
Hog-Nosed Snake	
Banded Gecko	

The Great Big Book of Super-Fun Math Activities   Scholastic Professional Books

Basilisk Lizard
(BAH-se-lisk)

Water Dragon

Sidewinder

Pygmy Rattlesnake
(PIG-me)

Hog-Nosed Snake

Banded Gecko
(GEH-ko)

Reptile Ruler

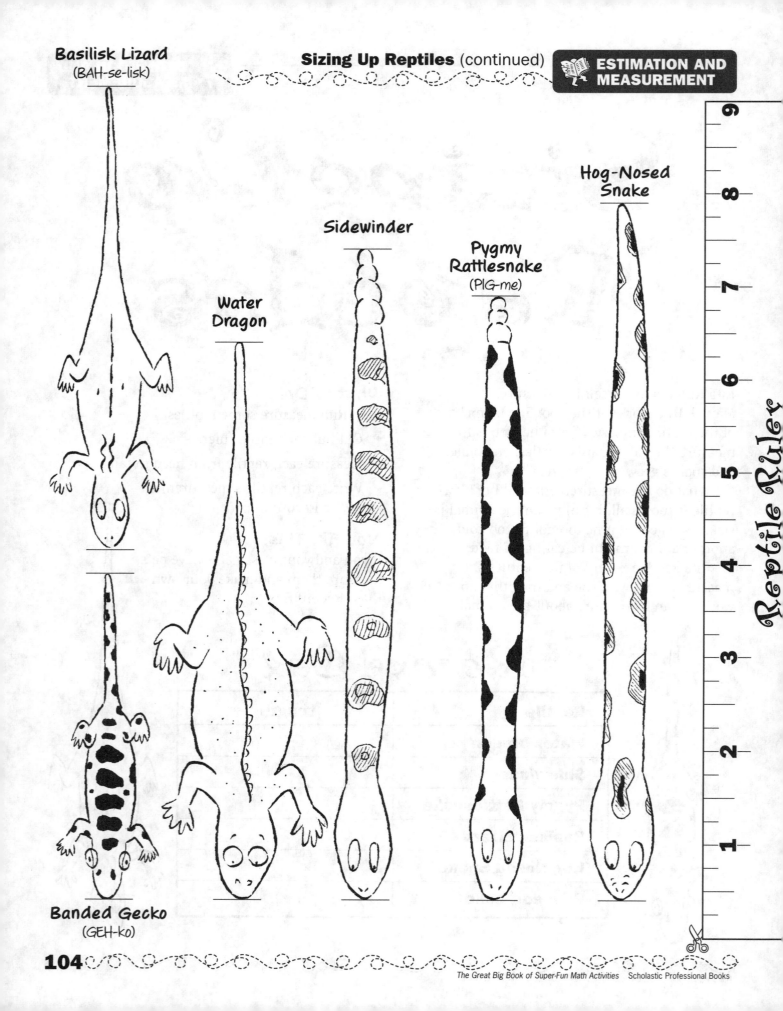

Ready, Set...A Measurement Rally!

✎ **Measuring length**

✎ **Giving and following directions**

⌖ Aim

Students read about car road rallies and then have their own rally by giving and following directions using measures of length.

Before the Activity

Copy and distribute page 106. Explain to students that they will be reading about a kind of race in which giving and following directions are very important. Have students describe some circumstances in which they had to give or follow directions.

During the Activity

Students can work on this activity in the classroom, the school building, or outside. For any location, students will have a safe, yet still challenging, rally if they keep the distances in their directions to fewer than 10 meters.

  Before the class gets started, talk about how team members can best work together. Mention that they can help each other measure and make sure they have written directions that are easy to understand. They can also check that they are following directions correctly.

After the Activity

Ask students: *How would the directions you give be different if your secret place was outside? If it was in a different neighborhood? If it was in a different town?* (For example, if the secret place was in a different neighborhood, it would be difficult to measure distances with a meterstick. Directions could be given in terms of walking or riding a bike.)

Extension _____

Have a rally in which students compete to follow directions in the shortest amount of time. Write one set of directions for all the teams to follow. Then time the teams as they follow the directions. If students use the directions at different times, make sure that they do not reveal to their classmates the secret spot you have chosen. Post the times in a chart and then have students order the times from the fastest to the slowest.

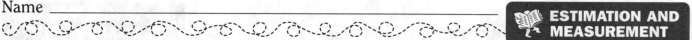

Ready, Set...
A Measurement Rally!

To race in a road rally, you don't need a fancy car or special driving skills. But you do need math. Each rally team is made up of a navigator and a driver. The navigator gets a set of directions that leads to a secret finish line. The team that gets to the right place in the right amount of time wins the race.

Rod and Rhonda Roadrace have won so many road rallies they can't count them all! Rod drives and Rhonda navigates. She uses the direction sheet to tell Rod how fast and how far to go.

During a rally, Rod has another set of rules to follow: the rules of the road. "A regular car race is held on a course where there is no other traffic," Rod explains. "In a road rally, you drive on public roads. If you get a ticket, you lose!"

Here are the directions I wrote.

From the doorway of the classroom, turn left and go down the hall three meters. Then go straight seven meters. Walk through two doorways and turn right. Walk six and a half meters. Then stop. Where do you end up?

You Need:

pencil and paper
meterstick or yardstick

What to Do:

Your class can have a rally—and you don't even need a car! In this rally, you'll be giving and following directions—just like Rhonda and Rod do.

- Work with a partner to make up a set of directions that leads to a secret spot. Measure the distances with the meterstick and write them down carefully.

- Exchange your direction sheet with another team. Use their direction sheet to find their secret spot. Did you find it? Did the other team find your secret spot?

On the Road with Measurement

✎ **Understanding measurement**

✎ **Using measurement words**

✍ Aim

Students use their knowledge of measurement to list objects in a travel scene that can be measured.

Before the Activity

Lead a short brainstorming session in which students identify some of the things they measure and explain why they measure them. Review measurement vocabulary, including units used for units used to measuring time, length/distance or height, volume, weight. Then copy and distribute pages 108–109.

During the Activity

Students can work on the activity individually or in groups. Those working in groups should make one list of items. Then they can divide the list among themselves or work together to match the items with the measurement words.

As they work on the activity, students may tend to focus on the more familiar measurements of length and capacity. Have them read the list of measurement words first if they need help extending their scope.

Ask students to compare their lists after they have completed the activity.

Extension

Have students draw a similar picture of a scene and the things they would bring from a real or imaginary vacation. They can then list the items that can be measured in their pictures and the words that can be used to describe the measurements.

⚷ ANSWERS

Answers will vary. Here is a partial list:

Map: miles, kilometers

Watch: hours, minutes, seconds

Calendar: days, months, years

Gas: gallons, liters

Baby bottle: ounces, milliliters

Dog: inches, pounds, kilograms

Juice and sunblock: ounces, milliliters, pints, quarts

BRAIN POWER: Jerome's family is in Cincinnati, Ohio, in the picture.

Name _____

On the Road with Measurement

Jerome and his family drove across the United States this summer. The car was certainly full! What was the most important thing they packed? Measurement! From reading maps to buying gas, the family measured all day long. Jerome says, "Measurement— don't leave home without it!"

What to Do:

Look at the picture of Jerome's family. List at least 20 items you could measure.

Then look at the **Measurement Words**. Decide which of the words tell how you could measure each item. List them next to each item.

Measurement Words and Abbreviations

millimeter/mm	ounce/oz
foot/ft	gallon/gal
quart/qt	yard/yd
pound/lb	year/yr
minute/min	day
kilometer/km	inch/in.
month/mo	mile/mi
kilogram/kg	meter/m
centimeter/cm	hour/hr
tablespoon/T	gram/g
pint/pt	liter/l

My soda can be measured in ounces, cups, pints, or liters. Now you try!

Trim off this strip and attach to page 109.

Attach to page 108 here.

BRAIN POWER
Use an atlas to find out where Jerome's family is in the picture.

Break the Ice with Perimeter and Area

✎ **Using a model**

✎ **Exploring perimeter and area**

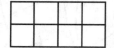 **ANSWERS**

1. Add four crackers (units).

2. The area will be 9.

3.

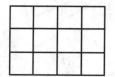

4. Possible answers: a square 4 units by 4 units with a perimeter of 16; a rectangle 2 units by 8 units with a perimeter of 20; a rectangle 1 unit by 16 units with a perimeter of 34.

5. Answers will vary, but any correct answer will use 24 units.

BRAIN POWER: One shape is a square made of 16 units.

🖋 **Aim**

Students use square crackers to explore how to find shapes with given areas and perimeters.

Before the Activity

Collect a minimum of 25 crackers or square counters for each student to use in this activity, and set aside a reserve of 100 crackers or counters for students to work with when answering the Brain Power question. Other ideas for square counters include square game chips, cut-out graph paper squares, and cardboard squares. Copy and distribute page 111.

During the Activity

Students can work through this activity individually, in small groups of three or four, or as a whole class.

For Question 2, have students work with their crackers to build a rink with the given dimensions. Then have students look at each other's constructions to see whether they are all the same shape and whether they all have four sides.

As students work with crackers to answer Question 3, watch for those who neglect to place crackers in the centers of the squares they build. Explain to these students that they have to cover a whole space with crackers to cover a whole space with ice. Point out that the area of a square with no crackers in its center will be less than that of a square filled with crackers.

To answer Question 5, students do not have to find all possible shapes. It is more important that they explore with their crackers to discover that shapes with the same area can have different perimeters. Encourage students to build both rectangular and nonrectangular shapes and to think about what would be some good shapes for ice-skating rinks.

After the Activity

Ask: *Why do you think two or more shapes can have the same area but different perimeters?*

Extension _____

For more practice with area and perimeter, copy and distribute page 112. Have students complete the activities for the Perimeter and Area Zoo page.

Name _____

Break the Ice With Perimeter and Area

Jessie is building ice skating rinks for her friends. She measures the size of each rink in two ways—**perimeter** and **area**. Perimeter tells the measurement **around** the rink. Area tells how many square units fit **inside** each rink. Some rinks have the same area but different perimeters. Try some building yourself!

You Need:
square crackers or square counters

Here's the rink Jesse built for Shawn. Its area is 4. Its perimeter is 8.

What to Do:
Use the square crackers to help you answer the questions. Then draw how the crackers look.

1. Shawn wants a bigger rink. He wants it to have a perimeter of 12 and an area of 8. What can you add to Shawn's rink? Draw what it will look like.

2. Gil also wants a rink with a perimeter of 12. But he wants to be square. What will it look like? What will its area be? Draw what it will look like.

3. The area of Rita's rink is 12. Its perimeter is 14. What does her rink look like? Draw it.

4. Sonia wants her rink to have an area of 16. She says it can be shaped like a square or a rectangle. What could the rink look like? What will its perimeter be? Draw it.

5. José wants a rink with an area of 24. It can be any shape. What are some of the shapes it could be? What are their perimeters? Draw one example.

> **≱BRAIN POWER≰**
> Draw a shape whose perimeter and area are the same number.

Perimeter and Area Zoo

A shape doesn't have to be a square or a rectangle to have perimeter and area. The animals in this zoo are different shapes. Can you find each animal's perimeter and area?

Remember: To find perimeter, count the sides of the units. To find area, count the number of whole units.

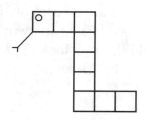

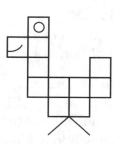

1. Perimeter _____

Area _____

2. Perimeter _____

Area _____

3. Perimeter _____

Area _____

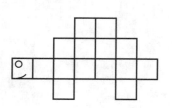

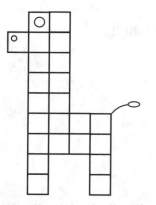

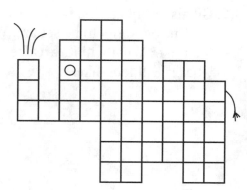

4. Perimeter _____

Area _____

5. Perimeter _____

Area _____

6. Perimeter _____

Area _____

Picnic Area

✎ **Using a model**

✎ **Finding area**

❀ Aim

Students find the area of picnic blankets by counting square units.

Before the Activity

Copy and distribute page 114. Hold a class discussion about area. Make a list on the board of situations where people need to measure area (landscaping, mapmaking, painting a wall, laying down carpet, covering a baseball field in the rain).

Remind students that area is a measure of the number of square units inside a shape. The area of each blanket in this activity is a number of square units.

During the Activity

Ask: *Can you find a faster way to find the area of these blankets than by counting each square?* (by multiplying the length of each rectangle by the width) If you want, share the formula for finding the area of a rectangle: $A = \ell \times w$.

Extension 1

Copy and distribute page 115. Invite students to complete In the Area. For any shapes that students color that are rectangles, have them apply the formula $A = \ell \times w$ to see that it accurately represents a way to find the area of a rectangle.

Extension 2

Have students find the area of various square and rectangular objects in the classroom by measuring their lengths and widths in inches or centimeters, then multiplying the two measurements together.

☛ ANSWERS

1. a and e (4); b and c (30); d and g (16)

2. a and d

3. a, b, and d

4. 124

Name _____

ESTIMATION AND MEASUREMENT

Picnic Area

These hungry ants have found the perfect "area" for a square meal!

What to Do:

Area measures the number of square units inside a shape. Find the area of each ant family's picnic blanket by counting the number of squares on the blanket. Then answer the following questions.

Remember—area is measured in square units, such as square centimeters. My blanket's area is four square units.

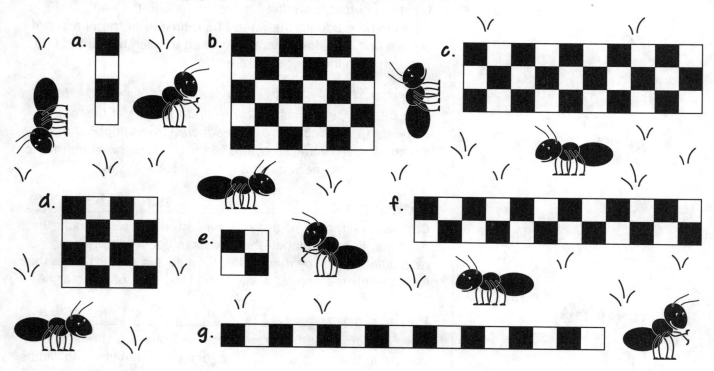

1. Which pairs of blankets have the same area?

_____ and _____

_____ and _____

_____ and _____

2. Which two blankets can you put together to make a rectangle with an area of 20?

_____

3. Which three blankets can you put together to make a rectangle with an area of 50?

_____

4. What is the total area of all of the ants' blankets?

_____

114

The Great Big Book of Super-Fun Math Activities Scholastic Professional Books

In the Area

Shapes with the same area can look very different! Color in two or more shapes that have the same area. The first one is done for you.

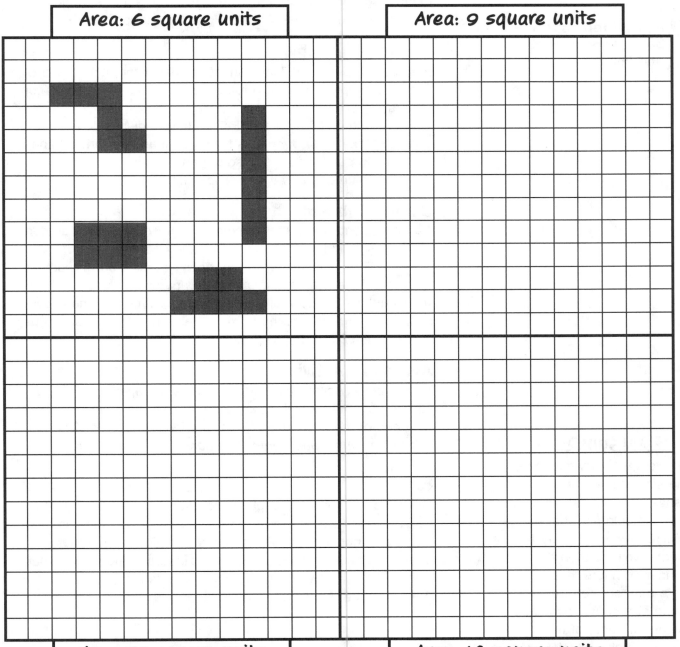

| Area: 6 square units | Area: 9 square units |

| Area: 12 square units | Area: 16 square units |

ESTIMATION AND MEASUREMENT

You "Can" Measure Volume

 **Understanding volume**

Using a scale

Finding relationships between surface area and volume

Aim

In this activity, based on an idea from author Marilyn Burns, students discover how two flat shapes with the same area can form three-dimensional shapes with different volumes.

Before the Activity

Prepare two 5-inch by 7-inch sheets of paper for each student. Gather a supply of beans, a roll of tape, a scale, and some containers.

Copy and distribute page 117. Initiate a discussion about volume. Make a list of objects that are measured with volume (juice, milk, paint, soup, and so on) and some words that describe volume (*cup, gallon, ounce, liter*).

During the Activity

Assist students while they assemble their "cans." Each student or group should have one tall "can" and one short "can."

Note: This activity, as written, does not measure the actual volumes of the two containers but compares them by weight. If you would like to incorporate measuring volume into the activity, simply measure the beans from the tall and short cans in cups or liters instead of weighing them.

After the Activity

Try the activity again with different sizes of paper, including a square pair. Ask: *Which cans seem to have more volume, the tall ones or the short ones? Can you find a pattern? What happens with cans made from two square sheets of paper?*

Extension

Make a class volume scrapbook or volume bulletin board. The display could include real-life examples of volume such as food labels or empty boxes, or pictures of containers and other three-dimensional shapes from magazines. For more great math activities, try Marilyn Burns's book *About Teaching Mathematics* (Sausalito, CA: Math Solutions Publications, 1992).

ANSWERS

Answers will vary depending on the size of the cylinder and usage of beans. In general, students should find that the shorter, wider cylinders have a greater volume than the taller, thinner cylinders, even if they were both created from the same size paper. Two square sheets of paper of the same size will make cylinders with the same volume.

Name _____

ESTIMATION AND MEASUREMENT

You "Can" Measure Volume

At the "You Can" Can Factory, workers just can't contain themselves—about volume!

Short cans, tall cans, shiny cans. How do you measure a can? One way is by measuring its volume. Volume tells how much a three-dimensional shape (like a can) can hold.

There's more to volume than meets the eye! Want to find out for yourself? Just visit the "You Can" Can Factory. Grab your paper and tape and let's get rolling!

You Need:
two 5-inch by 7-inch sheets of paper
tape
dried beans
empty container
scale

What to Do:

1. Roll one of the sheets of paper into a "can" by matching the two long edges and taping them. Try not to overlap the edges.

2. Do the same with the other sheet, this time matching the two short edges. You now have one tall can and one short can.

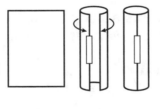

3. Do you think one of the cans has more volume? Or do you think both cans will hold the same amount? Write your guess here:

   I think _____

   _____

4. Put the tall can in the container. Fill the can to the top with or beans. Then slowly remove the can so that the beans stay in the container. Weigh the container and the beans together.

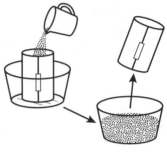

   Weight of container and beans from the tall can = _____

5. Empty the container. Follow step 4 to find the weight of the beans in the short can.

   Weight of the container and beans from the short can = _____

6a. Were the two volumes different or the same?

   _____

b. Which can has more volume?

   _____

7. Try this experiment again with two 3-inch by 10-inch sheets and two 5-inch by 5-inch sheets.

8. Can you think up a rule that explains why one can holds more than the other does? Write your rule on a separate piece of paper.

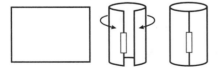

The Great Big Book of Super-Fun Math Activities Scholastic Professional Books

Volume Pops Up Everywhere!

✎ **Using a model**

✎ **Estimating volume**

🕊 Aim

Students use popcorn and containers to explore and estimate volume.

Before the Activity

Copy and distribute page 119. You may want to review the difference between two- and three-dimensional shapes. Some students may believe that they would be able to hold a circle, triangle, square, etc., if the shape were cut out of paper. Use a shape cut from paper to demonstrate that the shape has thickness, even though it is quite thin. Explain that flat shapes are two-dimensional and are formed from lines on a flat plane. Shapes that have thickness are three-dimensional.

During the Activity

To complete this activity, students can work individually or in groups of three or four people. If they work in groups, each student in the group should make an estimate for Questions 1, 2, and 4, and students should work together to compare their estimates and discuss the ideas in Question 3.

After the Activity

Remind students that this activity explored finding, comparing, and using the volumes of hollow shapes. Explain that we also use volume to measure solid shapes. Ask students how they could use what they know about finding the volume of a hollow shape to figure out the volume of a solid shape.

🔑 ANSWERS

Students' estimates will vary according to the size of the cone, cup, drink box, and pie plate, and the estimation methods they use. These are by no means the "right" answers but answers we felt were reasonable based on our own tools and methods.

1. Answers will vary.
   Answers will vary.
   6 cones

2. 5 cups

3. the cup

4. $5\frac{1}{2}$ drink boxes

Volume Pops Up Everywhere!

Look around your classroom. Do you see any of the shapes shown here?

Cylinder

Cube

Cone

These shapes are three-dimensional. That means that they are solid—you can touch them with your hands. (You can't hold a two-dimensional shape like a circle, square, or triangle.) We measure three-dimensional shapes in a special way—using volume. Volume tells how much the shape can hold inside.

Ready to learn about volume? Let's go!

You Need:
2-lb bag of unpopped popcorn
ice cream cone
empty drink box with top cut off
empty 8-oz yogurt cup
8- or 9-inch pie plate

1. Start with the cone and the yogurt cup. How many cones do you think it will take to fill the cup with popcorn?

_____ cones

Fill the cone with popcorn. Then pour it into the cup. Keep filling the cup until you think it's half filled. Do you want to change your guess?

New guess: _____ cones

Now finish filling the cup. How many cones did it take?

_____ cones

2. How many cups of popcorn do you think it will take to fill the pie plate? Start pouring popcorn from the cup to the pie plate. When you think the pie plate is half filled, guess again. Then fill it all the way. How many cups did it take?

_____ cups

3. Which do you think holds more, the cup or the drink box? How could you find out? Test your ideas. Which holds more?

_____

4. How many drink boxes do you think it would take to fill the pie plate? Try it.

_____ drink boxes

Now pop the popcorn, fill the cone with ice cream, and have a volume party!

> ⚡ **BRAIN POWER** ⚡
> Try more volume experiments with other containers.

Skating and Trading

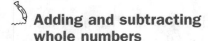 **Understanding place value**

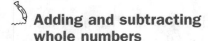 **Adding and subtracting whole numbers**

 Regrouping

 ## Aim

Students add and subtract with regrouping as they play a board game. The game gives students concrete experience with regrouping and helps them connect the concrete experience to the abstract symbols as one member of each team solves problems with counters while the other member solves the same problems with paper and pencil.

Before the Activity

Copy and distribute pages 121–122. Review the directions on page 121. Then practice playing the game with students to make sure they understand the roles of the trader and writer. Draw a sample tally sheet on the board to show students what the writer's work should look like. For example:

$$
\begin{array}{r}
25 \\
+\ 4 \\
\hline
29 \\
-10 \\
\hline
19
\end{array}
$$

Ask students why the first number is 25. (That's the number each team starts with.) Then ask what space the team must have landed on first. (A "RAD! 4 ONES" space.)

During the Activity

If students haven't had much experience with regrouping, have them play the game with base-ten blocks, base-ten strips, or bean sticks. Once they have had more experience, encourage them to play with different-color counters, chips, or play money.

After the Activity

Ask students: *How did you use mental math to play the game? Did trading help you to add and subtract? How? How is what the trader and writer do similar? How is it different?*

Skating and Trading

You Need:

3 kinds of counters or chips:
  30 of one color (worth 1 point each)
  30 of a second color (worth 10 points each)
  30 of a third color (worth 100 points each)
2 different coins (or other game pieces)
paper and pencils
paper clip

Object:

To be the team with more points at the end of the game.

Number of Players:

4—2 teams of 2 players each

To Begin:

- Make 3 piles of counters (1 for each color). That's the bank.

- One player on each team is the **trader**. The trader collects and gives back counters. The other player is the **writer**. The writer keeps track of the team's points.

- The trader on each team collects 2 tens counters and 5 ones counters. The writer writes 25 on top of the paper.

- Each team chooses a game piece and puts it on START.

- Make a spinner using a pencil, a paper clip, and the number wheel on the game board. Spin to see which team goes first.

TRADING RULES

- If you collect 10 ones, trade them for 1 ten. If you need ones to subtract, trade 1 ten for 10 ones.

- If you collect 10 tens, trade them for 1 hundred. If you need tens to subtract, trade 1 hundred for 10 tens.

To Play:

- Each turn, spin and move the number of spaces shown. (More than one team can land on a space.)

- On a RAD! space, the trader collects counters from the bank. The writer adds the points to the team's total.

- On a WIPEOUT space, the trader returns counters to the bank. The writer subtracts the points from the teams's total.

- Check your work. Make sure the writer's total matches the total shown by the trader's counters.

- The game ends when one team runs out of counters or reaches FINISH. (You don't have to land on it exactly.) The team that has more points wins.

COMPUTATION

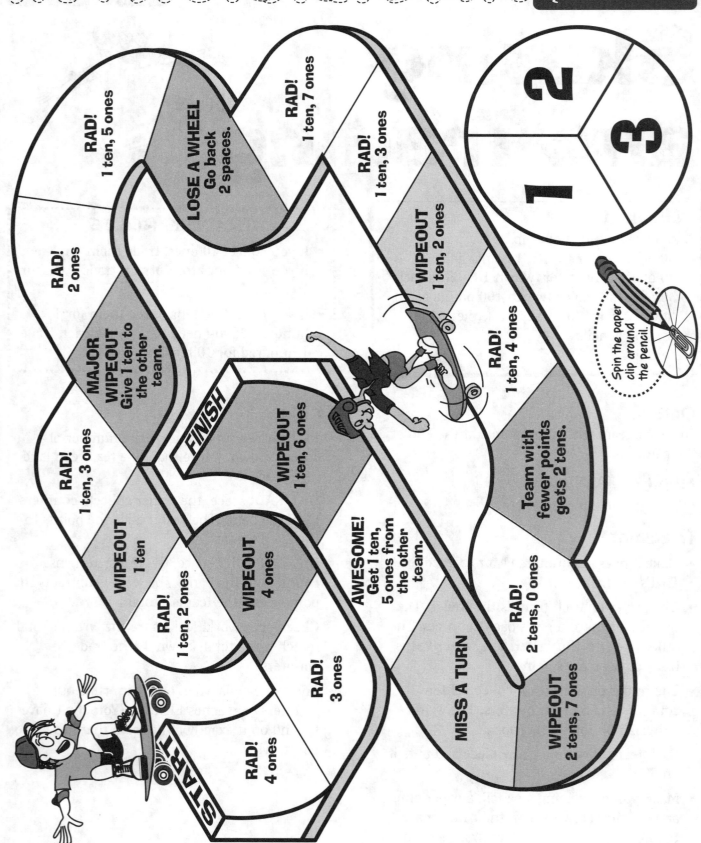

Spin the paper clip around the pencil.

1 2 3

RAD!
1 ten, 5 ones

LOSE A WHEEL
Go back
2 spaces.

RAD!
1 ten, 7 ones

RAD!
1 ten, 3 ones

RAD!
2 ones

WIPEOUT
1 ten, 2 ones

MAJOR
WIPEOUT
Give 1 ten to
the other
team.

RAD!
1 ten, 4 ones

RAD!
1 ten, 3 ones

FINISH

WIPEOUT
1 ten, 6 ones

Team with
fewer points
gets 2 tens.

WIPEOUT
1 ten

RAD!
1 ten, 2 ones

WIPEOUT
4 ones

AWESOME!
Get 1 ten,
5 ones from
the other
team.

RAD!
2 tens, 0 ones

RAD!
3 ones

MISS A TURN

WIPEOUT
2 tens, 7 ones

RAD!
4 ones

START!

 **COMPUTATION**

Apple Add-Up

✎ **Adding whole numbers with and without regrouping**

🖈 Aim
Students practice basic addition facts as they play an apple-picking game of luck and skill.

Before the Activity
Copy and distribute two copies of page 124 to each pair of players. If necessary, review addition of one-digit and two-digit numbers.

During the Activity
Encourage students to use mental math rather than paper and pencil to find the combinations of numbers that equal the numbers on the spinner. Discuss strategies they can use to plan ahead as they play.

⚷ ANSWERS
BRAIN POWER: Answers will vary. You might encourage students to keep a list of their moves in order to defend their strategy.

Apple Add-Up

Spin the paper clip around the pencil.

Spinner: More than 30 | Equal to 15 | Less than 25 | Less than 15 | Equal to 25 | More than 15

You Need:
small counters
pencil
paper clip

Object:
To cover more apples than the other player.

Number of Players: 2

To Play:

- Each player gets a copy of the apple tree game board. Decide who will go first.

- Take turns spinning. (Look at the picture to see how to use the spinner.) After spinning, cover **two** apples on your tree with the counters. The two numbers on the apples must add up to a number that matches the spinner. **Example:** Player 1 spins "Equal to 15." Player 1 can cover 7 and 8, 5 and 10, 2 and 13, or any other combination of two apples that totals 15. Player 2 spins "More than 15." Player 2 can cover any combination of two apples that totals more than 15.

▶ Once your counters are on the board, you can't move them!

▶ If you can't cover two apples to match the spinner, you're out. The other player wins.

⇒ BRAIN POWER ⇐
Tell about a strategy you used to cover the most apples.

Jungle Jam

 Adding and subtracting whole numbers

Aim

Students add and subtract whole numbers as they play a jungle board game.

Before the Activity

Copy and distribute pages 126–127. Have students tape the two pages together to make the game board. You can laminate the game board for durability.

During the Activity

As students play the game, one person can be the scorekeeper, or each person can tally his or her own score. Though students may use a calculator to total their scores, suggest that they play a few rounds with pencil and paper to help practice their computation skills. To help students develop a sense of how their scores will increase or decrease, suggest that they say the number they hope the spinner will land on before they spin it.

After the Activity

Ask students: *Would you want to "swing down the vine" in this game? Why or why not?*

Extension 1

To increase the difficulty of Jungle Jam, add 100 points to each space on the game board. For example, the first four spaces will become "+119," "+117," "+115," and "+113." Players should start with 120 points.

Extension 2

For practice adding and subtracting integers, students can play the game using a number cube numbered 1–6 instead of the spinner. If students need help keeping score, have them keep track with colored counters—one color for positive numbers and one for negative numbers. Remind them that if their score is negative, they should add colored negative counters when they land on a number with a minus sign and remove colored negative counters when they land on a number with a plus sign.

Jungle Jam

You're lost in the jungle. There's only one way to get home—
add and subtract along the path!

You Need:
game piece for each player
pencils and paper
paper clip

Object:
To get out of the jungle with the
most points.

Number of Players:
2, 3, or 4

To Play:
▶ Decide who will go first. Each
player starts with 20 points.

▶ Take turns spinning. After
you spin, move ahead the
number of spaces shown on
the spinner.

▶ Add or subtract the number
marked on the space where
you land. Keep a total of your
points on paper as you play
the game.

▶ If you land on a SWING
DOWN VINE space, follow the
vine to the space where it
ends. Start on that space on
your next turn.

▶ The game ends when each
player lands on or passes
END. The player with the
most points wins.

Spin the paper
clip around
the pencil.

1 2
3 4

START
You have
20 points.

+19

+17

+15

Tiger gives
you a ride.

+13

Trim off this strip and attach to page 126.

END

−6

SWING DOWN VINE

+5

Monkey steals your food. −1

+13

−9

Z

+11

Take a rest under a banana tree. +5

Z

+3

+14

DANGER

−4

QUICKSAND! −5

−8

+10

+4

SWING DOWN VINE

Parrot gives you the wrong directions. −8

−2

−3

Take a swim +6

Attach page 125 here.

Compute With Candy Codes

 Using a code

Understanding whole number operations

Aim

Students use a candy code to explore symbolic number representation and to solve equations.

Before the Activity

Copy and distribute pages 129–130. As a warm-up exercise, and to prepare students for using the code in this activity, have them list combinations of two or more addends that give specific sums.

During the Activity

Have students look for patterns in the Candy Code. Help them notice that the shapes for the numbers 1–5 repeat in the code, and that all numbers greater than 5 have one ⬭ candy in them. While students use the code to solve the equations, encourage them to find more than one way to show their answers by drawing various combinations of candy shapes that will represent the answers.

After the Activity

Ask students: *If one candy-coded number uses more pieces of candy than another, does that mean that the first number is greater than the second number? Why or why not? Give an example to prove your answer.*

Extension

Give students a 25-square grid made from 1-inch squares. Then have them use the Candy Code to put a coded number in each square of the grid. Working from left to right across each row, students should show all the numbers from 1 to 25. When students have filled the grid, have them write about the patterns they notice.

ANSWERS

How students represent the answers will vary. Accept any answer, as long as the student can justify it according to the Candy Code.

1. 12

2. 72

3. 1

4. 100

5. 2

6. Answers will vary. Any number less than 24 is correc

7–13. Answers will vary.

Compute with Candy Codes

Math is sweet when you solve it with candy!

CANDY CODE

●	★	◆	∩	▭	◑▭	★▭	◆▭	∩▭	▭▭
1	2	3	4	5	6	7	8	9	10

What to Do:

Look at the Candy Code above. Each candy or group of candies in the code stands for a number.

For example, one ◆ stands for a 3. Two ▭ stand for a 10.

The number 16 is not in the code.
How could you show 16? You could show it like this: 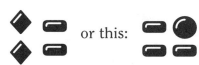 or this:

Once you've found ways to make numbers in the code, you can solve equations.
Draw your answers using candy shapes.

1. ★ × ◑▭ =	2. ◆▭ × ∩▭ =
3. ∩ + ▭ = ▭▭ −	4. ▭▭ × ▭▭ =
5. ◆▭ ÷ ∩ =	6. ◆ × ◆▭ >

Use the Candy Code to show . . .

7. an addition equation.

8. a subtraction equation.

9. a multiplication equation.

10. a division equation.

11. a fraction.

12. an equation that equals more than 100.

13. your age three different ways.

Write some candy equations for your friends to solve.

⭆BRAIN POWER⭇
Use your favorite candy to make up your own Candy Code. You can use different shapes or different colors.

Sled Dog Math

✎ **Using whole-number addition, multiplication, division**

✎ **Finding combinations**

🗝 **ANSWERS**

1. 72 ÷ 3 = 24; 24 × 4 = 96; 96 × 2 = 192. So the team is 72, ÷ 3, × 4, × 2.

2. 240

3. Sets of teams that equal the same number:

36 ÷ 3 × 5 ÷ 2 = 30
36 ÷ 12 × 5 × 2 = 30
72 ÷ 6 × 5 ÷ 2 = 30
36 ÷ 6 × 5 × 2 = 60
72 ÷ 3 × 5 ÷ 2 = 60
72 ÷ 12 × 5 × 2 = 60
36 ÷ 3 × 4 ÷ 2 = 24
36 ÷ 12 × 4 × 2 = 24
72 ÷ 6 × 4 ÷ 2 = 24
36 ÷ 6 × 4 × 2 = 48
72 ÷ 3 × 4 ÷ 2 = 48
72 ÷ 12 × 4 × 2 = 48

4. 12 teams equal zero.

5. There are 48 different teams.

🎯 **Aim**

Students make "teams" of sled dogs by computing with whole numbers.

Before the Activity

Copy and distribute pages 132–133.

During the Activity

Have students practice finding a few dog teams before they answer the questions. Suggest that they keep track of the math used for each team so they can use it to answer the questions. Students may not find all the possible combinations of teams to answer Question 5. However, finding all the combinations will help them to answer Questions 1–4. If you want them to find all the combinations, encourage students to think about how they can work in an organized way to do so. Suggest that they talk to other students, or that they start with finding all combinations for the number 72 lead dog and then all for the number 36 lead dog.

Extension

Have students make their own groups of dogs for sled teams and then find all the combinations of teams that can be made.

Sled Dog Math

Meet our two lead dogs—36 and 72! They'll head up the dog teams in the Math Mushers Dogsled Race. We need you to put the teams together. How? Add, multiply, and divide! All set? Mush!

You Need:
4 counters
paper and pencil or calculator

What to Do:

- Each dog team needs four dogs: one lead dog and a dog from each of the other three groups: striped, spotted, and checked. Start with a counter on one of the lead dogs.

- Pick one dog from each of the other groups to make a team. Use the counters to mark each dog in the team. Always move left to right.

- As you pick your dogs, follow the directions on their jackets. Write down the math that you do on scratch paper. The answer will be what that team equals.

Now that you know how to pick a team, figure out:

1. Which dog team equals 192?

_____

2. What is the highest number any of the dog teams can equal?

_____

3. Are there three teams that equal the same number? If so, what are they?

_____

_____

4. How many teams equal zero?

_____

5. How many different teams can you find?

_____

I started with 36 and then picked striped ÷ 6. Then I picked spotted × 4, and checked × 2.
36 ÷ 6 = 6
6 × 4 = 24
24 × 2 = 48
This dog team equals 48!

I started with 36 also. But I'm picking ÷ 3 next.

The Great Big Book of Super-Fun Math Activities Scholastic Professional Books

COMPUTATION

Divided House

 Dividing whole numbers

 LANGUAGE ARTS CONNECTIONS:
Reading a play
Writing in math

Aim

Students use counters to divide whole numbers as they read a play.

Before the Activity

Copy and distribute pages 135–136.

During the Activity

Have students use their counters to model the division problems that appear in the play as preparation for using the counters to answer the questions. Encourage students to devise their own methods of forming equal groups of counters. Then have students describe the methods they discover. (Some methods students may find: Create four groups with one counter in each group, then keep adding one counter to each group until you run out; make four groups that appear to have the same number of counters, count how many are in each group, and adjust if necessary to make the groups more equal.) After students solve the division problems with counters, encourage them to write number sentences to represent the problems.

On the chalkboard, write this number sentence to represent the first division problem in the play: $24 \div 4 = 6$. Ask students what each number represents. (The 24 represents 24 peanuts or 24 kids at the party; 4 represents 4 equal groups of 4 tables; 6 tells how many peanuts are in each group or how many kids should sit at each table.)

After the Activity

Ask students why they think we call the operation "division."

Extension

Have students write a short description of a situation in which they or someone they know had to share a number of things that could not be shared equally. Students should tell how they solved the problem, and why they chose the solution they did.

ANSWERS

1. 5 kids

2. 9 kids

3. 6 kids

4. 3 bowls

5. Answers will vary. Possible answers: The 30 kids could use 6 tails instead of 9, and have 5 kids share each tail. Or 18 kids could share 6 tails (with 1 tail going to every 3 kids), and 12 kids could share the remaining 3 tails (with 1 tail going to every 4 kids).

Name _____

Divided House

CHARACTERS

Stiff-Knee, 9-year-old girl
Misspell, Stiff-Knee's younger sister
P.J., Stiff-Knee's older sister
Tanny, Stiff-Knee's father
Messy, Stiff-Knee's uncle

Stiff-Knee: My life is over!

Tanny: What's the matter?

Stiff-Knee: My party starts in one hour and the tables aren't set up yet!

Messy: We'll help you.

Tanny: How many kids should sit at each table?

Stiff-Knee: Let's see. 24 kids will be at the party.

Messy: And you have 4 tables of the same size.

P.J.: Divide the 24 kids into 4 equal groups. That will tell you how many kids to put at each table.

Misspell: I'm only three years old. I can't divide.

Tanny: Without my calculator, I have a hard time myself.

Stiff-Knee: Here, Dad. Use these peanuts to help you.

Tanny: I'm not hungry.

Stiff-Knee: Don't eat the peanuts, Dad. Use them to solve the problem. Take 24 of them. Pretend they're the 24 kids at my party.

P.J.: *(to herself)* I always thought her friends were nuts.

Stiff-Knee: Divide the 24 peanuts into 4 equal groups.

Tanny: There are 6 peanuts in each group!

Stiff-Knee: That's right. That means 6 kids should sit at each table. *RING! (Stiff-Knee answers the phone.)*

Messy: Who was that?

Stiff-Knee: Ann, Dan, Fran, and Jan. They can't come. How rude!

Tanny: They have to come! I already counted them! Now how will we know how many kids sit at each table?

Stiff-Knee: Relax, Dad. Have a peanut.

P.J.: Have 4 peanuts. One for each kid who's not coming. You'll have 20 peanuts left.

Stiff-Knee: Put the 20 peanuts into 4 equal groups.

Tanny: I think I've got it. Each table should have . . . *RING!*

Stiff-Knee: Hold that thought, Dad. That might be more of my "nutty" friends, now . . .

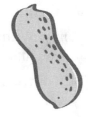

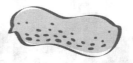

What to Do:

Help Stiff-Knee set up. Use peanuts or other counters to help you.

1. So far, Stiff-Knee expects 20 kids to come to her party. How many kids should sit at each of the 4 tables?

   _____

2. That was the school band on the phone. P.J. invited them to the party! That means 36 kids will be there in all. How many kids should sit at each table?

   _____

3. Tanny gets 2 more tables. Now there are 6 tables. How many of the 36 kids should sit at each table?

   _____

4. Stiff-Knee fills 18 bowls with potato chips. How many bowls should she put on each of the 6 tables so that each table has the same number of bowls?

   _____

5. The party starts. 30 kids want to play pin-the-tail-on-the-uncle. But there are only 9 tails. Explain how you think the kids should share the tails.

   _____

   _____

   _____

   _____

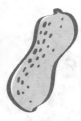
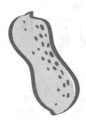

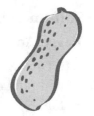

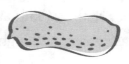

 COMPUTATION

Heart to Heart Division

 Understanding division with remainders

Aim

Students use their knowledge of division facts to get a remainder and move ahead in a division game.

Before the Activity

Copy and distribute pages 138–139. Review division with remainders if necessary. Point out that in this game moves are determined by choosing the divisor that will give the highest remainder. Therefore, players may want to try several division problems before choosing a divisor.

During the Activity

Make sure players in each group understand the rules. You may elect to set a time limit on each turn if players are taking too long to answer.

Extension

Students can make their own theme board games using these or their own rules.

LOVE U 4EVER

UR GR8

Heart to Heart Division

The winner of this division game remainders...uh, remains to be seen!

You Need:
counter for each player
pencil and paper

Object:
To be the first player to reach the last heart, without going past it.

Number of Players: 2 or more

To Play:

♥ Each player starts on the number 13. This is the first number you will divide.

♥ Decide who will go first.

♥ Each heart has a number or instructions on it. Use those numbers or instructions to move around the board. Here's how:

Look at the number on the heart you land on. Divide the number on the heart *by any number you choose* from 1 to 9.

Whatever remainder you get after doing the division is the number of spaces you get to move. So pick your numbers carefully!

♥ The player who ends up exactly on the last candy heart, without going past it wins! If you don't reach the end on an exact number, keep choosing a number until you get the remainder you need.

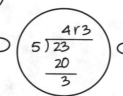

I landed on 23 and I choose to divide by 5.

$$5\overline{)23} \quad \begin{array}{r} 4\,r3 \\ \hline 23 \\ 20 \\ \hline 3 \end{array}$$

Since the remainder is 3, I get to move 3 spaces.

 **COMPUTATION**

Mining for Multiplication

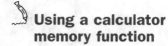 **Using a calculator memory function**

Multiplying and adding money amounts

Aim

Students learn to use the memory function on a calculator.

Before the Activity

Copy and distribute pages 141–142. You will need a calculator and a counter for each player. Familiarize yourself with the memory function key procedures on your class's calculators. Check if the activity's instructions work for the calculators you will be using. If not, instruct the class how to use the memory function on their particular calculators.

To practice working with the memory function key and multiplying with decimals, demonstrate on the chalkboard or use an overhead projector to show an equation such as this one:

$$2 \times \$1.84 \rightarrow M+ \rightarrow 4 \times \$.99 \rightarrow M+ \rightarrow$$
$$6 \times \$.31 \rightarrow M+ \rightarrow 5 \times \$4.72 \rightarrow M+ \rightarrow MR$$

Point out that the = key is not used at all; the M+ and MR keys are used instead.

During the Activity

Walk around the room to help students who are having difficulty. Encourage students to try to find the total for each mine shaft. Students may find it helpful to trace the entire length of each mine shaft with their fingers before entering the math problems.

Extension

Invite students to use a supermarket circular to find prices of different grocery items. Use the memory function to keep a running total of a large list of groceries, including multiple purchases of the same items.

ANSWERS

From left to right, the totals of the six shafts are:
Shaft 1: $50.00
Shaft 2: $140.00
Shaft 3: $150.00
Shaft 4: $100.00
Shaft 5: $100.00
Shaft 6: $100.00

Mining for Multiplication

Your calculator can help you strike gold!

Looking for fun? Head for Wickenburg, Arizona! Every year, the folks there get together for "Gold Rush Days," a celebration of Old West history. If you drop by, be sure to catch the rodeo, the parade, and the carnival—and don't forget to pan for gold!

Can't make it to Arizona this year? Don't worry. You can remember the gold rush by playing this calculator memory game!

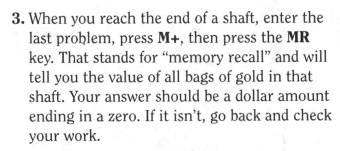

You Need:
calculator
counter

What to Do:

1. Place a counter at START. Enter the first multiplication problem (4 × $.50) on your calculator. Don't press the = key to find the answer. Instead, press the **M+** key. The **M** stands for "memory." Pressing the **M+** key tells your calculator to remember that product and add it to the total.

2. Choose a mine shaft to follow. Use your counter to mark your place. As you come to each bag of gold in the shaft, enter the multiplication problem and press **M+**. Repeat this step until you reach the end of a shaft.

3. When you reach the end of a shaft, enter the last problem, press **M+**, then press the **MR** key. That stands for "memory recall" and will tell you the value of all bags of gold in that shaft. Your answer should be a dollar amount ending in a zero. If it isn't, go back and check your work.

4. After you get to the end of a shaft, press **C** to clear your answer. Then start a new one! Which shafts have the same amount? Which shaft should you mine for the greatest amount?

COMPUTATION

Calculate a Happy Chinese New Year

Understanding operations with whole numbers: addition, subtraction, multiplication, division

Aim

Students read about the Chinese calendar and compute with whole numbers.

Before the Activity

Copy and distribute pages 144–145. Have students tape the two pages together to make the number path.

During the Activity

Students can use paper and pencil to record their calculations, or for an added challenge, they can try to move along the path using mental math.

After the Activity

Ask: *If you and a partner pick the same number to start, do you end up with the same number?*

Extension 1

Have a computation race in which two or more students start with the same number and race to compute their way along the path. Students should write all their computations as they go. The winner is the first person who gets to the end of the path with all of the correct computations written down.

Extension 2

To find out when a specific animal's year occurred or will come again, subtract or add 12 from the years on the list. This can be done indefinitely. By doing this, you can have students figure out which animal's year it was or will be for any year on the Gregorian calendar (for example, the year 1776; the year 3000).

Calculate a Happy Chinese New Year

Everyone loves to celebrate New Year's Eve. But once January 1 is past, you don't need to hang up your party hat. You can still celebrate Chinese New Year. It doesn't come until January 23.

On the Chinese calendar, each year is named after one of 12 animals. For example, 1987 was the Year of the Rabbit. 1993 was the Year of the Rooster. The animals are all on your game board.

What to Do:

▶ Pick any number and write it in the first rooster, by START.

▶ Follow the animals around the board. Do what their sign and number tell you. Keep track of your total on scratch paper.

▶ Every time you get to a rooster, you should get the number you started with as the answer. If you don't, go back and check your work.

▶ After you finish, play again with a different number. Want a challenge? Try using a 3-digit number.

COMPUTATION

Which Animal Are You?

Find the year you were born on this chart.
Which animal sign were you born under?
Which animals are others in your family?

Rooster	1981	Rabbit	1987
Dog	1982	Dragon	1988
Pig	1983	Snake	1989
Mouse	1984	Horse	1990
Cow	1985	Sheep	1991
Tiger	1986	Monkey	1992

÷ 2

− 6

+ 50

x 6   ÷ 3   ÷ 2   − 39

− 11

x 10

+ 46

÷ 2   − 23   ÷ 5

Attach page 144 here.

COMPUTATION

Divide the Signs

✎ Dividing whole numbers

✎ **LANGUAGE ARTS CONNECTION:** American Sign Language

Aim

Students learn the numbers from 1 to 20 and signs for operations in American Sign Language, then use the signs to practice math equations.

Before the Activity

Copy and distribute pages 147–148. Explain to your class that American Sign Language (ASL) is used by the hearing impaired and is a language of its own, like English, Spanish, or Japanese. Have students practice each of the signs on the chart several times before solving the math problems. Ask: *Do you see a pattern in the numbers 1 though 20? Can you guess how some higher numbers might be formed?*

During the Activity

While signing problems F through K, help students form each sign slowly and clearly. Make sure they remember to sign the "divided by" and "equals" signs.

Extension

Expand students' knowledge of ASL by inviting them to research the numbers up to 100. They then will be able to sign and practice many more division and multiplication facts. You might suggest the book *The Joy of Signing* by Lottie L. Riekehof (Springfield, MO: Gospel Publishing House, 1983).

ANSWERS

A. 8 + 3 = 11

B. 13 − 6 = 7

C. 5 × 2 = 10

D. 12 ÷ 3 = 4

E. 18 ÷ 3 = 6

F–K. Observe students' formation of signs.

Divide the Signs

You know that 6 ÷ 3 is equal to 2. But did you know that   also equals 2?

Those hand signals stand for "six," "divided by," and "three" in American Sign Language (ASL). ASL is used by hearing impaired people and the people who communicate with them. The signs are easy to learn. So lend a hand and sign away!

What to Do:

Use the chart that shows the numbers 1 to 20 in ASL. The chart also shows the addition, subtraction, multiplication, division, and equals signs. Complete the sign language equations below. Write each answer in number form. Then change the number equations into ASL. Make sure you sign the answer in ASL, too.

A.  = _____

B.   = _____

C.  = _____

D.  = _____

E.   = _____

Now try signing these division problems in ASL.

F. 7 ÷ 1 = _____

G. 12 ÷ 6 = _____

H. 15 ÷ 3 = _____

I. 9 ÷ 9 = _____

J. 16 ÷ 4 = _____

K. 20 ÷ 5 = _____

The Great Big Book of Super-Fun Math Activities   Scholastic Professional Books

Numbers and Signs in American Sign Language

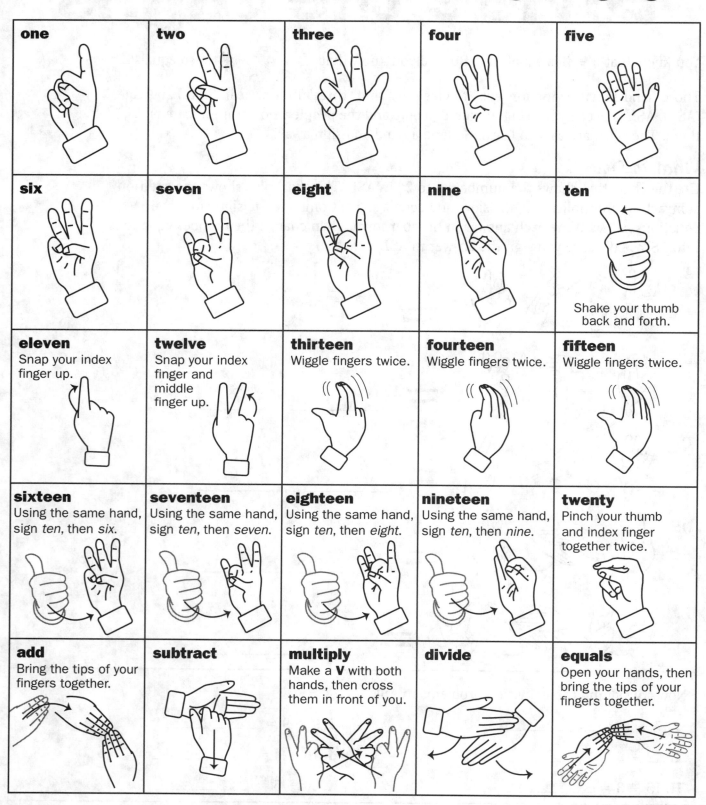

one	two	three	four	five

six	seven	eight	nine	ten
				Shake your thumb back and forth.

eleven	twelve	thirteen	fourteen	fifteen
Snap your index finger up.	Snap your index finger and middle finger up.	Wiggle fingers twice.	Wiggle fingers twice.	Wiggle fingers twice.

sixteen	seventeen	eighteen	nineteen	twenty
Using the same hand, sign *ten*, then *six*.	Using the same hand, sign *ten*, then *seven*.	Using the same hand, sign *ten*, then *eight*.	Using the same hand, sign *ten*, then *nine*.	Pinch your thumb and index finger together twice.

add	subtract	multiply	divide	equals
Bring the tips of your fingers together.		Make a **V** with both hands, then cross them in front of you.		Open your hands, then bring the tips of your fingers together.

The Great Big Book of Super-Fun Math Activities Scholastic Professional Books

A "World" of Averages

 Finding averages

Whole-number addition, division

Aim

Students compute averages to learn about averages at Walt Disney World.

Before the Activity

Explain to students that they will be learning about averages in Walt Disney World. Ask if they have heard of the word *average* before and how the word was used.

There are three types of averages: the *mean*, *median*, and *mode*. The mean, which students learn about in this activity, is computed by adding all of the numbers in a given set and dividing the sum by the number of elements added. Use counters to model the example problem in order to demonstrate finding the mean. Show separate groups of 10, 8, and 6 counters to stand for the hours walked each day. Then rearrange the counters until each group has an equal number. The number of counters in each group after rearranging into equal groups is the same as the number in each group after finding the mean.

Copy and distribute page 150.

During the Activity

Check that students are dividing their totals by the correct number of figures in each problem.

Reinforce the idea that the averages in the story reflect things that happen in Walt Disney World in a single day. If any class members have visited Walt Disney World, ask them to share any experiences that relate to the averages in the story.

After the Activity

Ask: *Why do you think the word* about *is used to describe the averages at Walt Disney World?*

ANSWERS

1. 100

2. 6,000

3. 1,013

4. 1,571

5. 4,247

6. 43,836

7. 15,033

8. 15,068

9. 1,000

A "World" of Averages

For many people, Florida's Walt Disney World is a magical place. You might say there's nothing average about it. But if you look closely, you can find lots of averages there!

What's an average? It's a number that describes a group of numbers. It isn't the biggest number in the group, or the smallest. It's somewhere in between. For example, the average number of people that visit Walt Disney World each day is about 77,000.

That doesn't mean that exactly 77,000 people visit the park every day. On a sunny day or a holiday, more than 77,000 people might visit the park. On a rainy day, fewer than 77,000 people might visit. But 77,000—the average—is about how many people visit on most days.

Want to find out more about an average day at Walt Disney World? Read on!

Finding an Average

Say you went on a three-day trip to Walt Disney World. How could you find the average number of hours you walked each day? Here's one way:

Add up the actual number of hours you walked each day:

10 hours + 8 hours + 6 hours = 24 hours

Then divide the total by the number of days you added up.

24 hours ÷ 3 days = 8 hours

You walked an average of 8 hours each day.

To find the average of any set of numbers, add all the numbers. Then divide the total by the number of numbers in the set. Example: to find the average of 40, 30, 22, and 20, first add. Then divide the total, 112, by 4. The average is 28.

What to Do:

By finding the average of each set of numbers below, learn more about what happens on an "average" day at Walt Disney World.

1. 25 and 175

   About _____ pairs of sunglasses are turned in to the Lost and Found in the Magic Kingdom every day.

2. 5,000 and 7,000

   You can choose from about _____ different food items.

3. 881; 924; and 1,234

   About _____ Mickey Mouse ears are sold.

4. 1,489; 1,584; and 1,640

   The monorail trains travel about _____ miles in and out of the parks.

5. 3,259; 4,039; and 5,443

   About _____ T-shirts are bought.

6. 10,660; 28,069; 58,392; and 78,223

   About _____ packets of ketchup are handed out.

7. 5,400; 10,000; 11,608; and 33,124

   About _____ hamburgers are sold.

8. 117; 3,274; 15,673; and 41,208

   About _____ pounds of potatoes are used to make french fries.

9. 35; 126; 780; 1,050; and 3,009

   About _____ Band-Aids are given out.

A Tasty Fraction Pie

- ✎ Using a model
- ✎ Subtracting fractions
- ✎ **LANGUAGE ARTS CONNECTIONS: Reading a story; completing a story**

⤳ Aim
Students use paper plate fraction wheels to model fractional parts of a whole as they follow the events in a story.

Before the Activity
Copy and distribute pages 152–153. You may want to identify the centers of the paper plates before you pass them out to students. To do this, mark the center of one paper plate by folding the plate in half and then in half again, like this:

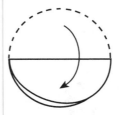 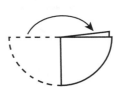

Unfold the plate and put a tack through the intersection of the folds. Then align your plate with the students' plates, and use the tack to make a hole in the center of each one.

During the Activity
Demonstrate how to turn the decorated plate to reveal the plain plate.

As students read through the story and show the different fractions, be sure they understand that the uncolored plate stands for the amount of pie that was eaten, while the colored plate represents the part of the pie that is left. For each stage of the story, ask students to name the fractional part of the pizza that was eaten and the fractional part that is left.

After the Activity
Have students share their story endings. Ask students: *Do you think you could still illustrate the events in the story if you turned your colored plate in the opposite direction? Why or why not? How can you use your fraction pie to find how many fourths equal one half?*

A Tasty Fraction Pie

Once, there lived a chef named Sheri. One morning, she emptied out all of her cupboards and made a magic pie—

Before you finish the story, make your own pie! Here's how.

You Need:
2 plain paper plates (each 8 inches)
crayons
scissors
glue or paste

What to Do:

1. Color the pizza pattern and paste it onto one plate. Cut along the dotted line, as shown.

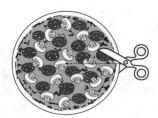

2. Mark the center point of the second plate.

3. Use a ruler to draw a straight line from the center of the second plate to its edge, like this.

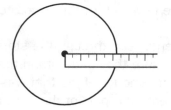

4. Cut along the lines on both plates.

5. Slip the two plates together at the slits, like this:

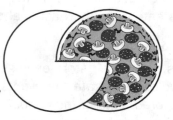

6. Now you have a magic fraction pie! And you are ready to go on with the story. Whenever you see a picture of Sheri's pie, make yours look the same.

The Amazing Fraction Pie

At noon, Sheri took her magic pie out of the oven. It was so pretty, she couldn't bear to cut it up. So Sheri put the whole pie on a table for everyone to see.

At 3:00, Sheri's cat, Sherlock, spotted the pie. To Sherlock, the pie looked tastier than meow chow! So he nibbled off $\frac{1}{4}$ of it. Now just $\frac{3}{4}$ of the magic pie was left.

At 6:00, Sheri's dog, Sam, sniffed the pie. It smelled better than a steak bone! So he put his paws on the table and took a big bite. Now only $\frac{1}{2}$ of the pie was left.

At 9:00, Sheri's friend Sarah stopped by for a snack. But Sheri was out shopping. So Sarah helped herself to a piece of the pie. Now $\frac{3}{4}$ of the pie was gone!

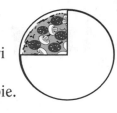

At 12:00, Sheri came home and ran to see her pretty pie. What do you think happened next? Write your own story ending here:

_____
_____
_____
_____
_____
_____

Fractions Under the Sea

Identifying fractions represented by symbols and pictures

Identifying fractional parts of a whole and of a group

✸ Aim

Students practice identifying fractions as they play a fraction bingo game.

Before the Activity

Copy and distribute pages 155–156. Each partner gets a different game board. If students need practice identifying fractions, have them identify the fraction shown in each square on the game boards before they begin playing.

Extension

After students have played the game several times, have them write a note to a friend describing one or two strategies they used.

Name _____

Fractions Under the Sea

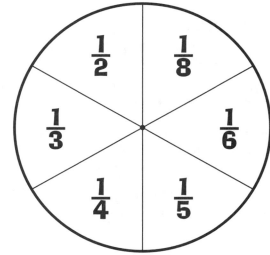

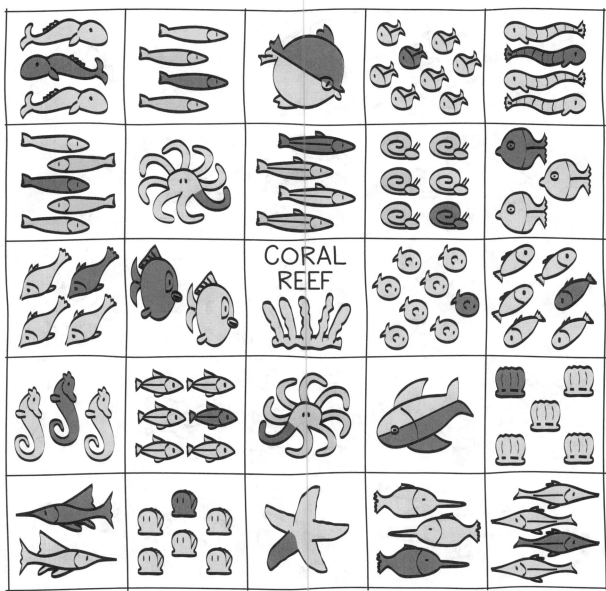

The Great Big Book of Super-Fun Math Activities   Scholastic Professional Books

You Need:
50 counters or beans
paper clip
pencil

Object:
To be the first player to cover a row on your fraction bingo card.

Number of Players: 2

To Play:
- Players each choose a card. Cover the Coral Reef box with a counter.
- Take turns spinning.
- After each spin, find a picture on your card that matches the fraction on the spinner. Cover that box with a counter. Cover only one box on each spin.
- There is more than one picture for each fraction. Choose carefully! The first player to cover a row wins. The row can go across, down, or diagonally.
- Switch cards and play again.

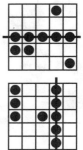

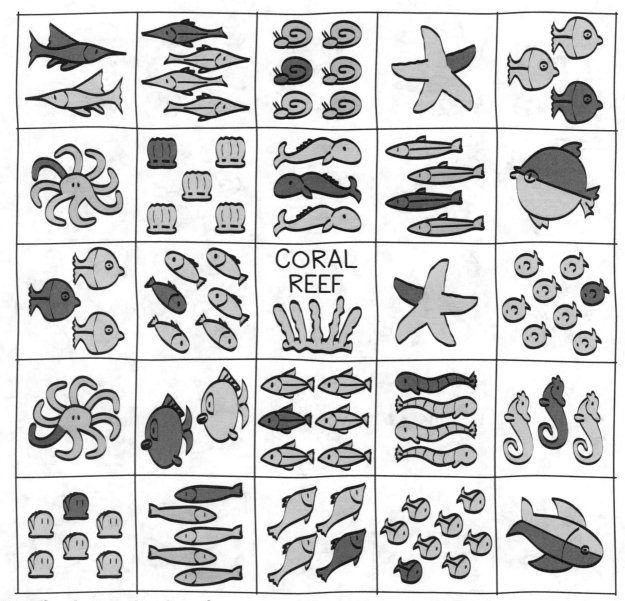

Wind-Blown Fractions

✎ **Rounding fractions**

✎ **Estimating fractional parts of a whole or parts of a group**

✐ Aim

Students look at a picture of broken kites. They decide whether the fraction remaining of each kite is closer to 0, 1, or ½.

Before the Activity

You can demonstrate fraction estimation by using fraction models of eighths, or a rectangular piece of paper cut into eight equal pieces. Show students the whole rectangle. Then hold up different numbers of sections. Each time you hold up a section, ask: *Am I holding almost the whole rectangle, almost none of the rectangle, or about half of the rectangle?*

Copy and distribute pages 158–159. You may want to have students tape the two pages together so that they can read the riddle sentence more easily. Review the directions and the hints for deciding whether the shaded portion of a kite is close to 0, 1, or ½.

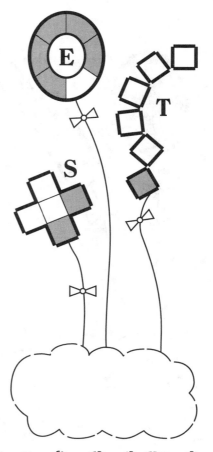

⚷ ANSWERS

The answer to the riddle ("Why did Kyle get an A on its math test?"): BECAUSE THE TEST WAS A BREEZE!

Wind-Blown Fractions

Kyle's kites are soaring in the March wind. But after a full day of flying, there's only a fraction left of each one. Look at the shaded part of each kite. That shows the part that is left. Estimate what fractional part is left and you'll untangle a riddle. Up, up, and away!

What to Do:

The clouds beneath the kites hold the answer to a riddle.

▶ Look at the fraction or number below each blank. Then look at the kites above that cloud.

▶ Pick the kite that is the closest to the fraction or number (0, $\frac{1}{2}$, or 1). Then write the letter of that kite on the blank.

▶ You won't need to use every kite. And some kites you'll use more than once. Some letters are already filled in for you.

Why did Kyle get an A on his math test?

T E E

S E A T

H S

B	C	U							
1	0	$\frac{1}{2}$	1	0	$\frac{1}{2}$	1	0	1	$\frac{1}{2}$	0

Trim off this strip and attach to page 159.

If almost none of a kite is left, the fraction is close to 0. If almost a whole kite is left, the fraction is about 1.

And if the amount left is somewhere in the middle, the fraction is about $\frac{1}{2}$.

Attach page 158 here.

W

A

R

S

I

A

B

E

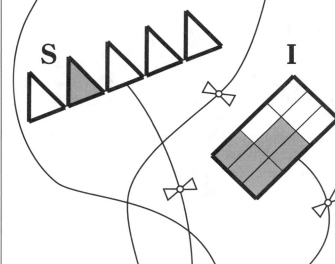

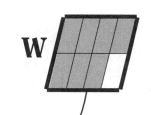

$$\overline{} \quad \overline{} \quad \overline{} \quad \overline{}$$
$$1 \quad 1\frac{1}{2} \quad 0 \quad 0$$

Z !

$$\overline{} \quad \overline{} \quad \overline{} \quad \overline{} \quad \overline{}$$
$$0 \quad \frac{1}{2} \quad 1 \quad 1 \quad 1$$

Peter's Pan Pizza Fractions

- **Understanding fractions**
- **Ordering like fractions**
- **LITERATURE CONNECTION: Reading a cartoon story**

Aim

Students order fractions to help a story character fix the signs in a pizza parlor.

Before the Activity

Copy and distribute pages 161–162.

During the Activity

Cut a paper "pizza" into fourths and choose two students to practice acting out the cartoon story by putting the pieces of pizza together.

After the Activity

Cut a large, circular piece of construction paper into as many slices as there are students in your class. Hand out one slice to each student and ask them to write one of the following statements on their slice:

"I like pizza a lot!"

"I don't like pizza."

"I've never eaten pizza."

After each student has filled in his or her slice, collect them all and arrange them back into a circle on the bulletin board. Put students' responses to each question together, and you'll form a pie chart, or circle graph. Ask: *What fraction of the whole pizza is one of our slices? What fraction of our class likes pizza? What fraction of our class does not like pizza? What fraction of our class has never tried pizza?*

Peter's Pan Pizza Fractions

Order fractions to put Peter's pizzeria back in order!

1 Hey, Peter, how big is a large pizza?

All my pizzas are this big, Suzie.

2 Huh?

I've only got one pizza pan, but you can get different-sized pizzas. I sell them by the fraction.

3 My $\frac{1}{4}$ pie has only one slice. The $\frac{2}{4}$ pie has two slices. The $\frac{3}{4}$ pizza has three slices. And the $\frac{4}{4}$ pizza is a whole pie!

4 $\frac{1}{4}$ $\frac{2}{4}$ $\frac{3}{4}$ $\frac{4}{4}$

See? I hung pictures of the different pizza fractions. You just...

Ooof!

5 Oh no! My pictures are all mixed up! Now nobody can order pizzas!

...unless we order the fractions!

6 It's easy to compare fractions if the denominators are the same. The one with the smallest numerator is the smallest fraction.

So $\frac{1}{4}$ is smaller than $\frac{3}{4}$!

⑦ And $\frac{2}{4}$ is between $\frac{1}{4}$ and $\frac{3}{4}$. So I can hang it here.

Now you've got the "hang" of it!

⑧ Thanks to fractions, you're back in action! Now we can sit and rest.

You sit first, Suzie...I've only got one chair.

What to Do:

Peter also uses fractions to sell his garlic bread, lasagna, and cake. He cuts bread into three pieces, lasagna into six pieces, and cake into eight pieces. A strong wind blew into Peter's restaurant and knocked over his displays. Draw a line from each picture to where it would go on the sign. The first one is done for you.

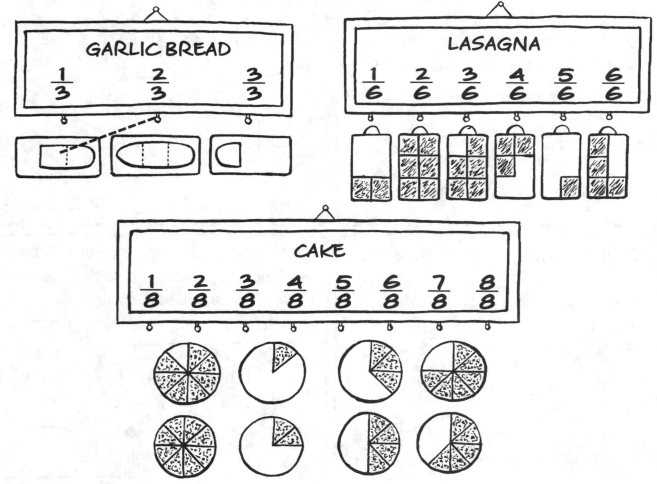

Handy Dandy Fraction Candy

✏️ **Adding fractions to make one whole**

✏️ **Using equivalent fractions**

🔑 **ANSWERS**

Here are six ways to make whole candy bars out of the fraction pieces. Your students may find more.

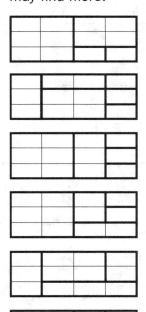

🎯 Aim

Students use pictures of candy bars to find fractions that add up to one whole.

Before the Activity

Copy and distribute page 164.

During the Activity

Point out that one whole candy bar contains 12 squares. Ask questions such as: *How many squares make up $\frac{1}{12}$ of the bar? How many squares make up $\frac{1}{6}$? Which two fractions make $\frac{1}{2}$ of the bar? What other fractions make up $\frac{1}{2}$?*

After the Activity

Invite volunteers to share their solutions.

Extension

Have students use the candy bars to illustrate the following situations:

- Gil ate twice as much of the candy bar as Jonah. What fraction of the candy bar did each of them eat? How much was left over? (Possible answer: Gil ate $\frac{1}{2}$, Jonah ate $\frac{1}{4}$, and $\frac{1}{4}$ was left over.)

- If Sandy joined them and they all ate the same amount, how much would they each have eaten? ($\frac{1}{3}$ each)

Have students work in pairs and invite them to create their own candy bar questions.

Name _____

Handy Dandy Fraction Candy

Use these candy bars to see just how sweet fractions can be!

You Need:
scissors

What to Do:

- Cut out the candy bars along the dashed lines.
- Work with a partner. Use both candy bars to do the activity.

1. Arrange some of the pieces this way to make a whole bar:

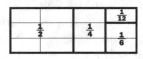

Here's how you can show that combination of fractions in an equation:

$\frac{1}{2} + \frac{1}{4} + \frac{1}{6} + \frac{1}{12} = 1$ whole candy bar

2. Can you find another way to make one whole candy bar without using the $\frac{1}{2}$ piece? What would it look like? How would you write it in a fraction equation?

3. How many ways can you use the pieces to make whole candy bars? (Each whole bar will have 12 pieces.) Draw a picture of each solution on a separate sheet of paper.

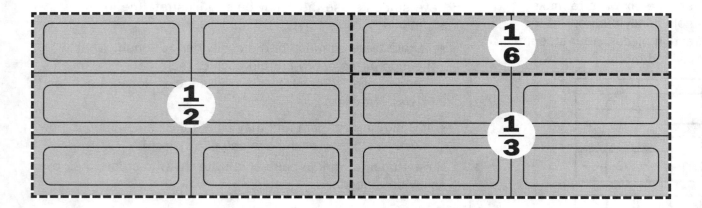

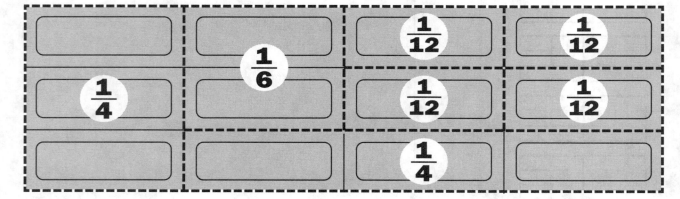

Fractions by the Dozen

 Using a model to explore equivalent fractions

ANSWERS

$\frac{2}{6}$ = 4 counters

$\frac{1}{2}$ = 6 counters

$\frac{4}{12}$ = 4 counters

$\frac{8}{12}$ = 8 counters

$\frac{3}{6}$ = 6 counters

$\frac{1}{4}$ = 3 counters

$\frac{2}{12}$ = 2 counters

$\frac{1}{6}$ = 2 counters

$\frac{2}{3}$ = 8 counters

$\frac{3}{12}$ = 3 counters

$\frac{9}{12}$ = 9 counters

$\frac{2}{4}$ = 6 counters

$\frac{4}{6}$ = 8 counters

$\frac{6}{12}$ = 6 counters

$\frac{3}{4}$ = 9 counters

Equivalent Fractions

2 counters = $\frac{1}{6}$, $\frac{2}{12}$

3 counters = $\frac{1}{4}$, $\frac{3}{12}$

4 counters = $\frac{1}{3}$, $\frac{2}{6}$, $\frac{4}{12}$

6 counters = $\frac{1}{2}$, $\frac{2}{4}$, $\frac{3}{6}$, $\frac{6}{12}$

8 counters = $\frac{2}{3}$, $\frac{4}{6}$, $\frac{8}{12}$

9 counters = $\frac{3}{4}$, $\frac{9}{12}$

One way to prove that two fractions are equivalent is by showing that they both fill the same amount of holes in the egg carton.

Aim

Students work with an egg carton and counters to discover equivalent fractions.

Before the Activity

Copy and distribute pages 166–167. You may want to review how to represent fractional parts of one whole and fractional parts of a group.

During the Activity

For fractions with denominators other than 12, students can place pieces of string or thin strips of paper across their egg cartons to help divide the cartons into equal parts. Remind students that the denominator of a fraction tells how many equal parts the carton should have, and the numerator tells how many of those parts should contain counters.

After the Activity

Ask: *How would you tell someone why the fractions $\frac{1}{2}$ are $\frac{4}{8}$ are equivalent?*

Extension

Arrange eight chairs in a horizontal row in front of the class, separate the class into two teams, and have them play an equivalent fractions game. To play, teams take turns having several members sit in the row of chairs to show a fraction of the row (such as $\frac{1}{2}$, $\frac{2}{8}$, $\frac{6}{8}$, etc.). Both teams list the fraction or fractions shown by the sitting students. Teams earn one point for every correct fraction they list. If the team with sitting students does not list a fraction, they should subtract one point from their score. This game can also be played with rows of 6, 9, 10, 12, 14, 15, 16, 30, 24, and 25 chairs.

Fractions by the Dozen

You Need: counters

What to Do:

Look at the fractions. Figure out how many counters you will need to fill that fraction of the egg carton. Put only one counter in each hole in the carton. For example, $\frac{1}{3}$ = 4 counters.

$\frac{1}{3}$ = _____ 4 counters

$\frac{2}{6}$ = _____

$\frac{1}{2}$ = _____

$\frac{4}{12}$ = _____

$\frac{8}{12}$ = _____

$\frac{3}{6}$ = _____

$\frac{1}{4}$ = _____

$\frac{2}{12}$ = _____

$\frac{1}{6}$ = _____

$\frac{2}{3}$ = _____

$\frac{3}{12}$ = _____

$\frac{9}{12}$ = _____

$\frac{2}{4}$ = _____

$\frac{4}{6}$ = _____

$\frac{6}{12}$ = _____

$\frac{3}{4}$ = _____

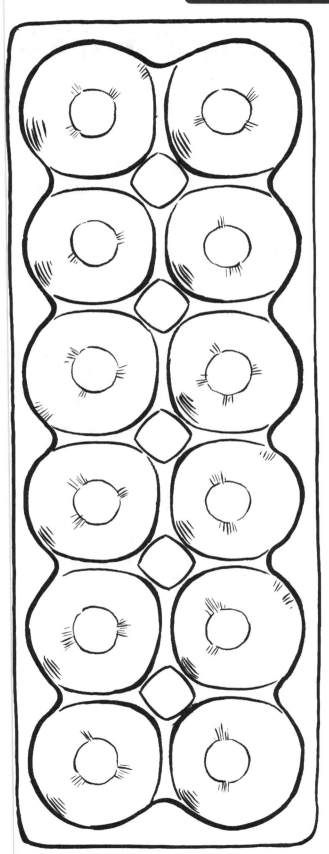

⚡ BRAIN POWER ⚡
The fractions that are made with the same
number of counters are equivalent.
Which equivalent fractions did you find?
How can you show that they are equivalent?

Fraction Carnival

✏ **Identify equivalent fractions**

🎯 Aim

Students color in balloons to learn about equivalent fractions.

Before the Activity

Copy and distribute page 169. Ask students to examine the fraction balloons and review halves, fourths, eighths, and sixteenths. Then review equivalent fractions with the class, particularly the equivalents for the fractions given on the spinner: $\frac{1}{8}$, $\frac{1}{4}$, $\frac{3}{4}$, and $\frac{1}{2}$. For each, elicit a list of equivalent fractions and write them on the chalkboard. Leave the list where students can easily refer to it as they play the game.

After the Activity

Ask: *Did you find a strategy that could help you win the game?* (Players should find that it is advisable to color in the biggest balloon pieces first, leaving the smallest pieces for the end of the game.)

Fraction Carnival

You Need:
crayons
pencil and paper clip

Come one, come all! The balloons at the Math Carnival are full of fun and fractions!

Object:
Be the first one to color in all of your balloons at the carnival.

Number of Players: 2

To Play:

▶ Each player chooses one group of balloons to color. Decide who will go first.

▶ Take turns spinning.

▶ The spinner will stop on a fraction. Color in any balloon pieces (in your group only) that equal that fraction. You can color in parts of more than one balloon during a turn.

▶ If you cannot use up the whole fraction in one turn, skip your turn.

The first person to color all of his or her balloons (with nothing left over) wins.

The spinner landed on $\frac{1}{2}$. I can color in one $\frac{1}{2}$ piece, or two $\frac{1}{4}$ pieces.

I spun $\frac{3}{4}$. I'm going to color in one $\frac{1}{4}$ piece, two $\frac{1}{8}$ pieces, and four $\frac{1}{16}$ pieces.

Spin the paper clip around the pencil.

$\frac{1}{8}$ $\frac{1}{4}$

$\frac{3}{4}$ $\frac{1}{2}$

Yo-Ho-Ho and a Map Full of Fractions

✎ **Finding equivalent
fractions**

✦➷ Aim
Students find equivalent fractions in a desert island game.

Before the Activity
Review equivalent fractions by drawing fraction pictures on the chalkboard, such as $\frac{6}{12}$, $\frac{1}{2}$, and $\frac{2}{4}$. Copy and distribute pages 171–172.

During the Activity
Make sure students know how to use the spinner (as shown in the game directions) by spinning a paper clip around the point of a pencil.

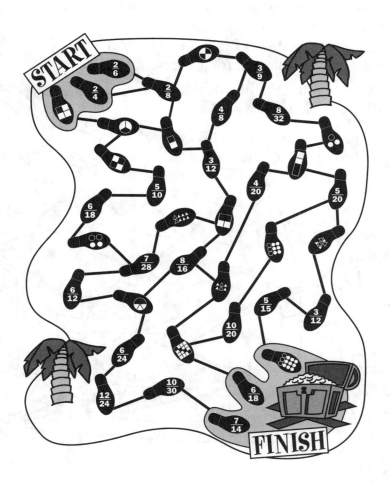

Yo-Ho-Ho and a Map Full of Fractions

Race your friends around a desert island to find equivalent fractions and a pirate's treasure.

You Need:
counter for each player
pencil and paper clip

Object:
To be the first to reach the treasure chest.

Number of Players: 2 or more

To Play:

▶ Decide who will go first. All players begin on START.

▶ Spin the spinner. Move to the closest footprint that is equivalent to the fraction that you spun. For example: $\frac{1}{2}$ is equivalent to $\frac{6}{12}$ or 🔘🔘 . If the fraction equivalent is not right next to the fraction that you are on, skip to the nearest footprint with the equivalent fraction.

▶ After you have moved your counter, it's the next player's turn. If you could not move to another space, you must wait your turn to try again.

▶ The game ends when the first player reaches the treasure chest at FINISH.

Spin the paper clip around the pencil.

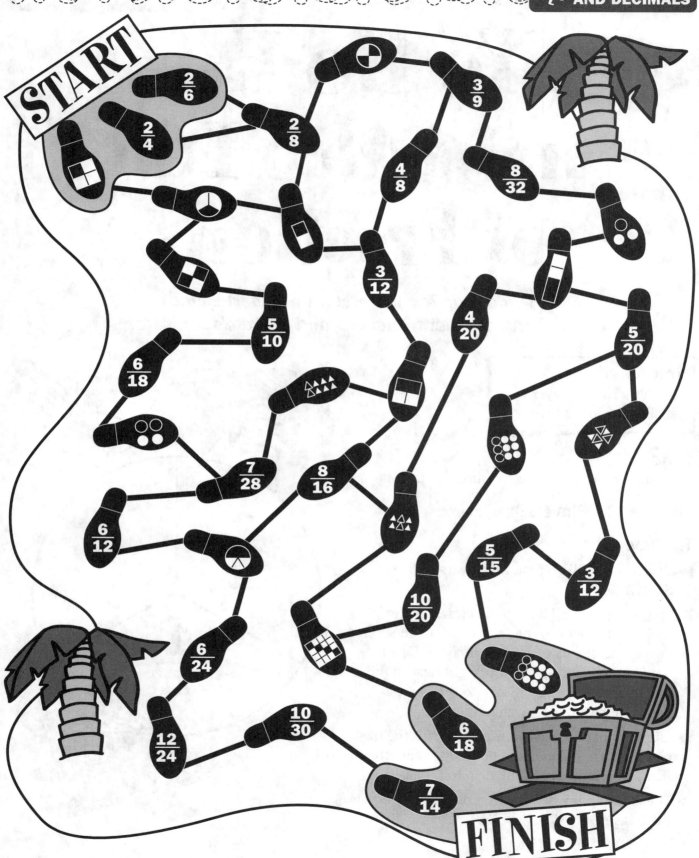

Filling Up on Fractions

REAL-LIFE MATH:
Increasing a recipe

Fraction addition

Aim
Students add fractions to increase a recipe for gorp (good old raisins and peanuts).

Before the Activity
To prepare students for the math in this activity, review adding fractions with like denominators. You may also want to review reducing fractions to lowest terms. Then copy and distribute page 174.

During the Activity
Read through the recipe with the class and have students identify the amount of each ingredient needed to serve 2 people. Have students look at the fractions they will add to increase each ingredient. Ask them what they notice about the fractions. Help students understand that they add the same fraction each time they want to increase the number of servings by 2.

After the Activity
Ask students: *Suppose you wanted to increase the recipe to serve more people. How could you figure out how much of each ingredient to use?*

If the denominators are the same, just add the numerators.
$$\frac{1}{5} + \frac{1}{5} = \frac{2}{5}$$

ANSWERS
Note: some answers reflect fractions rewritten in lowest terms.

Serves 4	Serves 6
$\frac{2}{6}$ or $\frac{1}{3}$	$\frac{3}{6}$ or $\frac{1}{2}$
$\frac{2}{4}$ or $\frac{1}{2}$	$\frac{3}{4}$
$\frac{2}{3}$	$\frac{3}{3}$ or 1
$\frac{2}{2}$ or 1	$1\frac{1}{2}$
$\frac{2}{2}$ or 1	$1\frac{1}{2}$

Filling Up on Fractions

You Need:
measuring cup
ingredients listed in the chart
large bowl and spoon

You've been mountain climbing all day. You're almost at the peak. You're hungry. Time for gorp! The letters in **gorp** stand for **good old raisins** and **peanuts**. It's a mixture of raisins, nuts, and sweets. Gorp gives you energy, and it's easy to carry. By the time you finish your gorp, you're ready to climb again. See you at the top!

What to Do:

The recipe below shows the amount of each ingredient you need to make enough gorp for 2 people. What if you want to feed 4 or 6 people? Add the fractions to increase the amounts. Then mix the ingredients together—and munch on gorp!

You can change the gorp recipe to suit your taste. What other ingredients would you add to your gorp?

How do you add fractions?

If the denominators are the same, just add the numerators.
$\frac{1}{5} + \frac{1}{5} = \frac{2}{5}$

If the numerator and the denominator are the same, the fraction is equal to 1.
$\frac{5}{5} = 1$

INGREDIENT	SERVES 2	SERVES 4	SERVES 6
Sunflower seeds	$\frac{1}{6}$ cup + $\frac{1}{6}$ cup = _____	+ $\frac{1}{6}$ cup = _____	
Raisins	$\frac{1}{4}$ cup + $\frac{1}{4}$ cup = _____	+ $\frac{1}{4}$ cup = _____	
Unsalted peanuts	$\frac{1}{3}$ cup + $\frac{1}{3}$ cup = _____	+ $\frac{1}{3}$ cup = _____	
Granola	$\frac{1}{2}$ cup + $\frac{1}{2}$ cup = _____	+ $\frac{1}{2}$ cup = _____	
Plain M&Ms®	$\frac{1}{2}$ cup + $\frac{1}{2}$ cup = _____	+ $\frac{1}{2}$ cup = _____	

Take Note of Fractions

✏ **Fraction addition**

✏ **MUSIC CONNECTION: Musical notation**

Aim
Students read about a fictional musical group, Fractured, to learn about how fractions apply to music. They label music measures with fractions and beats.

Before the Activity
Copy and distribute pages 176–177. Discuss with the class the notes and rests in the Take Note! box. Talk about the number of beats each note or rest is worth. You may need to explain the concept of a rest (a break in the music). Encourage students who play instruments to share what they know about notes and rests.

During the Activity
As students mark each measure with beats and fractions, point out that the fractions in each measure will add up to one whole.

After the Activity
If possible, ask a music teacher or anyone who can play a musical instrument to play each measure on page 177.

Extension
Obtain real sheet music. Have the class look at the music and pick out the notes and symbols they recognize.

ANSWERS
2. 1 + 2 + 1 + 1 + 2 + 1 = 8
3. 2 + 2 + 1 + 1 + 1 + 1 = 8
4. 4 + 1 + 2 + 1 = 8
5. 4 + 1 + 1 + 1 + 1 = 8
6. 1 + 1 + 2 + 1 + 2 + 1 = 8

Take Note of Fractions

Meet the hot new band, Fractured. They sing. They dance. And their new album is coming to a record store near you. What makes Fractured so popular? Fans like the way they look—and the way they sing. Most of Fractured's songs are written by group members.

Making music takes more than just talent. It also takes fractions! How? Think of a sentence in a book. It's divided into words. A musical sentence is divided into measures. And just like a word is made up of letters, a measure is made up of notes.

Notes are named after fractions: half note, quarter note, eighth note.

The notes create the beat of a song. The beat makes a song sound fast or slow. The number of notes in a measure may vary, but the beat always stays the same.

Fractured member Dina Mite says, "When I work on a song, I'll set a beat and then start writing. I think that some of our best songs started with a good beat."

What to Do:

Here are six measures from a song Dina wrote for the group's album *Fractured Beat*. Add up the notes in each measure. Here's how:

▶ Find each note in the Take Note! box.

▶ Under each note, write the fraction it stands for. Above each note, write the number of beats it stands for.

▶ Add up the beats. Each measure should add up to eight beats. The first one is done for you.

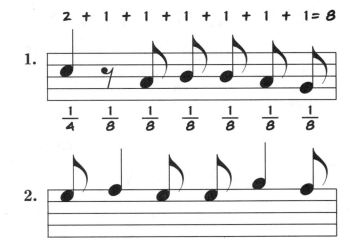

TAKE NOTE!

Notes are like a code. Each note stands for a certain number of beats.

♪ **This is an eighth note ($\frac{1}{8}$). It counts as 1 beat.**

♩ **This is a quarter note ($\frac{1}{4}$). It counts as 2 beats.**

♩ **This is a half note ($\frac{1}{2}$). It counts as 4 beats.**

𝄾 **This is an eighth rest ($\frac{1}{8}$).* It counts as 1 beat.**

𝄽 **This is a quarter rest ($\frac{1}{4}$).* It counts as 2 beats.**

▬ **This is a half rest ($\frac{1}{2}$).* It counts as 4 beats.**

* Rests are pauses between notes that are not played.
  But they are still counted as beats in the measure.

The Great Big Book of Super-Fun Math Activities   Scholastic Professional Books

Decimals Around the Diamond

Comparing decimals

Aim

Students compare decimals in the form of famous baseball players' batting averages and rank them from highest to lowest.

Before the Activity

Copy and distribute page 179. Refer students to the information about decimals in the box. Give them several decimal numbers (for example, .5, .68, .245) and ask volunteers to read the decimals. Then explain how decimals relate to fractions. The farthest place value on the right of a decimal number would be the denominator in its fraction equivalent. For example, Cal Ripken's average of .262 is the same as the fraction $\frac{262}{1,000}$. That means, for every 1,000 times Ripken would come to bat, he would get 262 hits.

Discuss with students that whenever they see a money amount, such as $2.47, they are looking at a decimal number. The decimal portion represents a fractional part of a dollar (100 cents). So $2.47 equals 2 dollars and $\frac{47}{100}$ of a dollar.

During the Activity

Here's a tip for students: When you are comparing decimal numbers with the same number of places, you can compare them as if they were whole numbers. Simply ignore the decimal points.

After the Activity

Send students on a "decimal scavenger hunt" through old newspapers and magazines. Have them cut out any decimals they find, glue them on construction paper, and label them as "tenths," "hundredths," etc.

Extension 1

Baseball fans in your class can pick their favorite players, track their batting averages in the sports pages each week, and compare them to some of the 1995 players' averages.

Extension 2

The First Book of Baseball by Benjamin Brewster (New York: Franklin Watts) is an excellent resource describing the rules and numbers of baseball for young readers.

ANSWERS

Here is the correct ranking from highest to lowest:
1—Tony Gwynn (.368)
2—Mike Piazza (.346)
3—Barry Larkin (.319)
4—Kirby Puckett (.314)
5—Frank Thomas (.308)
6—Mo Vaughn (.300)
7—Barry Bonds (.294)
8—Cal Ripken, Jr. (.262)
9—Ken Griffey, Jr. (.258)
10—David Justice (.253)

Decimals Around the Diamond

Take a swing at batting averages to see who was the best hitter in baseball.

Baseball fans always argue who the best player was. Some say it was Ken Griffey, Jr. Others insist it was Cal Ripkin, Jr. Still others claim it was Barry Bonds. Everybody seems to have a favorite!

When it comes to finding the best hitter, though, no one can argue with batting averages. The batting average shows how often a baseball player gets a hit. It is a 3-digit decimal number, and looks like this: .328, .287, .311, .253. The larger the batting average is, the better the hitter is.

Decimals are numbers between 0 and 1. They are written to the right of the ones place. Decimals always have a decimal point to the left of them.

.325

decimal point · tenths place · hundredths place · thousandths place

What to Do:

Read the chart of baseball players' batting averages from 1995. Rank the batting averages. This means number the batting averages in order from highest to lowest. (See Home Plate for help.) Write the numbers 1 to 10 in the boxes next to the names—1 for the highest average, 10 for the lowest. Ready? Play ball!

Rank	Player (Team)	1995 Batting Average
☐	Cal Ripken, Jr. (Baltimore Orioles)	.262
☐	Barry Bonds (San Francisco Giants)	.294
☐	Mo Vaughn (Boston Red Sox)	.300
☐	Barry Larkin (Cincinnati Reds)	.319
☐	Kirby Puckett (Minnesota Twins)	.314
☐	Tony Gwynn (San Diego Padres)	.368
☐	Ken Griffey, Jr. (Seattle Mariners)	.258
☐	Mike Piazza (Los Angeles Dodgers)	.346
☐	Frank Thomas (Chicago White Sox)	.308
☐	David Justice (Atlanta Braves)	.253

HOME PLATE

To rank decimal numbers:
- Start at the left.
- Compare the digits in the same place.
- Find the first place where the digits are different.
- The number with the smaller digit is the smaller number. EXAMPLE: Rank .317 and .312

.317
↕ ↕ ↕
.312

So .312 is smaller than .317.

Decimal Deliveries

 Decimal addition

SOCIAL STUDIES
CONNECTION:
Reading a map

Aim
Students read a map and add decimals to find the shortest routes for a balloon delivery service.

Before the Activity
Copy and distribute pages 181–182. Have students practice adding tenths. Point out that adding money is one way of using decimals that they are already familiar with.

During the Activity
Have students look over the map before they answer the questions. Stress that each distance on the map refers to only one line between two points and thaht the map is not drawn to scale.

Though students may use a calculator to compute the distances in this activity, encourage them to add some of the decimals with paper and pencil to ensure that they understand the process. Suggest that students write the decimal point in the sum before they begin to compute. They can trace routes on the map with colored pencils, crayons, or markers.

After students answer the questions, have them compare answers. This will help them check that they have found the shortest route and will show them alternate answers to the questions.

After the Activity
Ask students: *What else would you need to think about if you wanted to plan the best balloon delivery route?*

Extension
The American Automobile Association offers its members a route-planning service that includes free maps. If you or one of your students' parents belongs to the AAA, have them prepare a series of maps for a trip from your town to a destination chosen by the class. Students can use the maps to check whether the AAA chose the shortest route or the most scenic route. They can also use the maps to plan side trips, to write stories about the trip to their destination, or to compute distances between towns and cities.

ANSWERS

1. 2.9 miles

2. He could take four routes. The shortest would be 18.2 miles: from Bergenfield to Oradell to Fair Lawn, and back to Bergenfield.

3. 31.2 miles, round-trip.

4. The shortest routes are: Bergenfield to Yonkers and back (27.6 miles), then to Oradell, to Maywood, and back (12.6 miles).

5. 51.8 miles, round-trip

Decimal Deliveries

Having a party? Don't forget the balloons—and the decimals!

Some people deliver furniture. Others deliver pizza. Darla Bennet tops them all. She delivers balloons! And she uses decimals to get the job done. Darla builds balloon sculptures for parties. She makes them at her store, Balloons To Go, in Bergenfield, New Jersey. What sculptures has Darla made? She's built Teenage Mutant Ninja Turtles, Batman, the Cowardly Lion from *The Wizard of Oz*, even Marge Simpson!

After a balloon sculpture is finished, it must be delivered. Darla and her drivers use a map to find each customer's town. Then they load the van and head for the party!

The distances on the map are written in decimal units called **tenths**. Tenths are another way of writing a fraction that has ten as a denominator. If a distance on the map is 7.1 miles long, that is the same as saying the distance is 7 and $\frac{1}{10}$ miles long. Darla adds up distances on the map. Then she can find the shortest way to get from her store to a party—and back again.

Darla has a good reason for planning ahead. "I can make more deliveries if I know a driver is going to be back on time," she says. "And I can make more people happy."

What to Do:

Use the map to help Darla make her deliveries. Add up decimals to find the shortest routes from her store and back.

Here's how to say decimal numbers. For .6 say "six tenths." For 4.3, say "four and three-tenths."

It's easy to add tenths. Just keep the decimal points lined up—even for your answer. Add as you usually do.

1. Darla has to deliver balloons to a party in Demarest, New Jersey. How far away is it from Balloons To Go?

_____

2. Darla sends a driver to Fair Lawn, New Jersey. How many routes could he take? Which is shortest?

_____

_____

_____

3. 250 balloons are going to a wedding in Fort Lee, New Jersey. And a balloon elephant is for a birthday party in Jersey City, New Jersey. How many miles will it take to make one trip?

_____

4. Saturday, Darla has to deliver balloons to Yonkers, New York, Oradel, New Jersey, and Maywood, New Jersey. What routes should she use?

_____

_____

5. Darla wants you to deliver . . .
   ✔ A balloon gorilla to the Empire State Building in New York City.
   ✔ 20 pom-poms to Giants Stadium.
   ✔ Two balloon clowns to Pearl River, New York.

   How many miles will her trip take?

_____

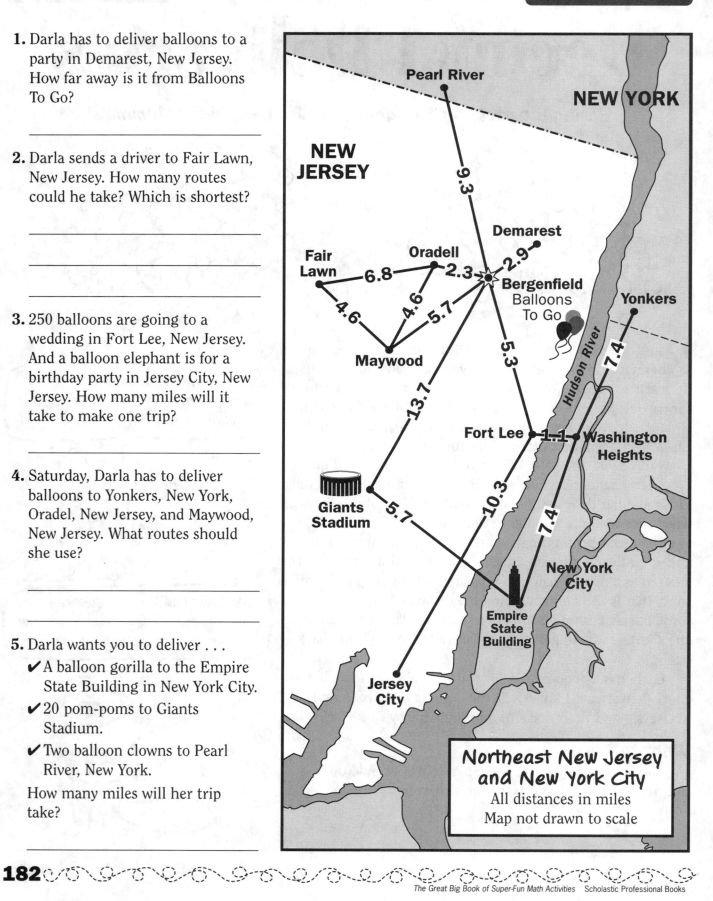

Northeast New Jersey and New York City
All distances in miles
Map not drawn to scale

The Great Big Book of Super-Fun Math Activities Scholastic Professional Books

Diving for Decimals

✎ **Reading and writing decimals**

✎ **Adding decimals**

✏ Aim

Students learn to add decimals in an undersea game.

Before the Activity

If students have not worked with decimals, you will need to discuss with them what decimals are and how to add them. Go over the pronunciation of *tenths* and *hundredths,* and explain that each successive place to the right of the decimal point is ten times smaller than the place to its left. (You may want to use dollars, dimes, and pennies as an example.) On the chalkboard, show some examples of how to line up decimal points in order to add decimals.

Copy and distribute pages 184–185. Before students begin playing the game, ask them to read through the rules. Then ask for a volunteer to explain the rules to the rest of the class.

During the Activity

If students are playing the game in groups, walk around and "visit" each group to make sure each student is adding his or her decimal scores correctly.

After the Activity

Have a class member look up the word *decimal* in the dictionary. Ask: *Why is the word* decimal *used to describe the numbers we talked about today?*

Extension

The Magic School Bus books, written by Joanna Cole and illustrated by Bruce Degen, are a fun way for younger students to learn about science topics such as the sea.

Diving for Decimals

Decimals add up to fun in this underwater game!

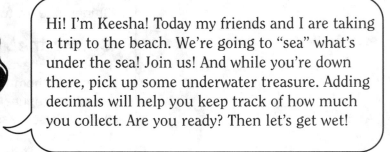

Hi! I'm Keesha! Today my friends and I are taking a trip to the beach. We're going to "sea" what's under the sea! Join us! And while you're down there, pick up some underwater treasure. Adding decimals will help you keep track of how much you collect. Are you ready? Then let's get wet!

You Need:
paper and pencils
paper clip

Object:
To get the highest number of pounds of treasure.

Number of players:
2 or more

To Play:

- Pick one of the four game piece characters. Cut out your game piece.

- Each player should take a piece of paper to keep track of your score.

- Spin to see who will go first. The player with the highest number goes first.

- When it's your turn, spin again. Move ahead that number of spaces.

- The decimal numbers on the board show how many pounds of treasure you've collected. When you land on a decimal number, add that number to your score.

- The first player to get back to shore gets a bonus of 5.2 pounds of treasure.

- Whoever gets back to shore with the most pounds of treasure is the winner.

To Add Decimals:

✔ Line up the decimal points in the numbers before you add.

✔ Add the same way you add whole numbers.

✔ Remember to write the decimal point in the sum! EXAMPLE: 2.14 + 1.47

$$
\begin{array}{r}
2.14 \\
+ 1.47 \\
\hline
3.61
\end{array}
$$

✔ If one number has fewer digits after the decimal point, you can add zeros to the right of the shorter number.

EXAMPLE: 5.3 + 1.12

$$
\begin{array}{r}
5.30 \\
+ 1.12 \\
\hline
6.42
\end{array}
$$

| **Carlos** | **Kim** | **Keesha** | **Allan** |

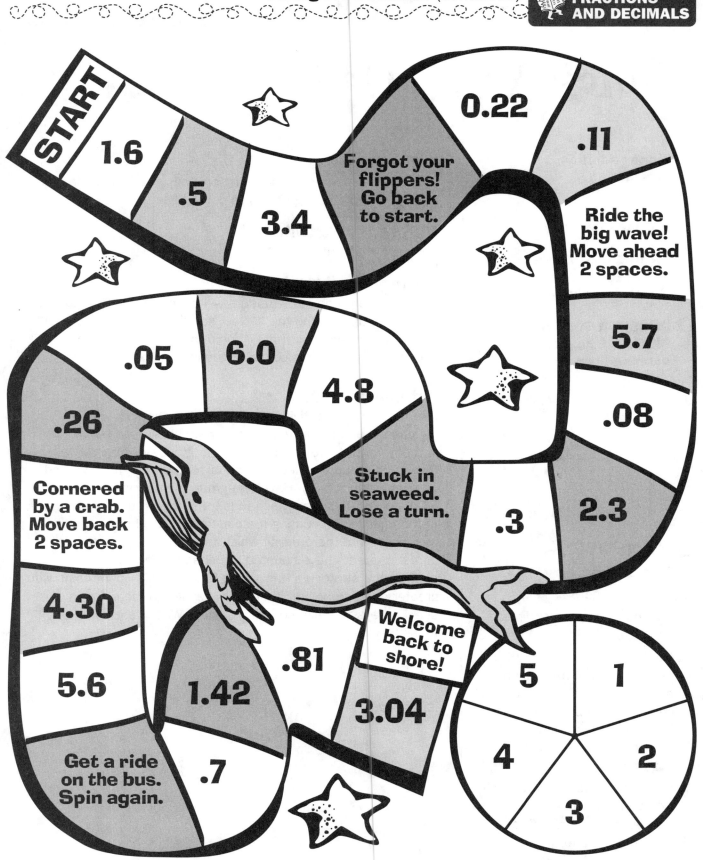

START

1.6

.5

3.4

Forgot your flippers! Go back to start.

0.22

.11

Ride the big wave! Move ahead 2 spaces.

5.7

.08

.05

6.0

4.8

.26

Stuck in seaweed. Lose a turn.

2.3

Cornered by a crab. Move back 2 spaces.

.3

4.30

5.6

1.42

.81

Welcome back to shore!

3.04

5   1

4   2

3

Get a ride on the bus. Spin again.

.7

Money Mysteries

 **Money addition, subtraction, multiplication**

Making change

PROBLEM-SOLVING STRATEGY: Guess and check

PROBLEM-SOLVING SKILL: Finding combinations

Aim

Students use the problem-solving strategy guess and check and practice making change to solve coin problems.

Before the Activity

Copy and distribute page 187.

During the Activity

To solve each problem, students will have to make a guess and revise it until they find the correct solution. Encourage students to record each guess. That will help them to organize their work and learn from each successive guess.

Extension

Use the following activity as a way for students to review counting change and to show students that change can be counted in many ways. Have students work in groups of three or four. Give each group a collection of quarters, dimes, nickels, and pennies (real or play). Have one group member pick up a handful of coins. Then have each student in the group find the value of the change by counting it aloud while the other group members write the order in which the coins are counted. When all the students have counted the change, have students discuss the strategies they used. Did students count coins with greater or lesser values first? Did they group the coins in special ways to make counting easier? What were some of those ways?

ANSWERS

1. 2 dimes and 1 nickel

2. 1 quarter and 3 nickels

3. 4 coins (1 quarter, 1 dime, and 2 pennies)

4. No, 5 coins that equal 28 cents could not have been buried. To make 28 cents, 3 coins have to be pennies. There is no way to make the remaining 25 cents with 2 coins.

5. Answers will vary. There are 24 combinations of coins that equal 35 cents. Check students' lists for accuracy.

6. and 7. Answers will vary.

Name _____

Money Mysteries

Solve these coin mysteries! Use real coins or play money to help you.

1. I have 3 coins. Together they're worth 25 cents. What are my coins?

_____

_____

2. I'm hiding 4 coins. All together they're worth 40 cents. But I don't have a dime! Can you guess my coins?

_____

_____

_____

3. I'm holding 37 cents. What is the smallest number of coins I could have?

_____

_____

_____

4. I buried 5 coins. Could I have buried 28 cents? Why or why not?

_____

_____

_____

5. I have some coins in my purse. I won't say how many. Together they are worth 35 cents. What coins could I have?

_____

_____

_____

6. Write your own mystery. Give it to a friend to solve.

7. On another paper, list a few ways you can make 35 cents. Compare your list with a friend's.

Make-a-Buck Challenge

How many ways can your class make one dollar using quarters, dimes, nickels, and pennies? Work together to find as many combinations as you can. Make a list. Then challenge another class to make a list too. See which class can make the most combinations. Each combination of coins must include at least one quarter, one dime, one nickel, and one penny.

Example:

GOOD	NOT GOOD
3 quarters 1 dime 2 nickels 5 pennies	3 quarters 1 dime 3 nickels

Carson's Coin Combinations

Making change

Finding combinations

LANGUAGE ARTS CONNECTION: Reading a play

ANSWERS

1. 16 coin combinations:
  4 dimes, 1 nickel, 5 pennies
  3 dimes, 3 nickels, 5 pennies
  3 dimes, 2 nickels, 10 pennies
  3 dimes, 1 nickel, 15 pennies
  2 dimes, 5 nickels, 5 pennies
  2 dimes, 4 nickels, 10 pennies
  2 dimes, 3 nickels, 15 pennies
  2 dimes, 2 nickels, 20 pennies
  2 dimes, 1 nickel, 25 pennies
  1 dime, 7 nickels, 5 pennies
  1 dime, 6 nickels, 10 pennies
  1 dime, 5 nickels, 15 pennies
  1 dime, 4 nickels, 20 pennies
  1 dime, 3 nickels, 25 pennies
  1 dime, 2 nickels, 30 pennies
  1 dime, 1 nickel, 35 pennies

2. 10 coin combinations:
  2 quarters
  1 quarter, 2 dimes, 1 nickel
  1 quarter, 1 dime, 3 nickels
  1 quarter, 5 nickels
  5 dimes
  4 dimes, 2 nickels
  3 dimes, 4 nickels
  2 dimes, 6 nickels
  1 dime, 8 nickels
  10 nickels

3. Machine 1

BRAIN POWER: There would be 42 combinations for Machine 1 and 18 combinations for Machine 2.

Aim

Students find different coin combinations with the same value.

Before the Activity

Each student or group will need at least 50 pennies, 10 nickels, 5 dimes, and 2 quarters to work through this activity. Copy and distribute pages 189–190.

During the Activity

Students can work in groups of three or four. Group members can work independently to find combinations and then compare their findings, or each can contribute to a group answer by finding combinations with certain conditions (for example, no quarters, no dimes, no nickels).

Encourage students to work systematically to find combinations. Suggest, for example, that they find all combinations that use one quarter, then all that use four dimes, then three dimes, and so on. Explain that making an organized list of combinations will help them be sure they have found all possible combinations. Students can record coin combinations they find on a chart with a column for each type of coin.

After the Activity

Ask students: *How can you be sure you have found all the combinations of coins that can go into either machine?*

Extension

To prepare a change-making game, write down 10 to 20 money amounts that are less than $5 on pieces of paper and put them into a container. Have students form pairs. Distribute 10 play quarters, dimes, nickels, and pennies to each team. To play, a dealer pulls an amount from the container and displays it. Each pair has 10 seconds to decide whether or not the amount can be made with the coins they have. Then partners should work together to make the amount. Pairs that make the amount earn a point for the round, as do pairs that correctly guessed that an amount could not be made.

Carson's Coin Combinations

You Need:

play money (quarters, dimes, nickels, pennies)

Characters

Bill, a high school student
Carson
Dalton ⎬ Bill's cousins
Erica

Bill: What's up? I keep putting change into these machines and I still can't get a print of my photo!

Carson: Maybe you are not placing the coins in the machine correctly!

Dalton: Here, let me try. Carson, put this change in for me!

Erica: Why don't you just read the signs? For Machine 2, you can put in any combination of quarters, dimes, and nickels. Machine 1 won't take quarters. And you have to put in at least one dime, one nickel, and one penny.

Carson: Oh, how exciting! It's like a brain teaser!

Dalton: You mean they won't take credit cards?

Bill: I get it! If I use Machine 2, I can put in one quarter and five nickels for a print. That's 50 cents.

Erica: And if you use Machine 1, you can put in two dimes, one nickel, and 25 pennies. But you can't use quarters!

Carson: Or if you use Machine 2, you can put in one 50-cent piece . . .

Bill: You egghead! These machines don't take 50-cent pieces!

Erica: Carson, you have to stick to the rules.

Dalton: This is too dull for me. I'll just wait in the car until you're all done.

Carson: What are these pictures of, anyhow?

Bill: They're shots of my father that I took to send to my friends back home.

Carson, Dalton, Erica: You mean to tell me these are "Pa Prints"?

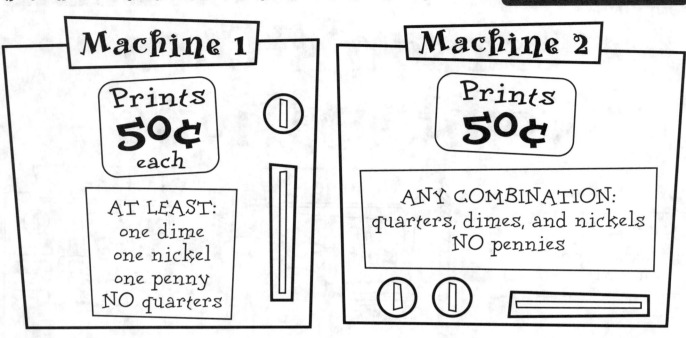

What to Do:

Use play money to help Bill and his cousins. List your ideas on another piece of paper.

1. Make a list of the coin combinations Bill could use in Machine 1 to make 50¢.
   How many can you find? Compare your list with a classmate's.

   _____

   _____

   _____

2. Make a list of the coin combinations Bill could use in Machine 2 to make 50¢.
   How many can you find?

   _____

   _____

   _____

   _____

3. Which machine takes more combinations?

   _____

> **⋛ BRAIN POWER ⋚**
>
> How many combinations could you
> make if the prints cost 75¢ each?

 **TIME AND MONEY**

Quick Change

🖊 **Addition and subtraction of money**

🖊 **Whole-number computation**

Aim

Students practice their money math while playing a board game.

Before the Activity

Copy and distribute pages 192–193. Remind students that to add or subtract amounts of money, they need to align the decimal points.

During the Activity

Provide students with play money, calculators, or pencils and paper. Remind students that after each player's turn, the other players must check his or her work. If they do not agree on the first player's answer, he or she must go back 2 spaces and wait until the next turn to move ahead again. Many of the moves on the game board involve 2-step problems. For example, in order to solve "A customer pays for a super salad and a shake with a $5.00 bill. What is her change?" students must first add to find the amount spent, then subtract the total amount from $5.00. As students play the game, talk with them about their solution strategies.

Extension

Obtain a takeout menu from a local restaurant. Have students rewrite the spaces in the Quick Change game board to make a new game based on the real-life menu.

Quick Change

When you work at Big Bob's Burger Bonanza, you need to make burgers—and change—fast!

You Need:
game piece for each player
play money or pencils and paper
pencil and paper clip

Object:
Become "Top Worker" by being the first to go around the game board.

Number of Players: 2, 3, or 4

To Play:
► Decide who will go first. Each player begins on START.

► Take turns spinning. Move your piece the number of spaces shown on the spinner.

► Each time you land on a space, follow the directions written there. If you answer a question, make sure the other players agree with your answer. If your answer is wrong, you must go back 2 spaces, then wait for your next turn.

► Use the menu board to find the price of each type of food. Use play money (or pencil and paper) to help you add and subtract money amounts.

► The game ends when the first player lands on or passes FINISH.

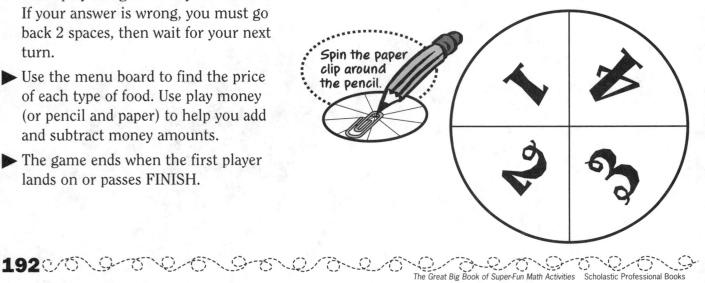

MENU BOARD

BURGER $1.50

JUMBO BURGER $1.79

CHICKEN SANDWICH . .$2.15

FRENCH FRIES $1.25

SMALL SODA . . . .$.69

SMALL SHAKE . . . .$.99

SUPER SALAD $2.39

JUICE . . . .$.55

APPLE . . . .$.49

BANANA . . . .$.45

Spin the paper clip around the pencil.

START

How much will a burger and french fries cost?

A customer pays $1.00 for a soda. How much change will he get?

The shake machine breaks, but you fix it. Move ahead 2 spaces.

A customer wants a shake and a chicken sandwich. How much will it cost?

A customer pays for a super salad and a shake with a $5.00 bill. What is her change?

A customer pays $3.00 for a jumbo burger and a soda. Does he get any change?

A customer praises your service. Move ahead 2 spaces.

A customer pays $10.00 for 2 orders of french fries and a Super Salad. What is her change?

You drop a shake! Go back 3 spaces.

You serve 10 customers in a row without making a mistake. Move ahead 3 spaces.

A customer pays for 2 jumbo burgers, 2 orders of fries, and 2 sodas with $10.00. What is his change?

A customer gives you $4.00 for 2 burgers and 2 bananas. Does he get change?

A customer pays for juice, an apple, and a chicken sandwich with $5.00. What is her change?

FINISH
You're the Top Worker!

You lose a customer's order. Lose a turn.

You give a customer the wrong change. Go back 3 spaces.

A customer orders 2 shakes, an apple, and a jumbo burger. How much will it cost?

Don't Hesitate–Estimate!

✎ **Rounding money amounts**

✎ **Finding sums and differences of money amounts**

✐ Aim
Students use their rounding and estimation skills to help a group of kids with their holiday shopping.

Before the Activity
Ask students if they have ever had to keep track of money or purchases without a calculator or pencil and paper. How did they deal with it? Did they use estimation?

To warm up for the activity, call out money amounts and have students round each one to the nearest dollar or half-dollar. If students are undecided about whether to round an amount up or down, explain that when estimating money, it is sometimes useful to round up, in order to avoid being short of money. After reviewing these tips for rounding money, copy and distribute page 195.

During the Activity
Be sure students understand that the answers to the problems include the word *about* because an estimate is not an exact answer.

Extension 1
Have students find the actual costs for each problem in the activity and then evaluate their estimates. How close were the estimates obtained with rounded numbers to the actual costs? How could the estimates have been closer?

Extension 2
For more practice rounding money amounts, have students round prices in a catalog or supermarket circular.

🔑 ANSWERS
1. $16; yes

2. $19.50; no

3. $16; about $4

4. $21.50; no. Answers will vary. Possible things Jessie could do are: make one painting for the whole family; buy paper that costs less money; or buy just one brush.

Name _____

Don't Hesitate—Estimate!

I just love buying gifts for my friends and my family.

I like it too. But shopping can be hard. How will I keep track of my money?

Easy—just estimate! Then you'll have a good idea of how much money you're spending—without using a pencil or calculator.

Great idea! Let's go shopping!

What to Do:

Each of the kids saved $20 to buy holiday gifts. Help them with their shopping and their estimating. Here's how:

▶ Read each problem. As you read each price, look at the last two digits.

If the digits are **more** than 50¢, round the price **up** to the nearest dollar. EXAMPLE: $3.79 is about $4.00.

If the digits are **less** than 50¢, round the price **down** to the nearest dollar. EXAMPLE: $6.25 is about $6.00

If the digits are **about** 50¢, make the price end in ".50." EXAMPLE: $9.49 is about $9.50.

▶ Try to add up the rounded numbers in your head. Write the rounded total at the end of each problem.

---

1. Sherman found some great gifts for his family. A hat for his dad costs $4.95. A pin for his mom will be $7.95. And a kite for his sister is $3.15.

   Sherman's total: about _____

   Will Sherman have enough money for all of his presents? _____

   (Remember: Each kid has $20.)

2. Gil's list is long! He found a toy truck for his younger sister for $2.05, and a book for his older sister for $1.89. He also saw a yo-yo for his younger brother at $2.55, a T-shirt for his older brother for $7.19, and a calculator for his parents that costs $5.99.

   Gil's total: about _____

   Will Gil have enough money left to buy his pet Lucky a dog dish for $1.40? _____

3. Sonia heads for Candy-by-the-Pound. All the candy costs $1.95 a pound. Here's her list:

Jessie	
Gil	1 pound of gumballs each
Sherman	
Dad	2 pounds of licorice
Mom	2 pounds of gummy bears
Baby Brother	1 pound of jelly beans

   Sonia's total: about _____

   About how much change will Sonia get back from $20? _____

4. Jessie would like to paint a picture each for her mom, her dad, her two sisters, and her brother. It will cost $3.15 for each sheet of fancy paper. The paint set costs $4.45. And she'll need two new brushes at $1.05 each.

   Jessie's total: about _____

   Will Jessie have enough money for her gifts? If not, what could she do? _____

   _____

Wise Buys

- Reading advertisements
- Comparison shopping
- Money addition, subtraction

Aim

Students read store advertisements and make purchasing decisions.

Before the Activity

Copy and distribute pages 197–198. Point out that some stores offer discount prices, but they might not offer other services (delivery, gift wrapping, return/exchange policy).

After the Activity

Have students share their shopping strategies.

Extension

Collect Sunday circulars, food ads, catalogs, menus, etc. Distribute them to individuals or groups of students and ask them to compare prices for similar items. Remind them to be sure to read the fine print for each store's or restaurant's pros and cons.

Wise Buys

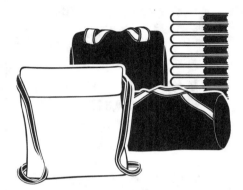

Buying gifts for family and friends, or things for yourself, can cost a bundle! But if you shop carefully, you might find a bundle of savings. Try this shopping spree. You'll practice buying gifts and making the best decisions about how to spend your money—before you use up the real stuff!

What to Do:

▶ Start with $100.

▶ Make a list of family members and friends you would like to shop for.

▶ Look at the ads. Each ad tells you the prices of different items and some facts about the store.

▶ Decide what you will buy for each person on your list. Read the ads carefully. Then decide at which store you will buy each gift.

▶ Keep a total of the money you spend. Make sure you don't go over $100.

J. P. Nickel's

We have helpful, friendly sales people!
You can return items for 7 days.
And we'll gift wrap for only $1.00 a package!

Sports Car Calendar: $10.00

African Adventure Cologne: $17.00
For men and women. 10-ounce bottle.

Koduck Disposable Camera: $8.00

 **Big-Time Watch: $20.00**
Guaranteed for one year.

Nylon Backpack: $15.00

Maple and Elm's Chocolate Logs: $4.50
24 pieces, in decorative tin box.

Baseball Caps: $13.00
American League teams only.

 **Paperback Books: $3.00**
Many titles.

BARGAIN Mart

MOVIE STAR CALENDAR: $9.00

Return items for store credit only. Gift wrap 50 cents a package.

MAPLE AND ELM'S CHOCOLATE LOGS: $10.00
24 pieces.

AFRICAN ADVENTURE COLOGNE: $18.00

WATCH: $7.00
OK brand. One-year guarantee.

BASEBALL CAPS: $4.00
Phillies, Mets, Cubs, or Giants only.

T-SHIRTS: 2 FOR $14.00
White only. All sizes.

KODUCK DISPOSABLE CAMERA: $7.00

NYLON BACKPACK: $12.00

PAPERBACK BOOKS: $2.50
Limited selection of titles.

Gifts-R-Us

Our sales people will help you shop. Return items for up to 30 days. Free gift wrap for all packages!

Two-Year Calendar: **$15.00**
Outdoor scenes.

African Adventure Cologne: **$20.00**
For men and women. 10-ounce bottle.

Koduck Disposable Camera: **$9.00**

Big Time Watch: **$25.00**
Guaranteed for 5 years.

T-shirts: **$20.00**
One of a kind!

Nylon Backpack: **$20.00**

Maple and Elm's Chocolate Logs: **$4.00**
24 delicious pieces.

Baseball Caps: **$16.00**
All major league baseball teams.

Paperback Books: **$3.50**
All the newest titles.

DISCOUNT DAVE'S

We don't have sales people-you serve yourself!
All sales are final. Sorry, no gift wrap.

 KITTEN CALENDAR: $8.00

NYLON BACKPACK: $11.00

AFRICAN ADVENTURE COLOGNE: $10.00 For men and women. 10-ounce bottle.

BASEBALL CAP: $8.00 No design.

KODUCK DISPOSABLE CAMERA: $6.00

Used, but in good condition.

PAPERBACK BOOKS: $2.00

WATCH: $15.00 No guarantee.

T-SHIRTS: $12.00 Extra-large only.

MAPLE AND ELM'S CHOCOLATE LOGS: $15.00
36 pieces.

Mall Math

- ✏ **Money addition and subtraction**
- ✏ **Comparing money amounts**

✐ Aim

Students play a board game in which they buy items at the mall to practice adding and subtracting with money.

Before the Activity

Copy and distribute pages 200–201. Suggest that students look over the items at the stores in the mall. Have them notice the prices of the items and which stores sell more or less expensive items.

During the Activity

After students have played the game a few times, they should begin to develop strategies for winning. The most evident strategy is that they can always try to buy the most expensive item at a store, and if they have to return an item, they can always return the least expensive item. Encourage students to write down their strategies for winning. Players can wait until the end of the game to find out how much they have spent, or each player can keep track of the amount he or she has spent as the game progresses. Adding purchases along the way gives students practice keeping a running total of expenses and comparing money amounts between players.

After the Activity

Ask students: *Can you tell who has won the game without adding at the end? How?*

Extension 1

One variation on this game is to try to spend the least money at the mall. Another is to have students start with $50 or $75 and try to play through an entire game without spending all of their money. If students think of other variations, they can play a few games and then, if their new rules work, share their games with the class.

Extension 2

Have students make their own similar game boards using items and prices from local stores. Students should use a wide range of prices.

Mall Math

You Need:
counters—a different color
  for each player
paper clip
pencils and paper

Object:
To spend the most money
at the mall.

Number of Players:
2, 3, or 4

To Play:

▶ Decide who will go first.

▶ Take turns spinning. After
  you spin, buy one item in
  the store shown on the
  spinner. Cover that item with
  one of your counters.

▶ Keep a total of the cost of your items
  as you buy them.

▶ If the spinner shows ANY STORE, cover any
  item on the board.

▶ If the spinner shows RETURN ONE ITEM, remove one of your
  counters from the board and subtract that amount from your total.
  (If you land on that space on your first turn, spin again.)

▶ Once an item is covered, it cannot be covered by any other player.

▶ If the spinner lands on a store in which all the items are covered,
  skip that turn.

▶ The game ends when every item has been covered. The player who
  has the highest total at the end of the game is the winner.

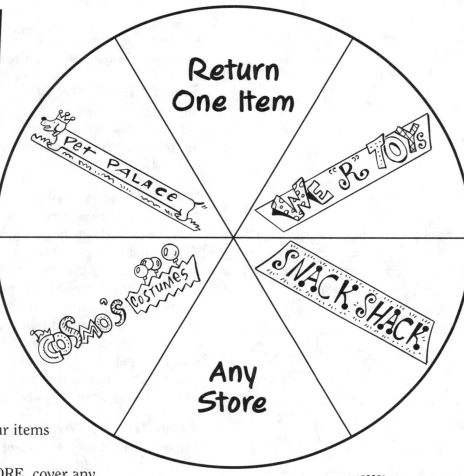

Spin the paper
clip around
the pencil.

WE "R" TOYS

$1.39	$7.98	$20.10
$4.49	$18.99	$5.59
$10.79	$3.45	$8.69

PET PALACE

$7.99	$12.19	$9.99
$1.29	$15.44	$20.03
$6.35	$17.49	$10.69

SNACK SHACK

$3.29	$2.50	$1.15
$2.66	$0.45	$0.79
$0.39	$0.59	$2.05

COSMO'S COSTUMES

$12.77	$2.33	$15.49
$9.97	$7.89	$11.01
$1.79	$10.50	$3.25

The Great Big Book of Super-Fun Math Activities Scholastic Professional Books

Be a Smart Shopper

 CONSUMER SKILLS:
Comparing costs, finding
the best buy

Reading a table

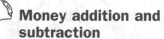 **Money addition and**
subtraction

✎ ANSWERS

1. $22.99, $22.99, $26.99

2. Shopsmart—$16.99;
Ed's Bargains—$21.99

3. $1.00

4. $1.00, $4.00

5. Answers will vary. Some students might say they would
shop at Dollardaze since it
has the lowest prices for
most of the items. Other students might pick the store
with the lowest price for one
item they want to buy.

❀ Aim

Students read a table of toy prices at three stores and use the
information to compare costs.

Before the Activity

Ask students tell about the considerations they make when
shopping for gifts for their friends. Encourage students to
describe the person to whom they are giving the gift, how they
think about the amount of money to spend, and how they
decide where to shop. Copy and distribute page 203.

During the Activity

Before they answer the questions, have students read the
labels on the table and be sure they understand that they
should read across each row in the table to find the cost of a
toy at the three different stores.

Students may find it easier to make comparisons and find
price differences if they write the toy prices in a vertical list.
You can help students with this process by working through
Question 2 on the chalkboard. Have students look at the three
prices and describe how they are similar (all have $.99, all have
a 2-digit number to the left of the decimal point) and how they
are different (each has a different number to the left of the decimal point). Then ask students what they would do to compare
the prices (compare the digits to the left of the decimal point).

Note that when finding price differences, some students will
be able to add or subtract using only the digits to the left of the
decimal point. Others will need to use the money amounts as
they are written in the table. Accept any approach that students
find useful.

If students need help with Question 5, have them circle the
best buy or buys in each row. Then they can make a visual comparison or make a tally to show how often each store has the
best buy.

After the Activity

Ask: *How does the table help you to compare prices? How can
you compare toy prices at the stores near your home?*

Name _____

Be a Smart Shopper

Smart shoppers always get B's—for bargains!

When it's time to buy a gift, every toy and game seems to say, "Buy me!" But don't buy a thing until you do some shopping homework. A great way to start is by comparing prices at a few stores.

Think you found a bargain? Hold on! You may have to do more studying. The store with the lowest prices might not be the best store for you.

It may be far away. It may not let you return a toy if it breaks. And the store may not be open when you want to shop.

Before you head for the mall, try your skills. We've made a table that shows the prices of some top toys and games at some imaginary stores. Use it to answer the questions.

TOY	Shopsmart	Dollardaze	Ed's Bargains
Battleship	$12.99	$11.99	$15.99
Spirograph	$9.99	$8.99	$9.99
Pictionary	$22.99	$22.99	$26.99
Etch-A-Sketch	$11.99	$7.99	$10.99
Silly Mr. Potato Head	$16.99	$19.99	$21.99
Play-Doh Fun Factory	$7.28	$6.99	$7.99
Playball Power Game	$9.59	$8.99	$9.99

1. How much does Pictionary cost at Shopsmart? At Dollardaze? At Ed's Bargains?

_____

_____

_____

2. At which store does Silly Mr. Potato Head cost the least? The most?

_____

_____

3. How much more does Spirograph cost at Shopsmart than at Dollardaze?

_____

4. How much less does Battleship cost at Dollardaze than at Shopsmart? Than at Ed's Bargains?

_____

_____

5. Which store would you shop at? Why?

_____

_____

_____

_____

Check, Please!

🖊 **Money addition and subtraction**

🖊 **Making change**

🖊 **REAL-LIFE SKILL: Reading a menu**

⌐ ANSWERS

1. Pizza 'n' Pasta; Fries-Days; Trendy's

2. Your meal might have been a sundae, milk, and the chicken fingers or the deep-dish pizza. Accept other answers that total $4.50.

3. Finnegan's has the best price at $2.75. The most expensive meal would be at Fries-Days.

4. Answers will vary.

5. Answers will vary. Students should give reasons for their answers.

⤳ Aim

Students read kids' menus from imaginary restaurants and compute with money.

Before the Activity

Copy and distribute pages 205–206. If necessary, remind students that computing with money is like adding and subtracting whole numbers, except that they should line up the decimal points before they add or subtract and remember to write the decimal point and dollar sign in the answer.

During the Activity

Have the class review the menus before they answer the questions. Point out that some of the menus have items in common.

Students should work backward to answer Question 2. Have them start with $4.50 and guess and check to subtract items until they reach the right combination. If they need a hint, tell them that a typical meal might include an entree, a beverage, and dessert.

If students need help with Question 3, rephrase the question so that they know they are looking for the least and most expensive combination possible at any of the restaurants.

After the Activity

Ask: *How might estimation come in handy at a restaurant?*

Extension 1

Tipping in restaurants is a great example of the math people use every day. Initiate a discussion about tipping—adding extra money onto the total bill to show appreciation for a restaurant's quality and service. Show students some of the different methods people use to figure tips (a tip table, doubling the tax, using the first three digits of the total and adding half to it).

Extension 2

Have students collect menus from some favorite local restaurants. They can make up their own math problems and also analyze which restaurant they would eat at and why.

Name _____

Check, Please!

Eating at a restaurant is a treat. It's also a great time to use money math. So before you get ready to order that burger, take a look at the menus on page 206. They're all kids' menus from imaginary restaurants. (A kids' menu has smaller portions—and smaller prices!) They'll help you practice your menu math—before you get stuck with the bill!

What to Do:
Use the menus and money math to answer the questions.

1. Which restaurant gives you the lowest price for . . .

... spaghetti? _____

... a meal that includes chicken? _____

... a hamburger and fries? _____

2. Your bill at Fries-Days comes to $4.50. What might your meal have been? _____

_____

3. You'd like to order a meal with a drink and dessert. Which restaurant has the best price? Which is

most expensive? _____

4. Ask two friends what they would order at one of the restaurants. Then decide what you would order. What is the total for all three of you? How much change would you get back from $20.00?

_____

_____

5. Which restaurant would you choose to eat at? Why? _____

_____

_____

Fries-Days

Hot Dog and Fries $1.95
Chicken Fingers and Fries . . $2.25
Hamburger and Fries $2.75
Grilled Cheese and Fries . . . $1.95
Deep Dish Pizza $2.25
Milk . . . . $ .75
Soda $1.25
Ice Cream Sundae $1.50

Trendy's

Hamburger and Fries $2.50
Cheeseburger and Fries $2.60
Grilled Cheese and Fries . . . $2.35
Spaghetti $2.70
Hot Dog and Fries $2.35
Chicken Basket and Fries . . $2.70
Shrimp Basket and Fries . . . $2.70
Milk, Lemonade, Soda . . . . . $ .55
Ice Cream Sundae $1.15

Pizza 'n' Pasta

Personal Pizza Pack $2.99
(includes personal-size pizza, drink in
take-home cup, surprise toy)
Kid's Salad $1.19
Spaghetti $1.79
Spaghetti and Meatballs . . . $2.19
Soda or Milk . . . . $ .79

Finnegan's

All meals served with a Jelly-O Pudding
Pop and a drink in a take-home glass.

Grilled Cheese and Fries . . . $2.75
Burger and Fries $3.75
Corn Dog and Fries $2.75
Popcorn Shrimp and Fries . . $3.75
Fish Sandwich and Fries . . . $2.75
Chicken Bites $3.75

The Great Big Book of Super-Fun Math Activities Scholastic Professional Books

 **TIME AND MONEY**

It's About Time

✏️ **Telling time to the hour, half hour, minute**

✏️ **Writing times using analog timepieces**

🏹 **Aim**

Students describe their daily schedules by drawing the hands on watch faces.

Before the Activity

Copy and distribute page 208.

During the Activity

Some students may find it difficult to draw the hour hand in its correct position for times that are between hours. Encourage these students first to use a pencil to draw the hour hand on the hour. Then have them draw the minute hand. To correct the position of the hour hand, students should estimate whether the minute hand is more or less than halfway between the hours.

🔑 **ANSWERS**

Answers will vary. Check to see that students have used a shorter hand to indicate hours and a longer hand to indicate minutes.

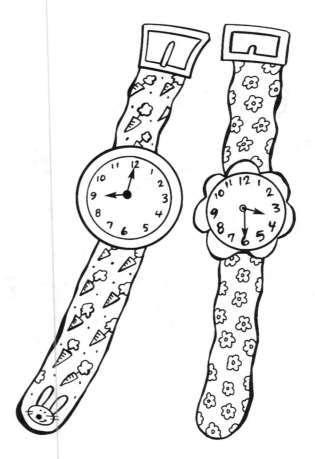

It's About Time

Telling time began as people watched day and night and the seasons change. Early timepieces included the hourglass, the sundial, and stone monuments that aligned with the rising sun or the full moon.

Today we have clocks and watches. Some have hands and numbers. These are called **analog** timepieces. Others, **digital** clocks and watches, have just numbers.

What to Do:

Give us a hand with these analog watches. While you're at it, give us two hands!

▶ Tell what time you usually do each activity. Write the time in the box.

▶ Draw the hands on the watch to show that time.

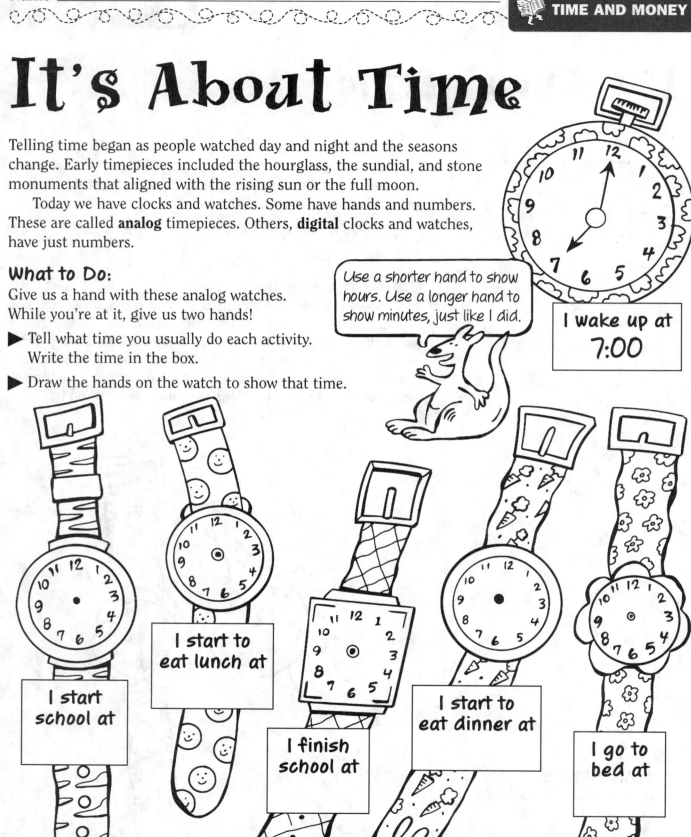

Use a shorter hand to show hours. Use a longer hand to show minutes, just like I did.

I wake up at 7:00

I start school at

I start to eat lunch at

I finish school at

I start to eat dinner at

I go to bed at

Places to Go, Things to Do

Reading a schedule

Finding elapsed time

LANGUAGE ARTS CONNECTION:
Writing in math

Aim
Students read and interpret a schedule.

Before the Activity
Copy and distribute page 210.

During the Activity
As they read the schedule, it may be helpful for students to find each time on a clock. They can also gain a better sense of Jessica's schedule if they talk or write about what they do on a typical weekday during the times listed. (See Extension 2.)

To answer Question 5, students must find the time elapsed between 1:30 and 4:30. After students find that these are the times class begins and ends, have them suggest ways to find the elapsed time. *(Methods include counting forward from 1:30 by hours; counting backward from 4:30 by hours; subtracting 4:30 – 1:30.)*

After the Activity
Ask students: *What does Jessica's schedule tell you about Juno's workday? Why might it be helpful for you to make a schedule of your own school day?*

Extension 1
Have students interview a parent, an older brother or sister, or a neighbor to find that person's schedule on a typical weekday. Students should write the schedule in the same form as the one in the activity. Invite students to give a short presentation of their findings to the class.

Extension 2
Invite students to list the different things they do during the day, and at what time. Remind them to list meals, different classes, and after-school activities. After they have made their lists, have students put them in chronological order to create a schedule for a typical weekday.

Once students' schedules are completed, discuss: Which activity takes the most time? How do students' schedules differ? How might their schedules be different on another day?

ANSWERS
1. 9:00 A.M.

2. 5:30 P.M.

3. In Jessica's room

4. 9:30 A.M., 10:30 P.M.

5. 3 hours

BRAIN POWER: Answers will vary. Possible answers: police horses, race horses, polo ponies, homing pigeons, watch-dogs, police dogs, circus animals, monkeys that help physically challenged people, zoo animals, animals in TV commercials.

Places to Go, Things to Do

For Juno, lending a helping paw is all in a day's work!

Hi. My name is Juno. I'm a dog. My owner is Jessica. She's my best friend in the whole world. The day I met Jessica was the happiest day of my life. I was 16 months old then. I'm almost seven years old now! Jessica goes to college. Someday, she's going to be a lawyer.

Every day, I go where Jessica goes—into classrooms, the library, even stores and places to eat. No, I'm not in college! Jessica is blind, and I'm her Seeing Eye dog.

Many people who cannot see use Seeing Eye dogs to help them. That's a big job for a dog! When I was younger, I went to a school for Seeing Eye dogs. I learned words like *forward, downstairs, left,* and *stop*. I learned to look both ways before leading someone across a street. I learned to wait for traffic lights to turn green before I walk. I can even tell if a tree branch is too low for a person to walk under!

Jessica has lots of places to go each day—and I help her. She holds my harness and says, "Go outside, Juno." When I'm in my harness, I can't play. I'm working!

Here's what we do on a really "ruff" day! After you read our schedule, use another sheet of paper to answer the questions.

1. At what time did Juno wake up?

2. When did Jessica eat dinner?

3. Where was Juno at 6:00 p.m.?

4. At what times did Juno eat?

5. How long is Jessica's English class?

Wednesday

9:00 A.M.	Jessica and I wake up.
9:30 A.M.	Jessica feeds me. Yum!
9:45 A.M.	Jessica brushes me.
10:00 A.M.	Jessica and I go to the computer room in her house. She works. and I sit under the desk.
11:30 A.M.	Jessica uses a cane to go downstairs for lunch. I stay in her room and chew my toy bone.
12:30 P.M.	Jessica takes a nap before class, but I want to play. I jump on her bed. "Down, Juno!" she says.
1:15 P.M.	We leave for school.
1:30 P.M.	English class starts.
3:15 P.M.	I yawn in class. The teacher looks at me.
4:30 P.M.	Class is over—time for a walk!
4:45 P.M.	Jessica checks for mail at her house and calls friends.
5:30 P.M.	She leaves me in her room and uses her cane to go downstairs for dinner.
6:30 P.M.	Dinner's over. Jessica takes me outside for a walk.
7:30 P.M.	Jessica and I walk to school for a meeting of disabled students.
9:30 P.M.	Jessica exercises in her room.
10:30 P.M.	Time for my dinner!
10:40 P.M.	Jessica takes a shower, then studies and listens to the TV.
1:00 A.M.	Bedtime. Jessica hugs me. Whew—what a day! I love being a Seeing Eye dog.

⇒BRAIN POWER⇐

What other animals that work with people can you think of?

How's Your Heart Rate?

- Reading a table

- Whole number multiplication

- SCIENCE CONNECTION: Understanding heart rate

Aim

Students read a table of animal heart rates, measure their own heart rates, and answer questions using information from the table.

Before the Activity

Copy and distribute page 212.

During the Activity

If students need help finding their pulses, have them make a loose fist with one hand and then bend that wrist in toward the elbow. In this position, students should be able to feel and see a tendon that runs along the length of the arm. The pulse can be felt at the wrist, just to the thumb side of that tendon.

Explain that human heart rates can differ greatly, depending on a person's age, physical fitness, and body type. To illustrate, have two students—one with a slow pulse and one with a fast pulse—count out loud or tap their feet along with their heart rates.

After the Activity

Ask students: *When are some times you have noticed that your heart beats faster or slower? Why do you think this is so?*

Extension 1

Have students use the information in the table and a metronome to play a heart rate game. Set the metronome to tick out the heart rate of an animal from the table. Have students guess which animal you have chosen. Award points for each correct guess.

Extension 2

For additional statistics resources, consult *Great Graphing* by Martin Lee and Maria Miller. (New York: Scholastic Inc., 1993).

ANSWERS

1. The canary's heart rate is the fastest. The gray whale's heart rate is the slowest.

2. Answers may vary. In general, the smaller the animal, the faster the heart rate.

3. A horse's heart beats 25–40 times per minute. It would fit between the elephant and the tiger. That answer would be logical because horse is larger than a tiger but smaller than an elephant.

4. Answers will vary.

How's Your Heart Rate?

You Need:
stopwatch or watch with a second hand
tennis ball

ANIMAL	HEART RATE (for one minute)
Canary	**1,000**
Mouse	**650**
Chicken	**200**
Cat	**110**
Dog	**80**
Adult human	**72**
Giraffe	**60**
Tiger	**45**
Elephant	**25**
Gray whale	**8**
You	

Animals have hearts that do the same job as a person's heart. An animal's heart beats all day long to pump blood through its body. What's different about an animal heart and a human heart? The number of times it beats in a day.

Each day your heart beats about 100,000 times. That's enough times to pump almost 1,500 gallons of blood throughout your body! By the time you are 70 years old, your heart will have pumped about 38 million gallons of blood. No wonder it's important to keep your heart strong and healthy!

The number of times a heart beats in a certain amount of time is called **heart rate**. Check out the table to find some average animal heart rates. Then follow the steps to add your heart rate to the table.

How to Find Your Heart Rate

- Place two fingers on your neck or your wrist. Move them around until you feel a pulse beat.

- Count the beats for 30 seconds. Have a partner time you with the watch.

- Multiply the number of beats by two. That number is your heart rate for one minute.

Hearts Are Hard Workers
To prove it, try this. Squeeze a tennis ball as hard as you can and let go. That's how hard your heart works to pump blood through your body. Now try to squeeze the ball for one minute to match your heart rate. Not too easy, is it?

Answer these questions about animals' heart rates, using the information on the table.

1. Which animal's heart beats fastest in one minute? _____

   Which beats slowest? _____

2. What do you notice about the size of the animal compared with its heart rate? _____

   _____

3. Where do you think a horse's heart rate might fit on the table? Explain your answer. _____

   _____

4. Which animal is your heart rate the closest to? _____

Graphing Trash

 **Reading a pictograph**

 **SCIENCE CONNECTION: Ecology**

Aim

Students read a pictograph showing a family's weekly trash output.

Before the Activity

Copy and distribute pages 214–215. Before students answer the questions, have them read the labels on the graph. Ask students to offer examples of the types of trash that would fall in each category. List their examples on the chalkboard.

During the Activity

To help students read the pictograph, have them look at the trash cans that represent paper trash. Ask what number they can count by to find the number of pounds of paper trash. (2) Students who are having difficulty finding the total number of pounds in a category can write a number sentence to represent the total. For the pounds of plastic trash, for example, a student can write:

$$2 + 2 + 2 + 1 = 7$$

Extension

Have each student log the kinds of trash his or her family throws away in one week. Ask students to use the pictograph on page 215 to estimate whether their families discard more or less than the weekly average. Ask students also to list the kinds of trash their families recycle.

ANSWERS

1. Paper

2. A family throws away more yard garbage than plastics.

3. 10 pounds

4. 🗑🗑🗑🗑🗑🗑🗑

5. Answers will vary A few additional ways to produce less garbage:

- Write on both sides of a piece of paper, or use the back for scrap paper.
- Use cloth instead of paper for towels and napkins.
- Bring a reusable bag to the grocery store.
- Buy food that comes in efficient containers.
- Buy things that can be reused or recycled.

Graphing Trash

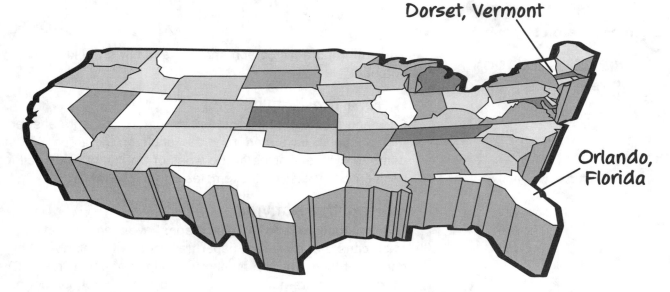

Dorset, Vermont

Orlando, Florida

Charlotte lives in the small town of Dorset, Vermont. She goes out of her way to pick up paper litter she sees. Lindsay is from the city of Orlando, Florida. You won't catch her throwing away a soda can.

Nine-year-old Charlotte and 10-year-old Lindsay live many miles apart. But they both **recycle**. Instead of throwing away an old newspaper or can, they try to see that it's used to make something new.

You won't find glass or plastic bottles in their trash, either. Lindsay and Charlotte's families separate things that can be recycled. Once a month, Charlotte's family brings them to a recycling center. In Orlando, Lindsay's separated trash gets picked up outside of her house by a special truck.

Why is recycling important? A family of four people throws away about 112 pounds of garbage a week. (That's about as heavy as two kids in your class!) Some places are running

out of room to dump all that trash. That's why many states have passed recycling laws.

When people recycle, there is less garbage to dump, bury, or burn. That helps keep our air and water clean. When paper is recycled, fewer trees have to be cut down. That saves forests and the animals that live in them.

"By recycling, my family doesn't waste the world's resources," says Charlotte. "It feels good to help the earth."

Kids Can Help

- Don't throw away what you can use again!
- Use the same lunch bag more than once. Or use a lunch box.
- Reuse plastic bottles for games or craft projects.
- Find out how your school can recycle paper and cans.

A FAMILY'S WEEKLY GARBAGE*

Paper	🗑🗑🗑🗑🗑🗑🗑🗑🗑🗑🗑🗑🗑🗑🗑🗑🗑🗑🗑🗑🗑🗑🗑
Yard Garbage	🗑🗑🗑🗑🗑🗑🗑🗑🗑🗑
Metal	🗑🗑🗑🗑🗑
Glass	🗑🗑🗑🗑⬗
Food	🗑🗑🗑🗑⬗
Plastics	🗑🗑🗑⬗
Other	🗑🗑🗑🗑⬗

Each 🗑 stands for 2 pounds (907 grams) of trash.

Each ⬗ stands for 1 pound (454 grams) of trash.

* Based on a family of four in the United States. Includes garbage thrown away at home, at work, in shops, and at school. Source: National Solid Wastes Management Association

What to Do:

Peek into a trash can. What will you find? The pictograph will give you an idea.
Use it to answer these questions.

1. What does a family throw away the most of each week? _____

2. Does a family throw away more plastics or yard garbage? _____

3. How many pounds of metal are thrown away each week? _____

4. Draw the trash cans you would need to show 14 pounds of trash on the graph.

5. In Kids Can Help are some ideas for ways you could cut down on garbage. Use the graph to come

up with more ways. List your ideas. _____

_____

_____

Don't Make a Mess—Take a Sample!

 Using a sample

 Reading and making a pictograph

ANSWERS

4. Answers will vary.

5. Answers will vary depending on the cereal used. If students conclude that there is more of one color or an equal amount of all colors, most of the pictographs in your class should show that to be true.

BRAIN POWER: Answers will vary. Using the idea of sampling, one way to estimate is to find the number of pieces of each color in some sample cups of cereal and to then find the number of cups in a box. Multiplying the number of cups by the number of pieces in each cup will give an estimate of the total number of pieces in the box. Encourage students to offer a variety of solutions.

Aim

Students learn to use a sample and make a pictograph to describe the distribution of colors in a box of colored cereal.

Before the Activity

Copy and distribute page 217. Discuss with students the meaning of the word *sample* and when it might be used. (sampling a taste of food; getting a sample of paint or carpet at the store; receiving a free sample in the mail)

The entire class can share one box of cereal for this activity. Use a type with more than two colors of cereal, such as Froot Loops, Trix, Kaboom, Lucky Charms, or Dino Pebbles.

During the Activity

Students can work individually or in groups. Begin by having students read to the end of Step 3. Then have them draw and label a pictograph. Remind students to list on their graphs all the colors of their cereal. After students complete Step 4, their three pictographs might look very similar or very different.

After the Activity

Ask: *Why did you need to make three pictographs? How does comparing graphs with your classmates help you to know about the colors in the box?*

Some students might not understand how the sample cupfuls of cereal they graphed stand for all the cereal in the box. Have students suppose that a box of cereal had many red pieces and few green pieces. If you picked out just a few pieces, they all could be red or green. Thus, the more cupfuls they take from the box, the more accurate that sample will be.

Extension

Tell students that to find out what a lot of people think about an idea or question, you could ask a few people, or a sample. Take a class poll. Have the students in each group answer a question such as: What is your favorite school subject? Groups should then tally their responses. Tally the results of the same question as a class. Then ask: *How did your group's results as a sample compare to the answers of the whole class?*

Don't Make a Mess— Take a Sample!

You Need:
box of colored cereal
measuring cup
piece of lined paper
crayons

Look into a box of colored cereal. How many colors do you see? Is there the same amount of each color? Or is there more of one color? To find out, you could dump out the whole box . . . but there's an easier way! You could use a **sample**—a little bit of cereal from the whole box. Looking at the sample will tell you more about how much of each color is in the box. And if you look at other samples, you'll have an even better idea.

A **pictograph** can help you organize your samples. (A pictograph uses pictures to show information.)

What to Do:

1. Fill the measuring cup with cereal to the $\frac{1}{2}$-cup line. This is your sample. Divide it into piles by color.

2. Line up the pieces in each pile.

3. Draw a row of circles on the lined paper for each row of cereal. Make sure that the number of circles on the paper matches the number of pieces in each row. Don't forget to label your pictograph!

4. Using new cereal from the box, repeat Steps 1, 2, and 3 two more times. Do your pictographs look the same or different? Write about what you see.

I'm not going to count the broken pieces.

I'm going to count two broken pieces as a whole.

COLORS OF CEREAL IN THE BOX
RED   OOOOOOOOOO
YELLOW OOOOOOOO
ORANGE OOOOOOOOOOOO

_____

_____

5. Now look at all of the pictographs in your class. Write about the colors of cereal in the box. Is there more of one color? Or do you think there is the same amount of each color? Why?

_____

_____

_____

⇒BRAIN POWER⇐
How many pieces of each color are in the whole box? How could you estimate?

Too Sweet to Eat?

 Making a real graph

REAL-LIFE CONNECTION: Reading food labels

Aim

Students make real graphs or pictographs showing the amount of sugar in one serving of different candies.

Before the Activity

Copy and distribute pages 219–220. You will need to provide a box of 3-gram sugar cubes for this activity. If you do not want to use real sugar cubes, have students draw cubes on their graphs instead. Students can work in pairs or small groups to complete the activity.

During the Activity

To help students make their graphs more precise, tell them to try to space the sugar cubes evenly within each column.

After the Activity

Ask: *Did you know that candy contained this much sugar? Why might it be important to be aware of the amount of sugar you eat every day? What could you do to cut down on that amount?*

Extension

Have students continue their investigation of sugar content in foods: for example, in breakfast cereals, soft drinks, cookies, and crackers. Have students share their findings with the school by posting their sugar cube graphs in the hallway.

ANSWERS

1. From the list provided in the activity, one serving of Chuckles has the most sugar (34 g). Goobers has the least sugar (16 g). Students' answers may vary depending on the candies they use.

2. Reese's Peanut Butter Cups would be even with Kit Kat.

3. Other foods that contain a large amount of sugar include ice cream, cookies, gum, soda, gelatin, soft drink mixes, and breakfast cereal. A good way to find out how much sugar is in a product is by checking its Nutrition Facts box.

Name _____

Too Sweet to Eat?

You decide. Make a graph to show how much sugar is in your favorite candies.

You Need:
box of 3-gram sugar cubes
poster board or heavy paper
glue
empty candy wrappers or boxes (optional)

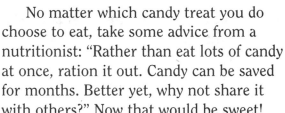

We all like to eat candy sometimes. What's so bad about candy, anyway? Nutritionists suggest that you should not eat a lot of candy. That's because candy contains sugar. And eating too much sugar can lead to tooth decay!

Just how much sugar is in one serving of your favorite candy? The Nutrition Facts box on the package will tell you. It looks like this:

Nutrition Facts	Amount/Serving	%DV*	Amount/Serving	%DV*
Serv. Size 1 bar	**Total Fat** 12 g	**18%**	**Total Carb** 28 g	**9%**
Calories 230	Sat. Fat 7 g	**34%**	Fiber 1 g	**4%**
Fat Cal. 110	**Cholest.** 5 mg	**2%**	Sugars 23 g	
*Percent Daily Values (DV) are based on a 2,000 calorie diet.	**Sodium** 60 mg	**2%**	**Protein** 3 g	
	Vitamin A 0% • Vitamin C 0% • Calcium 8% • Iron 0%			

The amount of sugar that a candy contains is listed in grams. The higher the number of grams, the more sugar in the candy. Making a sugar cube graph will help you see how your favorite candy stacks up.

No matter which candy treat you do choose to eat, take some advice from a nutritionist: "Rather than eat lots of candy at once, ration it out. Candy can be saved for months. Better yet, why not share it with others?" Now that would be sweet!

Candy List

Candy	Sugar in Grams
Goobers	16 g
Gummy Bears	20 g
Kit Kat	21 g
Reese's Pieces	23 g
Nestle's Crunch	24 g
Butterfinger	29 g
Chuckles	34 g

What to Do:

▶ Look at the Candy List. Start your graph by drawing pictures of the candies in the list on your poster board. Or tape empty candy wrappers or boxes onto the poster board, like in the sample graph.

▶ Check the Candy List to find out how many sugar grams are in each candy. If your candy is not on the list, find the sugar grams in its Nutrition Facts box.

▶ Now start your graph. Each sugar cube will stand for 3 grams of sugar. How many cubes will you need? Divide the total amount of sugar grams in each candy by 3. (Ignore any remainders.) Then glue the correct number of sugar cubes next to each candy on your graph, or draw sugar cubes to show each amount in a pictograph.

▶ After you have finished your graph, answer these questions.

1. Which candy bar has the most sugar? Which has the least?

_____

_____

2. Reese's Peanut Butter Cups contain 21 grams of sugar. Where would you put them on your graph?

_____

_____

3. What other foods do you eat that might contain a lot of sugar? How could you find out how much sugar they have?

_____

_____

_____

SAMPLE PICTOGRAPH	
Candy	Amount of Sugar in One Serving
	☐☐☐☐☐☐

TREASURE THOSE TEETH!

Keep your teeth and gums strong by forming healthy habits like:

✔ Avoiding foods with lots of sugar.

✔ Brushing and flossing after every meal.

✔ Using a fluoride toothpaste.

✔ Visiting your dentist every six months.

Out-of-This-World Graphs

✏ **Constructing a bar graph**

✏ **Understanding weight in relation to gravity**

✏ **Decimal multiplication**

✏ **SCIENCE CONNECTION: Astronomy, physics**

✏ **LANGUAGE ARTS CONNECTION: Writing in math**

❦ ANSWERS

1. The bar graph shows students' weight on the moon and different planets.

2. 10 pounds

3. Answers will depend on students' Earth weight.

4. About 2.5 times more

5. Students' weights should be about the same on Saturn, Uranus, and Neptune.

6. Answers will vary. Students should give reasons for their choices.

➳ Aim
Students construct a bar graph showing what they would weigh on different planets.

Before the Activity
Copy and distribute pages 222–223.

During the Activity
To reinforce concepts of weight, have students write the unit (pounds) in their answers to the questions.

For Question 4, students can compute with the numbers they wrote beneath each bar on the graph, or they can use the scale at the left of the graph to estimate the difference.

After the Activity
Ask students: *How did you use the graph to answer the questions?*

Extension 1
Draw a class bar graph to show and compare students' weights on the different planets.

Extension 2
Have students research why the planets have different gravity. They can also find out what the weather is like on each planet and how long it might take a modern rocket to travel to each planet. The book *Planets, Moons, and Meteors: The Young Stargazer's Guide to the Galaxy*, by John Gustafson (New York: Julian Messner, 1992) is a helpful resource.

Out-of-This-World Graphs

Future astronaut Mandy Mark weighs about 80 pounds on Earth. But if she found a way to live on Mars, she would weigh only 30 pounds!

Would she shrink? Not at all. Weight is really the measure of the amount of gravity pulling on you, not your size. What you see on a scale is only what you weigh on Earth.

The amount of gravity is different all over the solar system. So Mandy's weight would be different on every planet. She would weigh much less on Pluto—and much more on Jupiter. Of course, Mandy couldn't weigh herself most of these places. But you never know where her next shuttle may take her!

How Much Would You Weigh on Mars?

Use a calculator to multiply your Earth weight by the decimal numbers below to see how much you'd weigh all over the solar system! Then graph your weight. Complete the bar graph on page 223 using the information from this table.

Mercury	.37
Venus	.88
Moon	.17
Mars	.38
Jupiter	2.64
Saturn	1.15
Uranus	1.15
Neptune	1.12
Pluto	0.04

What Would You Weigh in Outer Space?

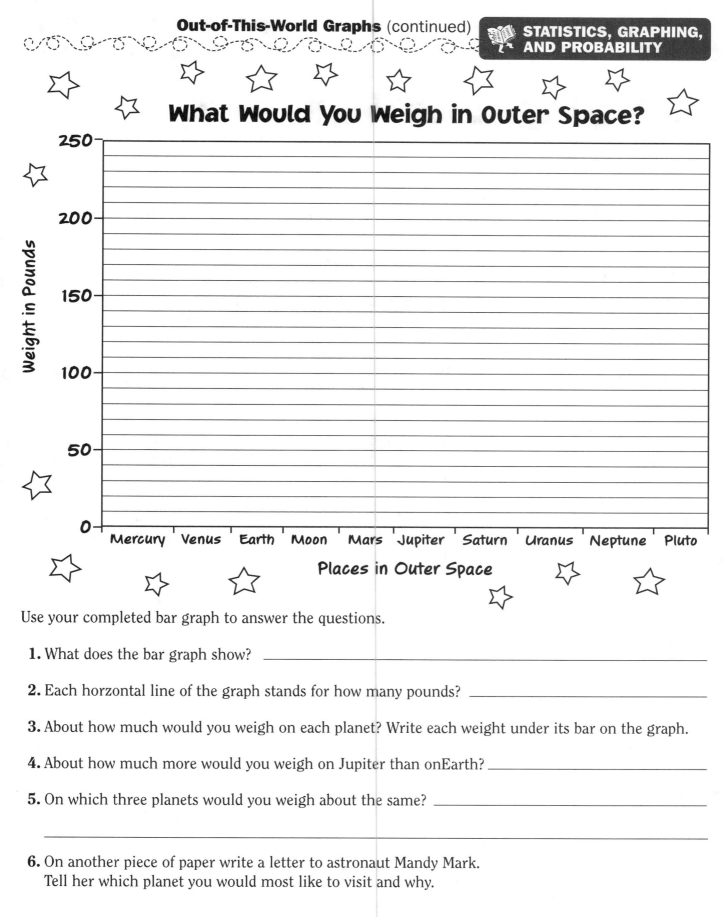

Use your completed bar graph to answer the questions.

1. What does the bar graph show? _____

2. Each horzontal line of the graph stands for how many pounds? _____

3. About how much would you weigh on each planet? Write each weight under its bar on the graph.

4. About how much more would you weigh on Jupiter than onEarth? _____

5. On which three planets would you weigh about the same? _____

_____

6. On another piece of paper write a letter to astronaut Mandy Mark.
Tell her which planet you would most like to visit and why.

Snacking with Statistics

 Taking a poll, using a representative sample

Making a bar graph

SOCIAL STUDIES CONNECTION: Geography

Aim

Students read bar graphs, take a poll, and compare their results to those in the article.

Before the Activity

Copy and distribute pages 225–226. Discuss the different areas of the United States shown on the maps in this activity. Ask your class to identify the region in which they live.

During the Activity

Ask: *How many people will each class member have to poll to make a total of 100?*

After the Activity

From the results of the schoolwide poll, ask: *Which is the favorite snack at our school? Which region is our school's result most like?*

Extension

Have volunteers write an article for your school newsletter with the results of your "favorite snacks" poll.

Snacking with Statistics

How do snacks stack up where you live?

If you brought some snacks to school, which kind would your friends finish first? As strange as it might sound, the answer might depend on where you live!

In most of the United States, potato chips top the list of favorite snack foods. However, tortilla chips are the number-one choice in the Pacific states. And folks in the Mid-Atlantic area can't get enough pretzels!

To see which snack foods are popular where you live, look at the bar graph in your region on the map. Do you and your school friends eat the same types of snack foods? To find out, take a poll. That's a quick way to learn what people think about something.

What to Do:

1. The bar graphs on each map show the favorite snack foods for every 100 people in that region. In order to compare your graph to the one in your region, make sure your class polls 100 students.

2. Make a list of the snacks students in your school eat. Be sure to include all of the snacks on our graphs, plus a space for other snacks. Example:

What's Your Favorite Snack Food?
Potato chips
Tortilla chips
Corn chips
Popcorn
Pretzels
Other kind of snack

3. Hand out 100 or more copies of the list. Ask students to circle their favorite snack.

4. Use the results of the first 100 lists you get back to make a bar graph.

5. Compare your graph with the one in your region. Do the students in your school reflect your region's snack tastes? Why or why not?

FAVORITE SNACK FOODS IN THE U.S.

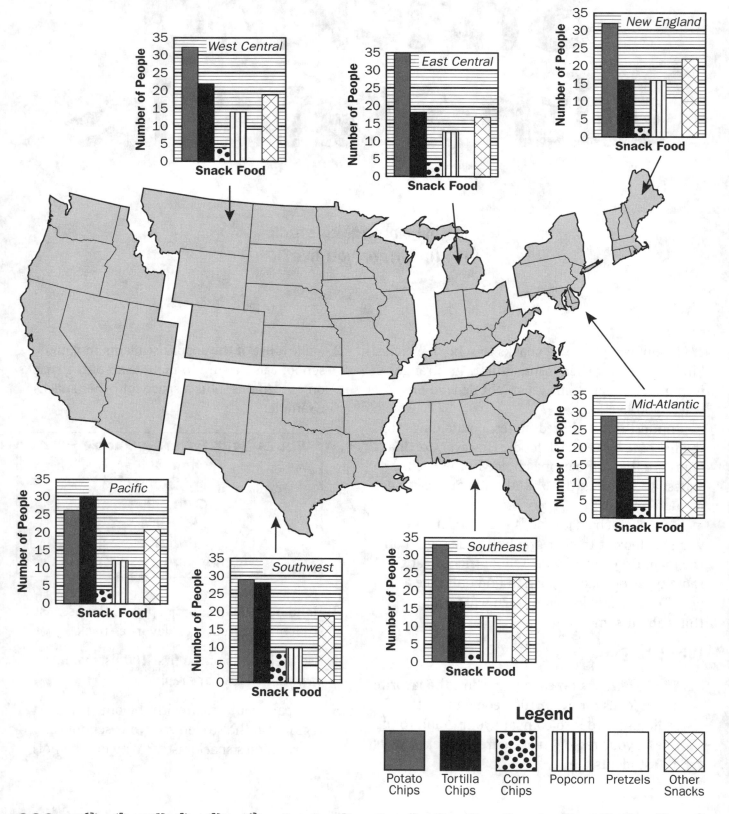

Legend

Potato Chips | Tortilla Chips | Corn Chips | Popcorn | Pretzels | Other Snacks

 **STATISTICS, GRAPHING, AND PROBABILITY**

Hot Dog—It's a Bar Graph!

 **Reading a list**

Completing a bar graph

Comparing money amounts

Money subtraction

🔑 ANSWERS

1. Dodge Stadium and County Stadium; $4.25

2. $1.25

3. $3.50; It is the price that appears most often on the graph.

4. Answers will vary. Possible answers include: the amount of profit the vendors need to make, the price of hot dogs in the area, how much it costs to buy and make the hot dogs.

5. Answers will vary. Students might suggest they would want to know the cost of tickets, souvenirs, other food, parking, and transportation to the stadium. To find these costs before the game, they could call the stadium or ask someone who has been there before.

🏹 Aim

Students use a list of hot dog prices at imaginary baseball stadiums to complete a bar graph and answer questions.

Before the Activity

Copy and distribute pages 228–229. Read through the graph with students. Have them notice that each amount on the scale at the left side of the graph is 25 cents more than the amount below it. If necessary, remind students how to subtract with money—line up the decimal points in each money amount and then subtract as you would with whole numbers.

During the Activity

If students need help computing with money or comparing money amounts, have them work with play money.

After the Activity

Ask students: *Does this graph make it easy to compare the prices of hot dogs at the different stadiums? Why do you think so?*

Extension

Have students research the costs of comparably sized hot dogs at local stadiums, restaurants, and/or convenience stores and have them make a list and a bar graph to show the different prices in your community.

Hot Dog— It's a Bar Graph!

Lets be frank—nothing's better than a hot dog at a baseball game. But watch out! While you're cheering for your favorite team, you might be paying an arm and a leg for your dog.

Check out the list for prices you might pay at some imaginary baseball stadiums. Then finish the bar graph!

What to Do:

Use the hot dog price list to finish drawing the bar graph. We did three for you. Then answer the questions.

I'm going to draw each bar a different color.

Pass the mustard.

HOT DOG PRICE LIST

PRICE	STADIUM
$4.00	Asterdome
$3.30	Bush Stadium
$3.75	Candlewick Park
$4.25	County Stadium
$4.25	Dodge Stadium
$3.50	Jack Stadium
$4.00	Olympia Stadium
$3.00	Riverback Stadium
$3.75	Shade Stadium
$3.50	Tree Brooks Stadium
$3.25	Veterinarians Stadium
$3.50	Wiggly Field

The Great Big Book of Super-Fun Math Activities   Scholastic Professional Books

How Much Does a Hot Dog Cost at a Baseball Game?

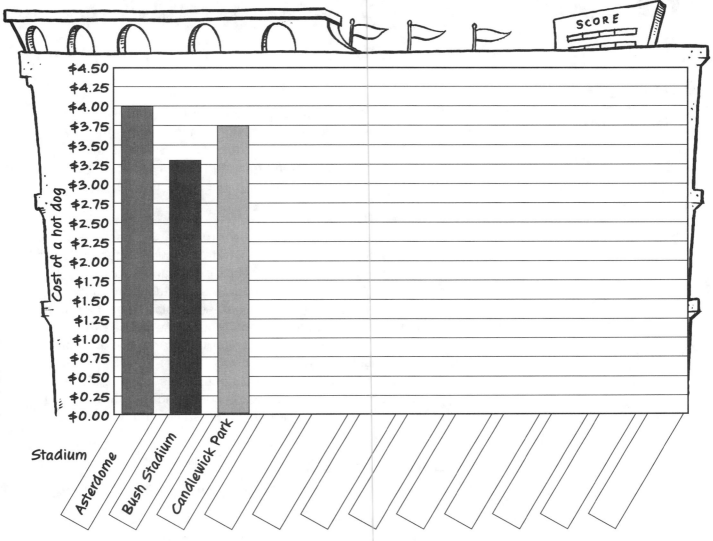

1. Where would you have to spend the most money for a hot dog? How much? _____

_____

2. How much more does the most expensive hot dog cost than the least expensive one? _____

3. According to this information, what is the most common price for a hot dog? How do you know?

_____

4. How do you think a stadium manager decides how much to charge for a hot dog? _____

_____

5. Say your class is going to see a baseball game. What other costs would you want to know besides

   the price of hot dogs? How could you find out? _____

_____

The Long and Short of Shadows

 Gathering data

Making a line graph

Measuring to the nearest inch

SCIENCE CONNECTION: Rotation of Earth

✒ Aim

Through direct observation, students will observe that as Earth rotates (causing the sun seemingly to move across the sky) their shadows become longer and shorter. Students will measure their shadows and record their observations on a line graph to show how the length changes over time.

Before the Activity

If you have a globe and a flashlight (or other light source) in your classroom, you can demonstrate the sun's effect on Earth during the day. Fold a piece of tape in half and attach it to the globe so that it will cast a shadow. Ask a student to turn on the flashlight (the "sun") and hold it steady. Hold the globe in front of the flashlight and turn it slowly. Your class will see that the shadow cast by the tape gets longer the farther it moves away from the flashlight's direct light.

Copy and distribute pages 231–232. Discuss the illustration and directions. Be sure students understand that they must stand on the same spot and face the same direction each time they take a measurement.

During the Activity

Have students work in pairs. Ask them to discuss and write down predictions before measuring their shadows. As students measure each other's shadows, be sure that they stand on the same spot each time and face the same direction (the shadows will fall in different directions and the lengths will change). Review the model line graph on page 232 before students begin creating their own line graphs.

Name _____

The Long and Short of SHADOWS

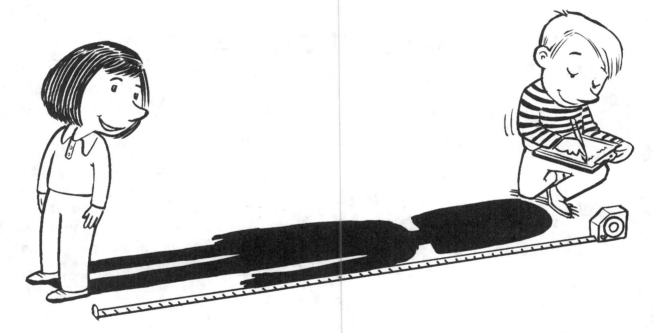

You Need:
tape measure
masking tape or chalk
graph paper
art supplies to decorate your graph

The sun makes the grass grow. It makes flowers grow. But did you know that the sun also makes your shadow grow—and shrink?

As Earth turns during the day, the sun seems to move across the sky. That makes the length of your shadow go from long to short and back again.

How much does your shadow change in one day? Make a line graph to find out. And don't worry about your shadow's ups and downs. No matter what, it will always stick by your side!

What to Do:

1. Work with a partner. Pick a sunny morning to start measuring your shadows. Find a flat area like a playground or parking lot. Mark a spot with tape or chalk. Be sure no tree or building will cast its shadow on your spot.

2. Ask your partner to stand up straight on the spot you picked. Measure your partner's shadow from where it starts at his or her feet to the top of the shadow's "head." Then have your partner measure your shadow.

3. Write down the time of day and the length of your shadow. This will be the start of your data—the information for your graph.

4. Try to measure each other's shadow at least three more times during the day. Be sure that you face the same direction each time you stand on your spot.

5. Use your data to make a line graph. Follow the hints on the sample graph below.

Sample Graph Data:

My shadow lengths
10:00 A.M.	66 inches
12:00 NOON	42 inches
2:00 P.M.	26 inches
4:00 P.M.	66 inches

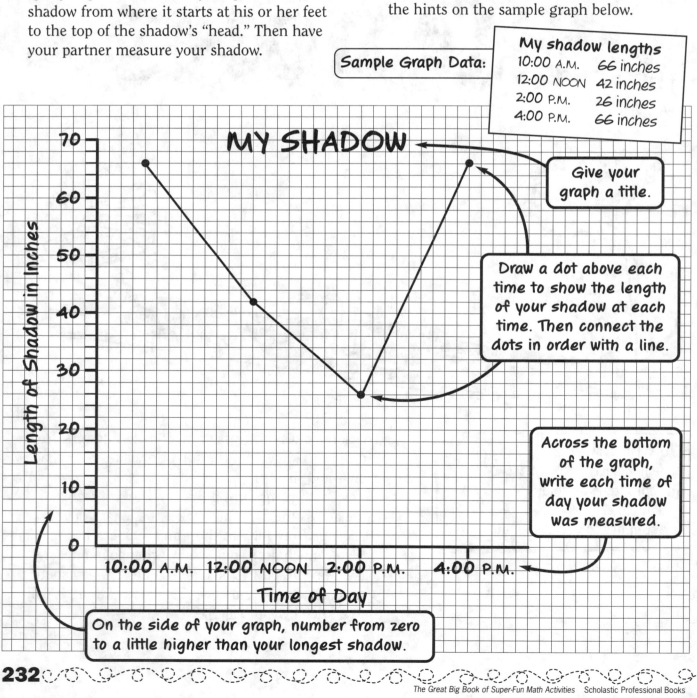

MY SHADOW

Give your graph a title.

Draw a dot above each time to show the length of your shadow at each time. Then connect the dots in order with a line.

Across the bottom of the graph, write each time of day your shadow was measured.

On the side of your graph, number from zero to a little higher than your longest shadow.

Length of Shadow in Inches

Time of Day

Sampling Cereal

 **Using tallies**

Constructing a frequency table

Estimating by taking a representative sample

Aim
Students take a sample of alphabet cereal and use tallies to keep track of the frequency with which each letter appears.

Before the Activity
You will need one box of Alpha-Bits cereal (or any generic alphabet cereal) for each four students. Copy and distribute page 234.

Talk about the word *sample* with your class. Ask: *Where have you heard the word* sample *before?* Explain that just as a sample of food will tell you how the rest of the food tastes, or a free sample of detergent will let you see how well a whole box cleans clothes, sampling a small amount of Alpha-Bits can tell you about the whole box. Review how to make tallies when counting; remind students that it is easier to total their tallies if they tally by fives, as shown under What to Do on page 234.

During the Activity
Remind students to set aside each piece of cereal they count. Do not put it back in the cup or pile.

After the Activity
Have students compare their results. Ask: *What do you think our samples tell us about the whole box?* (The more similar the samples, the more likely they are to represent those amounts of letters in the box.)

Extension

Have students use graph paper to turn their frequency tables into bar graphs. They may choose to draw the bars in order of most to least occurrences instead of in alphabetical order.

ANSWERS
4. Answers will vary.

5. Answers will vary.

BRAIN POWER: One way to answer this question is first to estimate or measure the number of cups of cereal in the full box. Next, multiply the number of each letter you counted in one cup by the number of cups in the box.

Sampling Cereal

Learn the ABCs of cereal by spooning up a sample!

You Need:
box of alphabet cereal such as Alpha-Bits
measuring cup
pencil and paper

Are there more Ps than Qs in a box of Alpha-Bits? How about the other letters? You could look at every piece of cereal in the box. But that could take a while. It might be dinnertime before you get to eat breakfast!

We've got a better idea. Take a sample. A sample is a small part of a larger group. Studying a sample can tell you a lot about the whole group. If you look at the letters in a small group of Alpha-Bits, you can get a good idea about what's in the rest of the box. That leaves only one more thing to figure out: who gets to eat the last bowl!

What to Do:

1. Measure out one cup of Alpha-Bits. This is your sample.

2. Pick one piece of cereal out of the cup. Then make a mark on the tally sheet next to the correct letter.

3. Do this for all of the Alpha-Bits in your sample cupful. Don't count broken pieces. (If you find more than one Alpha-Bit of the same letter, just mark it again on your tally sheet like this: |||| ||.)

4. Which letters have the most tally marks on your sheet?

_____

5. How does your tally sheet compare to your

classmates' sheets? _____

_____

Tally Sheet

A: _____
B: _____
C: _____
D: _____
E: _____
F: _____
G: _____
H: _____
I: _____
J: _____
K: _____
L: _____
M: _____
N: _____
O: _____
P: _____
Q: _____
R: _____
S: _____
T: _____
U: _____
V: _____
W: _____
X: _____
Y: _____
Z: _____

⇒ BRAIN POWER ⇐
How could you use your sample to estimate how many of each letter are in the whole box?

Worldwide Weather Graph

✎ Making a bar graph

✎ SOCIAL STUDIES CONNECTION: Reading a map

✎ SCIENCE CONNECTION: Weather and climate

✎ REAL-LIFE CONNECTION: Using a newspaper

⤳ Aim

Students gather data and graph the temperature of a world city for a week.

Before the Activity

Cut out and post the weather forecasts from your local newspaper for seven consecutive days. Copy and distribute pages 236–237. Since most of the places on the weather chart are listed by city rather than by country, you can incorporate social studies into this activity by showing students how to look up the cities in a world atlas and find the countries where they are located. (For further mapreading practice, have students locate these countries on a globe.) Make a list of the cities and countries (for example, Acapulco, Mexico; Athens, Greece; Bangkok, Thailand) and post the list to help students decide which city they would like to track.

During the Activity

Students may need some assistance as they draw bars on their graphs. Make sure that they are graphing only the high temperature for each day.

Extension 1

Save the graphs until winter or spring. Then repeat the activity, using new daily high temperatures for the same cities.

Extension 2

If students have worked with averages, ask them to find the average high and average low weekly temperature for their city.

Extension 3

Use the following resource for further information about weather: *The Sierra Club Book of Weatherwisdom* by Vicki McVey (San Francisco: Sierra Club Books, 1991).

⚷ ANSWERS

Students' bar graphs will vary according to the cities they choose. In general, cities nearer to the equator will be warmer than the cities nearer to the north and south poles.

Name _____

Worldwide Weather Graph

You Need:
a week's worth of newspapers
crayons or colored pencils

Say you could travel to any city in the whole world. Before you left on your trip, you'd need to know what to pack! Would a T-shirt and shorts be okay? Or would you need a parka and mittens?

Before you stuff your suitcase, take a tip from us. Make a bar graph to compare the temperature of your vacation spot every day for a week. Then you'll know if it's chilly in Chile, or balmy in Bombay!

What to Do:

1. First, gather your data—the information you want to graph. Find the weather page in a newspaper. It shows the temperatures for cities in other countries. (You can read a sample of one of these lists here.) Pick a city from the list, or another city you'd like to visit.

   Look up that city's highest temperature in the newspaper every day for a week. Write it down.

2. Now use your data (the list of the city's daily highest temperatures) to make a bar graph. Use the blank bar graph from your teacher. Follow the hints on the sample graph below.

3. On a world map, mark the cities you and your classmates picked. Where are the hotter cities located? Where are the colder cities found?

City	Today high/low
Acapulco	89/80
Athens	101/75
Bangkok	92/76
Beijing	85/72
Berlin	79/62
Budapest	92/66
Buenos Aires	61/41
Cairo	93/70
Dublin	62/53
Frankfurt	71/53

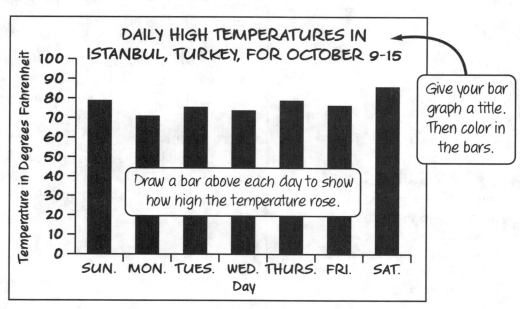

DAILY HIGH TEMPERATURES IN ISTANBUL, TURKEY, FOR OCTOBER 9-15

Give your bar graph a title. Then color in the bars.

Draw a bar above each day to show how high the temperature rose.

Temperature in Degrees Fahrenheit

SUN. MON. TUES. WED. THURS. FRI. SAT.
Day

STATISTICS, GRAPHING, AND PROBABILITY

Title: _____

Temperature in Degrees Fahrenheit

100
90
80
70
60
50
40
30
20
10
0

SUN.   MON.   TUES.   WED.   THURS.   FRI.   SAT.

Day

Tune in to Double Bar Graphs

✎ **Reading a double bar graph**

✎ **Conducting a survey**

✎ Aim

Students read a double bar graph displaying results from a 1997 Scholastic survey showing kids' five favorite television programs.

Before the Activity

Copy and distribute pages 239–240. Discuss the difference between a single bar graph and a double bar graph. Explain that a double bar graph is similar to a single bar graph, but that each bar is split into two bars. On the bar graph on the activity page, each bar is split into boys' votes and girls' votes. The purpose is to easily make comparisons.

During the Activity

Be sure that students understand the significance of the numbers on the vertical axis of the graph.

Ask: *What do the numbers on the left side of the graph stand for?* (number of respondants to the survey) *What is the highest number of votes that could be shown on this graph?* (110) *How many votes are between each horizontal line on the graph?* (10)

After the Activity

Have students add the boys' and girls' vote totals for each show on the graph. Then have them rank the shows to see which was the most popular overall. (1—*Home Improvement;* 2—*Full House;* 3—*The Simpsons;* 4—*Fresh Prince of Bel Air;* 5—*Rugrats*) Students can make a single bar graph to display their results.

Extension 1

Have students look through magazines and newspapers for a double bar graph. (*USA Today* prints several different types of graphs each day.) Post the double bar graphs on a bulletin board.

Extension 2

Copy and distribute We All Scream for Double Bar Graphs! on page 241 to give students more practice in making and reading double bar graphs.

✐ ANSWERS

1. b

2. c

3. c

4. a

5. b

6. b

BRAIN POWER Answers will vary.

Tune in to Double Bar Graphs

Does your family fight over who gets to hold the TV remote control? Everybody likes to watch something different on TV. The graph on page 240 shows the results of a poll of kids taken in 1997. One favorite show of many kids was *The Simpsons*. "It's a funny cartoon that makes me laugh," Jared Rampersaud said, "and it doesn't have too much violence." Amy Haynsworth, age 10, of Johns Island, South Carolina, preferred *Home Improvement*. "My Dad likes tools a lot, and I watch it with him," Amy said.

Look at the double bar graph to find out what other shows kids liked to watch.

What to Do:

In 1997, a survey asked kids about their favorite TV shows. The top five shows are on the double bar graph. The gray bars show how many boys voted for each show; the black bars show the number of girls' votes. Use the graph to answer the questions. Circle the correct answers.

1. Which is the favorite TV show of girls?

   a. *Full House*

   b. *Home Improvement*

   c. *Rugrats*

2. Which is the fifth favorite TV show of boys?

   a. *Home Improvement*

   b. *Rugrats*

   c. *Full House*

3. About how many boys picked *Home Improvement* as their favorite show?

   a. 100   **b.** 80   **c.** 60

4. About how many more boys than girls picked *The Simpsons* as their favorite show?

   a. 25   **b.** 50   **c.** 75

5. About how many more girls picked *The Simpsons* than picked *Rugrats*?

   a. 25   **b.** 10   **c.** 40

6. According to this graph, which statement do you think is true?

   a. The total number of boys and girls who picked *Home Improvement* is greater than 200.

   b. More boys than girls like cartoons.

   c. Reruns are more popular than all of the new shows.

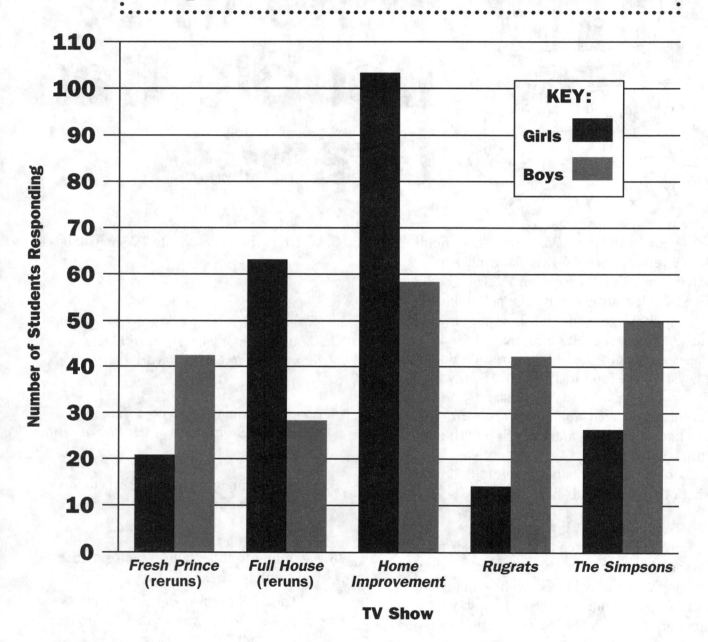

Top Five Favorite TV Shows

KEY:

Girls ▮

Boys ▮

Number of Students Responding (y-axis: 0, 10, 20, 30, 40, 50, 60, 70, 80, 90, 100, 110)

Fresh Prince (reruns)   *Full House (reruns)*   *Home Improvement*   *Rugrats*   *The Simpsons*

TV Show

⇒ BRAIN POWER ⇐

Take a survey of favorite TV shows in your own class. Draw a double bar graph to show the results.

Name _____

We All Scream for Double Bar Graphs!

Our Featured Flavors:
Marvelous Mint!
Great Grape!

Vanna Lah owns her own ice cream shop. She keeps things simple by selling only two ice cream flavors: Marvelous Mint and Great Grape. But keeping track of how much ice cream she's sold isn't so simple for Vanna. Can you help her out?

Here's the scoop: Use the information at right to make a double bar graph. Draw two bars above each month on the graph. One bar will show how many gallons of Marvelous Mint Vanna sold. The other will show how many gallons of Great Grape she sold. Here's a hint: Use two different colors to draw your bars—one for Marvelous Mint, and the other for Great Grape. Don't forget to color in your graph's key, too.

Information for Graph:
Gallons Sold Each Month

NOVEMBER
Marvelous Mint: 10 gallons
Great Grape: 8 gallons

DECEMBER
Marvelous Mint: 13 gallons
Great Grape: 12 gallons

JANUARY
Marvelous Mint: 9 gallons
Great Grape: 11 gallons

FEBRUARY
Marvelous Mint: 12 gallons
Great Grape: 12 gallons

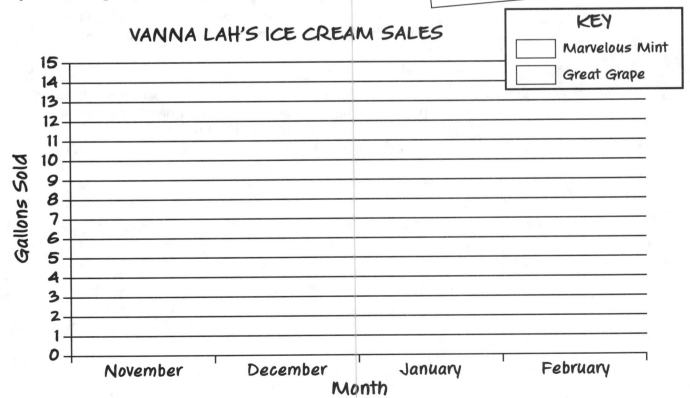

VANNA LAH'S ICE CREAM SALES

KEY
Marvelous Mint
Great Grape

Gallons Sold

November   December   January   February

Month

A Heart-y Graph

Gathering information

Making a line graph

SCIENCE CONNECTION:
Measuring heart rate

Aim

Students make line graphs showing the change in their heart rates from resting to working and back to resting.

Before the Activity

Have a stopwatch or a clock with a second hand ready. Each student will also need room to move around. Copy and distribute pages 243–244. Demonstrate finding a heart rate. (Refer to the instructions in the box on page 243.) Practice finding a resting heart rate with the class until everyone is able to do so.

During the Activity

SAFETY TIP   Any students who are unable to do strenuous exercises can still take their resting heart rates.

Extension 1

Have each student research one "heart-y" fact in an encyclopedia and write it on a heart-shaped piece of construction paper. Display the graphs and heart facts on a bulletin board.

Extension 2

For more information on the heart, or to inquire about school programs, contact your local American Heart Association or the National Association at 1-800-AHA-USA1 or www.americanheart.org

A Heart-y Graph

You Need:
stopwatch or watch with a second hand

Valentine's Day is February 14. That's why February is American Heart Month! Our hearts sure deserve the attention. After all, they pump blood through our bodies night and day without ever taking a break.

How hard does your heart work for you? Make a line graph to find out. A line graph shows changes in information over time. Your line graph will show the change in your heart rate from when you're at rest to after exercising.

What to Do:

1. Use the blank graph. Then read How To Find Your Heart Rate.

2. Sit quietly for about five minutes, then find your heart rate. Mark it with a dot on the line above "resting" heart rate on the graph.

3. Time for a workout! Run in place, do jumping jacks, or bend and touch your toes. Do this for exactly four minutes. As soon as you stop, find your heart rate again. Mark it on the graph above "working" heart rate.

4. Sit quietly for two minutes, then find your heart rate. Mark it on the graph above "recovery" heart rate.

5. Connect the three points on your graph with a line. Now your line graph shows how your heart rate changes from resting to working and back again.

HOW TO FIND YOUR HEART RATE

♥ Place two fingers on your neck or wrist. Move them around until you can feel your pulse.

♥ Count the beats for 15 seconds while a friend times you with the stopwatch.

♥ Multiply the number of beats by 4. That number is your heart rate for one minute.

Heart-y Facts

♥ Your heart is about the size of your fist. It beats about 100,000 times a day.

♥ When you were a baby, your heart beat about 140 times a minute!

♥ As you grow, your heart grows, too. But your heart rate decreases.

Give Your Heart a Hand

Make every month American Heart Month by keeping your heart strong and healthy. Here are some ways you can help your heart:

♥ Exercise every day by walking, bicycling, running, or playing outdoors.

♥ Eat three balanced meals a day. If you like to snack, choose fruits, vegetables, popcorn, or pretzels instead of candy or cookies.

HEART RATE GRAPH

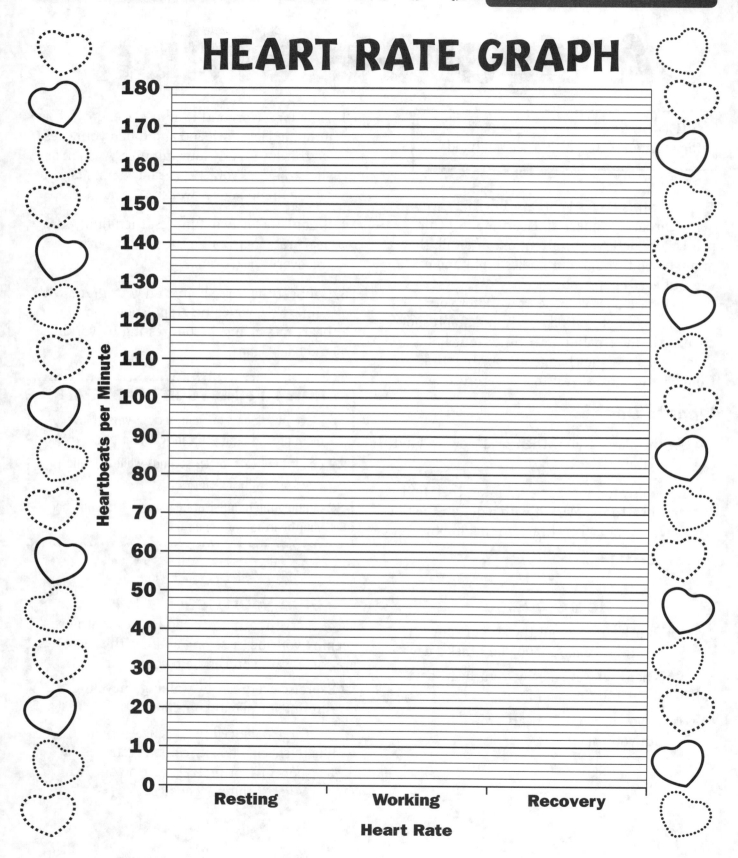

Heartbeats per Minute

180
170
160
150
140
130
120
110
100
90
80
70
60
50
40
30
20
10
0

Resting   Working   Recovery

Heart Rate

The Great Big Book of Super-Fun Math Activities   Scholastic Professional Books

Great Game Graph!

✎ **Reading a circle graph**

➵ Aim
Students read a circle graph showing the number of hours a day kids spend playing video games.

Before the Activity
Copy and distribute page 246. Explain to students that circle graphs show parts, with each part representing a ratio of part to whole. Many have parts expressed in percents. The circle graph in this lesson shows part to whole. Be sure students understand that the entire circle stands for 100 kids, and that each "slice" of the circle stands for a fractional part of 100. For example, the number of students who play video games each day for less than one hour is $\frac{43}{100}$.

After the Activity
Ask: *What other types of graphs can you name?* (pictographs, single and double bar graphs, line graphs) *Can you describe how the information on this circle graph would look if it were in the form of a bar graph?*

Extension 1
Have students look for other examples of circle graphs in newspapers and magazines. (*USA Today* is an excellent resource, as are many weekly newsmagazines.) Display the graphs on a bulletin board or in your math center.

Extension 2
This activity could lead to a basic introduction of percents. Explain that, just like the numbers of kids on the graph, a percent represents a number out of 100. The entire circle stands for 100%.

🔑 ANSWERS
1. 15 kids
2. 3 hours a day
3. Less than 1 hour a day
4. 6 or more hours a day
5. Less than $\frac{1}{2}$
6. Answers will vary.

BRAIN POWER Answers will vary.

Name _____

Great Game Graph!

How Long Kids Play Video Games Each Day

How much time do kids really spend playing video games? Read the circle graph to find out. Then, when you answer the questions, try to get the high score!

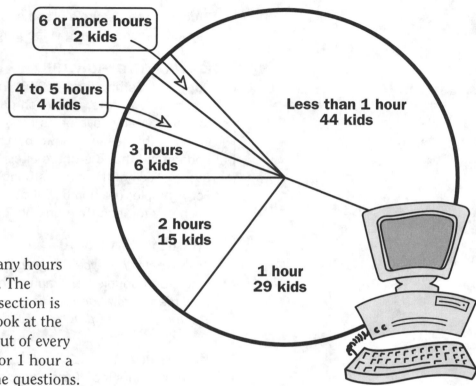

6 or more hours
2 kids

4 to 5 hours
4 kids

3 hours
6 kids

Less than 1 hour
44 kids

2 hours
15 kids

1 hour
29 kids

What to Do:

The circle graph shows how many hours kids play video games each day. The number of kids shown in each section is out of 100 kids. For example, look at the bottom section. It shows that out of every 100 kids, 29 play video games for 1 hour a day. Use the graph to answer the questions.

1. How many kids out of 100 play video games for 2 hours a day? _____

2. How many hours a day do 6 out of 100 kids play video games? _____

3. For how long does the largest group of kids play video games each day? _____

4. For how long does the smallest group of kids play video games each day? _____

5. Do more or less than $\frac{1}{2}$ of the kids play video games for less than 1 hour a day? _____

6. Think of the amount of time you play video games each day. What is the section of the graph where you would be?

_____

> ⤳ **BRAIN POWER** ⤳
> Do you think you and your friends spend too much time playing video games? Why or why not?

STATISTICS, GRAPHING, AND PROBABILITY

A Tidal Wave of Trash

 Reading a circle graph

LANGUAGE ARTS CONNECTION:
Writing in math

ANSWERS

1. Plastic

2. Glass

3. Metal; Answers will vary. Some metals that can be found on the beach are: soda cans, car parts, and toys.

4. Paper, glass, and metal.

5. Answers will vary. Students may suggest that plastic makes up most of the beach trash because plastic does not break down as quickly as other products. Some kinds of plastics that people throw away include: plastic bags, food wrappers, food containers, plastic or Styrofoam picnic products, six-pack rings, and milk and water bottles.

Aim

Students read and answer questions about a circle graph showing the breakdown of trash collected on U.S. beaches.

Before the Activity

Copy page 248. Explain to students that they will be reading about the kinds of garbage that is found on beaches in the United States. Have them name a few kinds of garbage they have found on a beach or lake shore, and what kinds of problems they think beach trash could cause. Then distribute page 248.

During the Activity

After students read through the article, explain that plastic trash is particularly dangerous to animals because they can get caught in it or try to eat it. For example, birds and other animals often mistake plastic objects for food and feed them to their young.

Help students identify the title of the graph and its labels. As they answer Question 2, help students see that they can compare the sizes of the sections in the graph, or they can compare the number of pounds shown in the labels. Point out that a circle graph makes it easy to compare data because we can look at the sizes of the sections without knowing the exact numbers they stand for.

After the Activity

Ask: *How does the circle graph help you to think about the data it shows? Do you think it's better to show this data in a circle graph or in a table? Why?*

Extension

Hold a class cleanup of your school grounds or playground. Have students separate and weigh each type of garbage they collect. To express the data as a circle graph, divide the weight of each type of garbage by the total weight of the garbage. A circle graph can then be drawn to reflect either percentages out of 100, or the ratios of pounds per 100 pounds.

A Tidal Wave of Trash

It's fun to find a pretty shell on the beach. It's not fun to find a plastic bag, a coffee cup, or a rotting sofa bed! But those things were part of the tons of trash that have washed up on some United States beaches.

Oceans, lakes, and rivers all have trash troubles. But the people at the Center for Marine Conservation in Washington, D.C. are trying to change that. That's why they hold a "Coastal Cleanup" every year. During each cleanup, kids and adults around the U.S. spend one day picking up beach junk. Mostly they find tons and tons of plastic—one of the worst kinds of beach trash.

What's especially bad about plastic? It doesn't rot like other garbage. A plastic fork tossed out today could last hundreds of years. And plastic floats. That makes it a danger to fish, birds, and other sea animals.

Cleanups are one way to protect beaches from trash. But there's another way: Don't litter!

What's in 100 Pounds of Beach Trash?

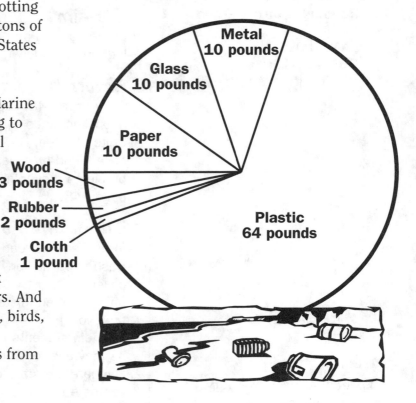

Metal
10 pounds

Glass
10 pounds

Paper
10 pounds

Wood
3 pounds

Rubber
2 pounds

Cloth
1 pound

Plastic
64 pounds

What to Do:

What kinds of trash are on America's beaches? The circle graph will give you an idea. It shows the types of beach garbage in every hundred pounds that were collected. Use it to answer the questions.

1. What is most beach garbage made of? _____

2. Was more glass or wood found on beaches? _____

3. Where would soda cans fit in on the circle graph? _____

What are some other things that fit in that group? _____

4. Which three groups make up about the same amount of the trash? _____

_____

5. Why do you think plastic makes up so much of the beach trash? List some kinds of plastic that

people throw away. _____

_____

Throw Around Some Statistics

✏️ **Making a double bar graph**

✏️ **Measuring distance in feet**

✏️ **SCIENCE CONNECTION: Air resistance**

⤵ Aim

Students estimate how far they can throw three objects of different weights, throw and measure the distances, then graph the results on a double bar graph.

Before the Activity

Have students work in pairs. Each pair will need a tape measure, two markers of different colors, and three objects of different weights. (This activity may need to take place outdoors.)

Copy and distribute pages 250–251. Introduce the activity by demonstrating each step. Roll out the tape measure and stand at the end. Ask: *How far do you think I can toss this rubber band?* Discuss reasonable estimates and locate where those estimates would be filled in on the graph. Throw the rubber band, measure the distance, and show where the distance would be filled in on the graph. Review the steps with the class and then have partners complete the activity and the questions that follow. Students should toss objects of approximately the same size but differing weights in order to relate weight and distance.

During the Activity

Instruct students to throw the objects underhand.

After the Activity

Discuss students' answers to Question 7. Ask: *Which object did you estimate that you could throw the farthest? Which object did you actually throw the farthest? Why do you think that might be so?* (In general, the heavier objects will travel farther because they are less affected by air resistance.)

Extension

If you're interested in finding statistics that students can graph for additional practice, check out *Comparisons* by the Diagram Group (New York: St. Martin's Press, 1980). This fascinating book contains loads of comparisons of the sizes and shapes of everything from buildings to insects.

Throw Around Some Statistics

Use a double bar graph to test your throwing arm!

You Need:
3 objects to throw
  (see What to Do)
2 markers of
  different colors
tape measure

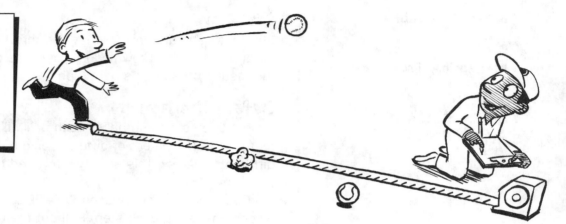

Here's the windup, and the pitch...hey, this isn't gym class, it's math class! Don't worry. You're going to combine the two. And you will use a double bar graph to do it!

Your double bar graph will show an estimate of how far you can throw an object. The graph will also show how far you can actually throw the same object.

What to Do:

1. Pick three things to throw. One object should be light, like a ball of crumpled paper. One object should be medium weight, like a tennis ball. The last object should be heavy, like a baseball.

2. Take a guess: How many feet do you think you can throw the light object? On the blank graph, draw a bar showing that distance. Color in the bar with the first marker.

4. Stand at a spot and throw the object in front of you. (Be sure not to throw any objects near people.) Have a partner measure the distance from your feet to where the object landed.

5. On the graph, make a bar showing that distance. Color it in with the second marker.

6. Now guess how far you can throw the medium and heavy objects. Then throw each object. Mark those distances on your graph.

7. Compare the distances shown on your graph.

Which object did you estimate you could

throw the farthest? _____

Which object did you actually throw the

farthest? _____

How close were your estimates to the actual

distances you threw the objects? _____

_____

If you're throwing an object that can bounce, estimate and measure only the first bounce.

THROWING DISTANCE GRAPH

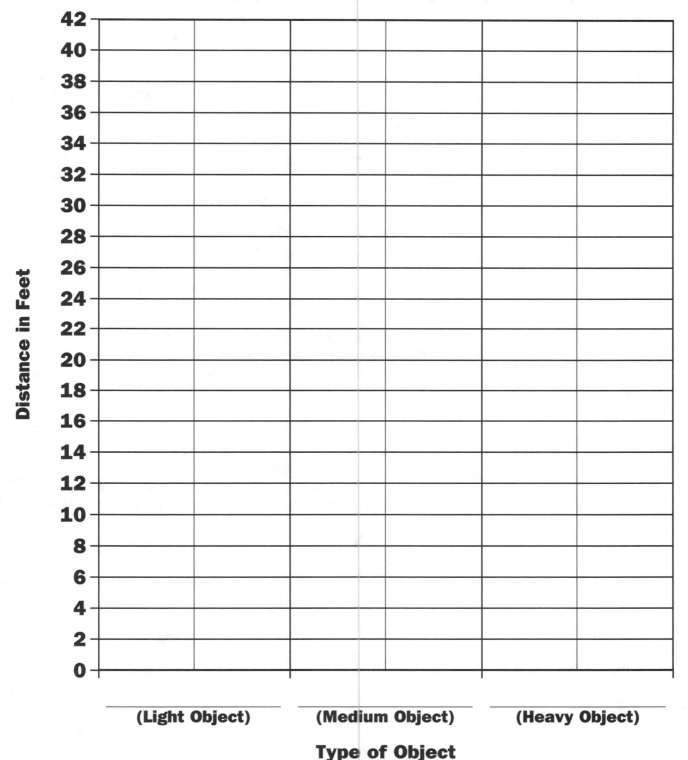

Distance in Feet

42
40
38
36
34
32
30
28
26
24
22
20
18
16
14
12
10
8
6
4
2
0

(Light Object)   (Medium Object)   (Heavy Object)

Type of Object

Shake, Rattle, and Roll!

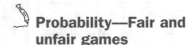

- Probability—Fair and unfair games

- Constructing a frequency table

Aim

Students test the probability of winning a number game and decide whether the game is fair or unfair. Note: This activity can also be completed with dice or number cubes.

Before the Activity

It may be easier for you to prepare the beans and juice boxes beforehand. Copy and distribute pages 253–254.

During the Activity

If students are working in pairs, one student can shake out the beans, and another can record the totals on the table. If students are working independently, each needs a box and beans and a copy of the table.

After the Activity

Discuss students' results and their answers to the questions. Ask: *Why do the tables look as they do? Which totals are most likely in this game? Which are least likely?*

Extension

Challenge students to find all the combinations of each possible score in the game. Ask them to relate this to their findings of most and least likely totals. They will see that the reason certain totals occur more frequently is because they have a greater number of possible combinations.

ANSWERS

1–4. Answers will vary. In general, the more times students spill out two beans, the more often the numbers in the middle of the graph will come up and the less often the numbers toward either end of the graph will come up.

Shake, Rattle, and Roll!

When is a game fair? When each player has the same chance of winning. Take a look at this number game

You will play the game by picking a number from 2 to 12. Then you shake two beans out of the box and add them up. If they add up to your number, you get a point. It's a fair game, right? Maybe—or maybe not!

It's all in the **probability**—the chance that a number will appear in the game. If one number seems to come up more often than another, the game may be unfair.

Here's how you can test the fairness of the bean game:

What to Do:

- Use the marker to label the beans. You need 2 sets of beans, each numbered from 1 to 6, as shown in the picture.

- Cut a hole in the top of the juice box small enough so that only one bean can go through it at a time.

- Put all 12 beans in the box. Shake the box until two beans come out. Add the numbers on the beans together. Mark an X on the bean table above the **total** of the two beans.

For example, if the two beans add up to 8, you will make an X on the graph above the number 8.

- Put the two beans back in the box. Shake two more out, and mark their total on the table. Repeat this until you have 10 X's on the table.

Take a look at your bean table. Do you see a pattern in the numbers? Do any of them appear more than once?

- Now shake out and total beans until you have 20 X's. What does your table look like now?

- Shake and total beans until you have 30 X's. Then compare your table with others in the class.

BEAN FREQUENCY TABLE

2	3	4	5	6	7	8	9	10	11	12

1. After 10 shakes, 20 shakes, and 30 shakes, do the tables look alike or different?

_____

2. Which numbers seem to appear most often? Which seem to appear least often? Why might this be so?

_____

_____

3. What might the tables look like with 50 X's? Try it!

_____

4. Do you think the bean game is fair or unfair? Why do you think so?

_____

_____

Fair... or Unfair?

 Probability with fair and unfair odds

 Aim

Students play games with different spinners and a penny to learn about probability.

Before the Activity

Copy and distribute pages 256–257.

During the Activity

As students play the games, their understanding of what is fair will begin to grow more complex. Games 1 through 4 will help them to see that a game is fair if the areas they can land on are equal in number and size. In Game 5, students should see that the game is set up fairly, because a penny has two sides and thus an equal chance of landing on heads or tails.

Game 6 is a bit tricky: Although there are an equal number of even and odd numbers, the even numbers are greater, so Player 1 will be more likely to win because he or she is likely to reach 50 first.

After the Activity

Ask students to discuss their findings about what makes a probability game fair or unfair.

Extension

Have students design their own spinner games that they think are fair. Then have them play the games with a partner to determine if they were correct in their judgments of fairness.

ANSWERS

Game 1: The game is fair, because both players have an equal amount of space to land on.

Game 2: The game is unfair, because Player 1 has a larger amount of space to land on.

Game 3: The game is fair, because both players have an equal number of spaces to land on.

Game 4: The game is unfair, because Player 2 has more spaces to land on.

Game 5: The game is fair, because a penny has two sides that are equally likely to come up on a toss.

Game 6: The game is unfair, because the even numbers are greater than the odd numbers.

Fair... or Unfair?

You Need:
pencil
penny
paper clip

Everyone likes to play games. But a game is no fun if it isn't fair. A game is fair if everyone playing has the same chance of winning. Play the games on these pages with a partner. Then decide which ones are fair and which are unfair. You might want to play some games more than once to help you decide.

GAME 1

Player 1 is "peanuts." Player 2 is "macaroni." Take turns spinning. The first player to land on his or her item 10 times wins.

Circle one: FAIR   UNFAIR

Explain your choice on a separate piece of paper.

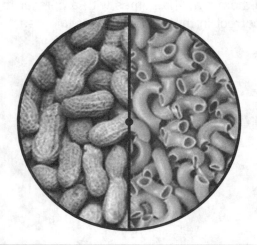

GAME 2

Player 1 is "peanuts." Player 2 is "macaroni." Take turns spinning. The first player to land on his or her item 10 times wins.

Circle one: FAIR   UNFAIR

Explain your choice on a separate piece of paper.

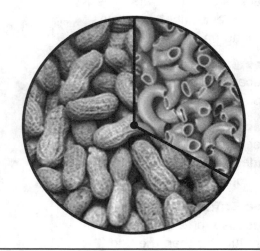

GAME 3

Player 1 is "gumballs." Player 2 is "Cheerios." Take turns spinning. The first player to land on his or her item 10 times wins.

Circle one: FAIR UNFAIR

Explain your choice on a separate piece of paper.

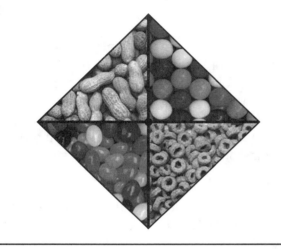

GAME 4

Player 1 is "Cheerios." Player 2 is "peanuts." Take turns spinning. The first player to land on his or her item 10 times wins.

Circle one: FAIR UNFAIR

Explain your choice on a separate piece of paper.

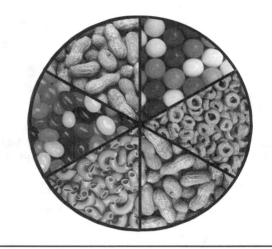

GAME 5

Get a penny. Player 1 is "heads." Player 2 is "tails." Take turns flipping the coin. The first player to get his or her side five times wins.

Circle one: FAIR UNFAIR

Explain your choice on a separate piece of paper.

GAME 6

Player 1 counts only even numbers. Player 2 counts only odd numbers. Take turns spinning. Keep a total of your scores. If you land on one of your numbers, add that number to your total score. The first player to pass 50 wins.

Circle one: FAIR UNFAIR

Explain your choice on a separate piece of paper.

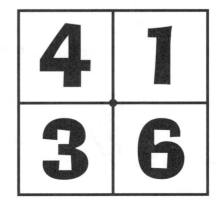

The Great Big Book of Super-Fun Math Activities Scholastic Professional Books

Great Groups!

 **Categorizing**

things with legs

Aim
Students classify items, based on shared attributes, from a group of pictures.

Before the Activity
Discuss some of the things that make all the members of your class belong to the same group. Some possible shared attributes include the fact that you are their teacher; all are in the same grade; all are humans. Copy and distribute pages 259–260. Choose one of the classification sets: for example, "things with numbers." Ask students to list items from the pictures, and from your classroom, that belong to that category.

During the Activity
Tell students that each group they make must have two or more things in it. Encourage students to work together and to write down their ideas for categories. Students should also list the items from the picture that belong in each category.

This activity can be used as a game in several ways: Have students find the most members of a given group in a given amount of time; have them find the most groups; have them make up the most other reasonable categories to which at least two members from the pictured items belong.

Extension
Have teams play a grouping and attribute game. To begin, each team should work together to make up five different groups (categories) of three people, places, and/or things that have something in common. The team should write each list of three on a separate piece of paper and also keep a "secret" piece of paper telling what the members of each group have in common. To play, teams take turns guessing what is common in another team's groups. Each team gets three chances to identify the common feature of a group. Teams score one point for each category (group name) they are able to identify. Allow the class to play several rounds of the game; encourage students to find items that have something in common yet may challenge others. Remind students that categories can be built around physical attributes, such as size, shape, and color; use; or function.

Great Groups!

How many ways can you group these items? Cut them out and move them into different groups. Find as many ways as you can. Then make a list of each group and the objects that belong in it. Use the ideas on these pages. Then make up your own great groups!

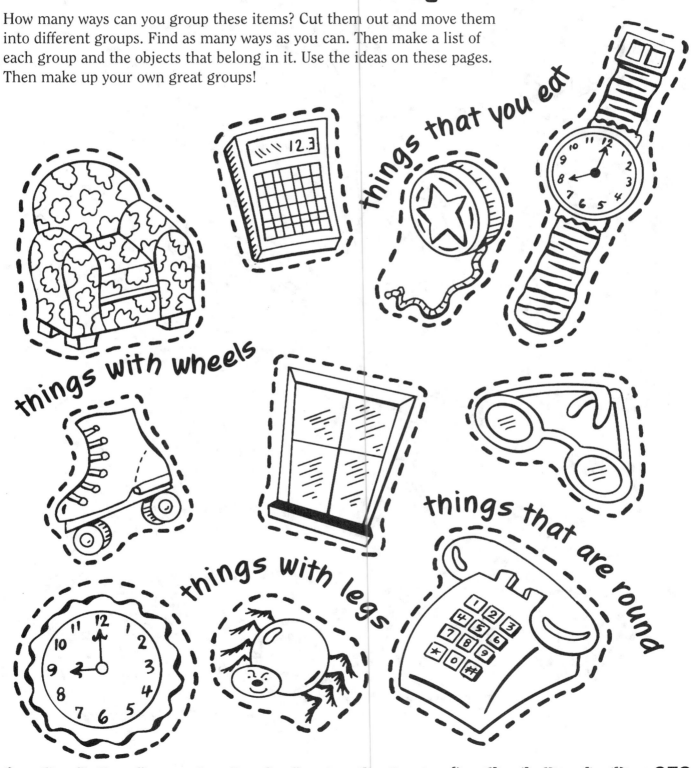

things you can see through

things with holes

things with numbers

things that hold something

LOGIC AND REASONING

Picture Yourself

✎ **Identifying attributes**

✎ **Reading a table**

✳️ Aim
By following a table, students identify attributes about themselves. They then use magazine pictures to illustrate their traits and complete a picture of store shelves.

Before the Activity
Copy and distribute pages 262–263.

During the Activity
Encourage students to cut out pictures that they like or that show something about themselves within each category. For example, if a student is looking for a toy, he or she could cut out a toy that has particular significance to him or her. That way, if students complete the activity again at a later time, they will be able to compare their stores and notice how they have changed.

Along with the completed store shelves, you may want to display the table to help students think about and compare the items in the stores.

LOGIC AND REASONING

Picture Yourself

Can you fill the shelves to give clues about yourself? Try it!

Why are the store shelves on page 263 empty? You can fill them. But don't put just anything on the shelves—follow the table below, and each item you find will stand for something about you. When you're done, the picture you create will be yours alone.

   Work alone, then with your classmates. Use the table to find the magazine pictures you need. Then paste or tape them to fill your shelves. When you are finished, put all of your stores up on the bulletin board.

You Need:
scissors
glue or tape
magazines for cutting

▶ Find a group of stores that have one item in common. Find stores that have two or three items in common, too.

▶ Choose one store. Tell about the person who made it. Then try to guess whose it is.

▶ Find your twin! Look for a store that has the same items as yours.

If...	Cut out a picture of...
1. you are a girl	a pair of shoes
you are a boy	a hat
2. you walk to school	a toy
you ride to school	a TV
3. you are less than 52 inches tall	an animal
you are 52 inches or taller	a plant
4. there are one or two kids in your family	a fruit
there are more than two kids in your family	a vegetable
5. your age is an odd number	a clock
your age is an even number	a telephone

The Great Big Book of Super-Fun Math Activities Scholastic Professional Books

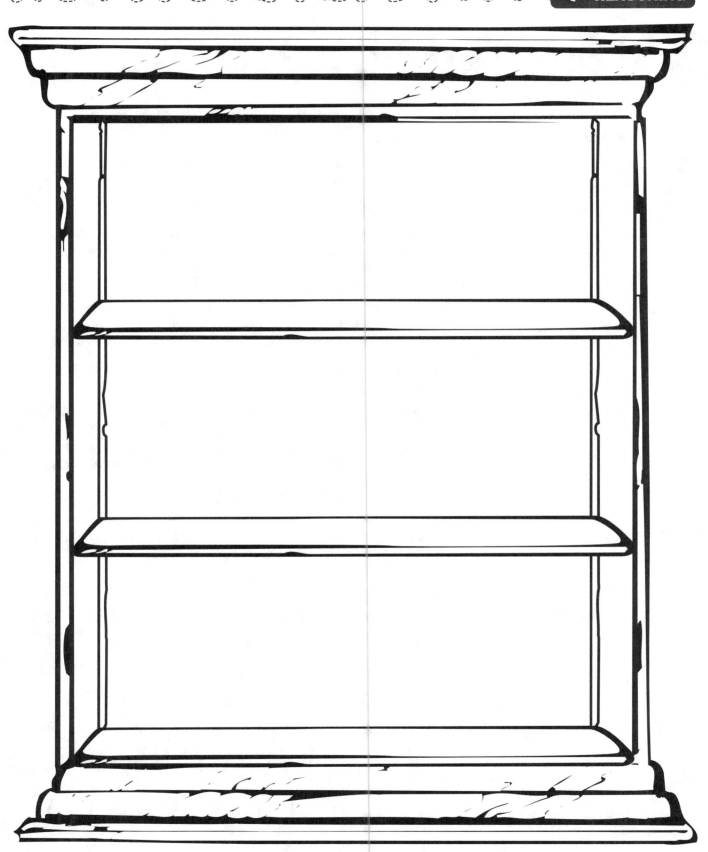

The Great Big Book of Super-Fun Math Activities   Scholastic Professional Books

LOGIC AND REASONING

A Math Tea Party

 Using strategic thinking

 **LITERATURE CONNECTION: Reading a story**

Aim

Students plan winning strategies as they play a board game with an Alice in Wonderland theme.

Before the Activity

If you like, establish the setting of this activity by reading aloud Chapter 7 of *Alice's Adventures in Wonderland*, "A Mad Tea-Party." Copy and distribute pages 265–266.

Provide each player or team with 10 counters. Each team should have its own color. It may be helpful to demonstrate how the game is played before students play it. Point out that jumping another player's "teacup" can be done only in a straight line, much like in checkers.

During the Activity

As class members play the game, they will become more adept at thinking a move or two ahead. Ask: *After playing the game a few times, have you found better ways to set up your counters at the beginning? What strategies have you discovered for winning?*

It is possible for two players to end up with one counter apiece, chasing each other around the board. Ask: *What will you do if this happens? Will you call the game a draw? Can you find a way to avoid this situation?*

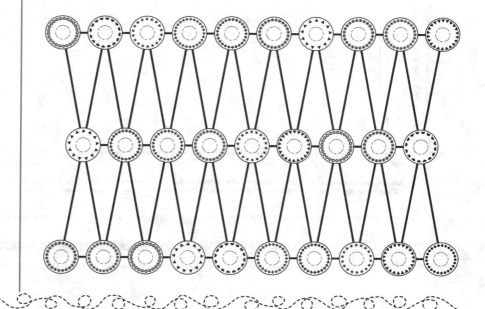

A Math Tea Party

In Lewis Carroll's most famous book, *Alice's Adventures in Wonderland*, a curious girl named Alice finds herself at a "Mad Tea-Party."

The guests at the tea party include a talking rabbit, a hatmaker, and a sleepy animal called a dormouse. Alice wonders: If there are only three guests at the party, why is the table set with so many cups and saucers? And why are all the guests racing around the table sipping tea from every cup?

Alice's friends may not be using logic, but you can. Pull up a seat at our Math Tea Party! One lump or two?

Object: To capture all of the other player's teacups.

Number of Players: 2 players or 2 teams of players

To Play:

► On the game board, set your teacups (counters) on any empty saucers you wish. Decide who will go first.

► Take turns moving one of your teacups to an empty saucer. You can move a teacup one space forward, backward, or diagonally along any line of the tablecloth.

► You can capture another player's teacup by jumping over it to an open saucer. You can jump only in a straight line. You cannot move your teacup and jump in the same turn.

Black captures one gray

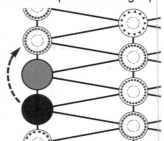

You Need:
10 counters of the same color for each player or team.

⊰ **BRAIN POWER** ⊱
Read the book *Alice's Adventures in Wonderland*. What are some of the different ways Alice uses logic?

► You can jump and capture more than one teacup in a row if there are enough empty saucers.

Black captures two gray

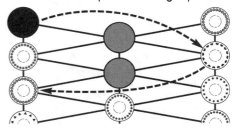

► You cannot jump over your own teacups.

► The game ends when one player captures all of the other player's teacups.

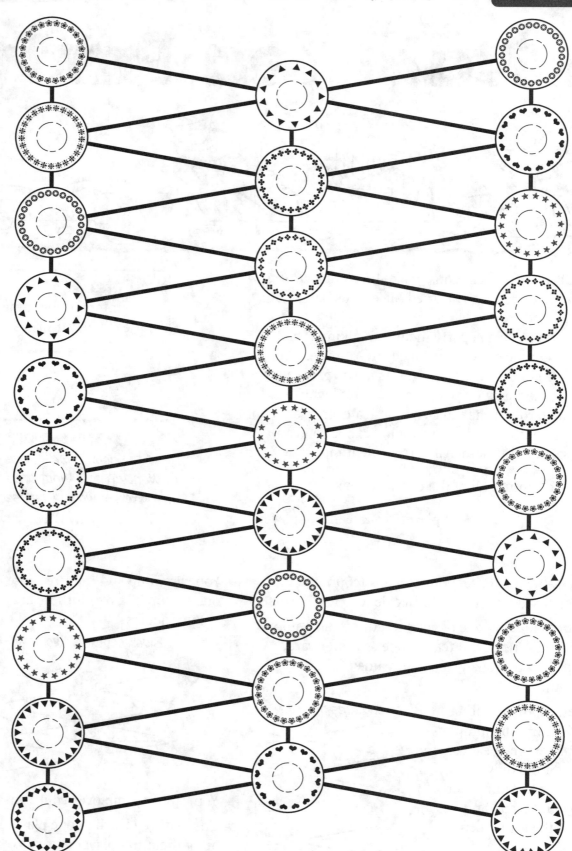

The Amazing Maize Maze

 Solving a maze

 PROBLEM-SOLVING SKILLS: Guess and check, working backward

ANSWERS

Here is one route through the maze:

Aim

Students work through a drawing of the amazing maize maze.

Before the Activity

Copy and distribute pages 268–269. Inform students that, when it was cut out of a cornfield in the summer of 1993, the real-life size of the Maize Maze was about 175 by 700 feet. Measure a large area such as the gym or playground, then use that as a guide to help students understand the size of the real maze.

During the Activity

Before drawing on the maze, students can choose a strategy and trace different routes with their fingers. Ask for volunteers to share successful strategies. Some will begin at START and try different paths; others may start at FINISH and work backward.

After the Activity

Invite students to design a large maze using masking tape on your classroom or gym floor. When students decide that it is sufficiently difficult, invite other classes to try it.

Extension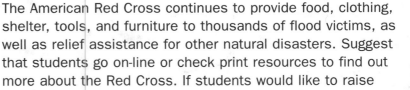

The American Red Cross continues to provide food, clothing, shelter, tools, and furniture to thousands of flood victims, as well as relief assistance for other natural disasters. Suggest that students go on-line or check print resources to find out more about the Red Cross. If students would like to raise money for this worthy cause, checks may be sent to: Flood Relief Fund, P.O. Box 37243, Washington, DC 20013.

Name _____

The Amazing Maize Maze

Trim off this strip and attach to page 269.

Meet Cornelius the Cobosaurus. He's about 700 feet long and has huge spikes on his back!

Don't worry—Cornelius isn't a real dinosaur. He's part of a maze big enough for people to walk through. In fact, the Amazing Maize Maze is listed as the largest maze in the world!

The maize maze was cut out of a cornfield one summer by students at Lebanon Valley College in Pennsylvania. Almost 7,000 people wandered through the maze the following fall. With their help, the college students raised more than $32,000 for the Red Cross's Corn Belt flood relief program.

The Great Big Book of Super-Fun Math Activities Scholastic Professional Books

Attach to page 268 here.

START

FINISH

What to Do:

Look at the drawing of the maze. Can you find your way from START to FINISH? Trace your path with a pencil. There's no need to rush. Maze designer Adrian Fisher says, "A good maze should be great fun. You should be able to solve it just before you've had enough."

We Love Combinations

 Finding combinations

 Making a list

Aim

Students develop probability and problem-solving skills as they color combinations on Valentine's Day cards.

Before the Activity

Discuss combinations with students to be sure they understand that a combination is the same regardless of the position or arrangement of the items. To demonstrate, pick two colors of chalk and draw a line of each color on the chalkboard. Ask students how many colors you have shown. (two) Ask students how many combinations you have shown. (one) Draw two more lines on the chalkboard, but this time switch the positions of the colors. Point out to students that the combinations of colors is the same.

Copy and distribute pages 271–272.

During the Activity

Students can do this activity individually or in groups of three or four. Explain to students that coloring the hearts on the cards is a way to keep track of all the combinations of two colors that can be made from a group of five colors.

After the Activity

Ask: *What are some ways you can be sure you did not repeat any combinations on the cards? What are some ways you can be sure you found all of the combinations?*

Extension

Write the following list of colors on the chalkboard: blue, yellow, red, green, orange. Challenge students to draw arcs to match pairs of colors. Have them first match blue to each of the other colors, then yellow, and so on. By counting the arcs students can learn how many combinations are possible.

ANSWERS

4. 10 combinations of 2 colors can be made from a group of 5 colors. Encourage students to find as many combinations as they can and to compare their combinations with other students'.

5. 10 combinations of 3 colors can be made from a group of 5 colors.

BRAIN POWER: 15 combinations of 2 colors can be made from a group of 6 colors.

We Love Combinations

You Need:
5 paper hearts, each one a different color
5 crayons or colored pencils, the same colors as the hearts

Welcome to the Value Valentines greeting card factory. No two of our cards are exactly alike. How do we do it? We use a different color combination on each card.

We're pretty busy around Valentine's Day. Help us out. Here's how.

1. Look at your five hearts. Pick out two colors. That's one combination.

2. Color the hearts on one of our Valentine's Day cards. Make the hearts on the card the same colors as the paper hearts that you chose.

3. Put all five hearts together again. Pick out a **different** combination of two colors. Use those colors on another card.

This is the same combination.

These are different combinations.

4. Each time you find a different combination, color it on a card. How many cards can you color?

5. We also make cards with three hearts, like this:

On a separate paper, see how many cards with three hearts you can make. Use your five hearts to find combinations of three colors. Remember: No two cards should have the same three colors.

⇒ BRAIN POWER ⇐
What if you had six hearts, each a different color? How many 2-heart cards could you make? Try it!

Valentine's Day Cards

Crazy Clothing Combinations

Making tree diagrams

Understanding combinations

Aim

Students use the problem-solving strategy of drawing tree diagrams to find clothing combinations.

Before the Activity

Copy and distribute pages 274–275. Students may not have seen a tree diagram before, so you may want to work through the example on page 274 with the whole class.

During the Activity

This activity lends itself well to group work. If you would like to make this activity a bit less challenging, have the groups figure out the answers to Questions 1, 2, and 3 using just Gary's hat, ties, and shoes (no suits). Then you can increase the difficulty of the activity by adding the suits and having each group rework the problems.

After the Activity

This activity can serve as an introduction to a study of combinatorics. Show students another way to find the number of combinations: multiply the number of choices for each piece of clothing. For example, Cathy has 1 necklace, 2 dresses, and 3 pairs of shoes. So we multiply 1 × 2 × 3, and find there are 6 possible combinations. Students can use the formula to double-check their tree diagrams.

Note: Students may be interested to know that the order of items on the tree diagram does not change the end result. For example, Cathy could have connected her necklace to the shoes, and the shoes to the dresses. She would have ended up with the same 6 outfit combinations.

ANSWERS

1. 12 combinations

2. 6 combinations

3. 4 combinations

4. Answers will vary.

BRAIN POWER: Answers will vary.

Extension

Discuss other times when you might use a tree diagram. (combinations of people to work in different groups, match-ups for sports tournaments, etc.)

Name _____

Crazy Clothing Combinations
Tree diagrams will help Cathy and Gary get dressed for the big dance!

WHAT TO DO:

Across town, Gary doesn't know what to wear, either! For each problem, use the list of his clothes to make a tree diagram. Remember: Connect the hat to each different tie. Connect each tie to each different suit. Connect each different suit to each different pair of shoes.

1. Draw a tree diagram using all of Gary's clothes. How many different clothes combinations did you find?

GARY'S LIST OF CLOTHES

HAT
top hat

SUITS
tuxedo
yellow spotted suit

TIES
bow tie
gold medal
orange tie

SHOES
Mush Puppies
Treeboks sneakers

2. Whoops! Gary's Mush Puppies shoes are covered with mud! Cross them off of the list of clothes. Now draw a new tree diagram. How many combinations did you find this time?

3. Gary forgot that he loaned his bow tie to his friend Clucky. Cross the bow tie off the list. (The Mush Puppies are still crossed off, too.) Now draw the new tree diagram. How many combinations are left?

4. What outfit do you think Gary should wear?

_____

_____

⇒ BRAIN POWER ⇐
Make your own list of crazy clothes for Cathy or Gary. Then make tree diagrams to see how many outfits they can wear!

Logic's in Bloom

✎ **Using strategic thinking**

⟿ Aim
Students find strategies to win a board game.

Before the Activity
Copy and distribute page 277. You may want to laminate the game boards for durability.

During the Activity
Students should discover winning strategies after playing the game several times. For instance, they may find that the first person to land on the middle space of the board has a greater chance of winning the game. Ask: *Does finding a strategy mean you will always win the game?*

Extension
Make a large Logic's in Bloom game board by placing masking tape on the floor of your classroom, or arranging desks in the same pattern as the flowers on our game board. Teams of four students can play against each other by having one person move the other three around the board. Team members should take turns being the "mover."

Name _____

Logic's in Bloom

Logic is "blooming" in this springtime board game!

You Need:
3 counters of the same color for each player or team

Object:
To be the first to cover three flowers in a row with your "bees" (counters). A row can be made across, up and down, or diagonally.

Number of Players:
2 players or 2 teams

To Play:

- Decide who will go first. Players take turns placing one bee at a time on an empty flower in the garden.

- After all six bees are on the board, players take turns moving one of their bees along any leaf to an empty flower.

- You can move only one bee at a time. You cannot jump over another bee.

- You can move your bee to only one other flower on each turn.

- The first player to get three bees in a row is the winner.

> **⇒ BRAIN POWER ⇐**
> Did you find a strategy
> to help win the game?
> Explain your strategy to a friend.

The Great Big Book of Super-Fun Math Activities Scholastic Professional Books

Logic Rules the Jungle

 Identifying attributes

 ART CONNECTION: Drawing imaginary creatures

Aim

Students explore attributes of imaginary animals.

Before the Activity

Copy and distribute pages 279–280.

During the Activity

After students come up with rules of their own, challenge them to write rules that include more than one trait. (For example, creatures that have three arms and three-pointed heads.)

Extension

Have students create their own weird jungle animals and write rules for them. Students can exchange animals and figure out the rules for categorizing them.

ANSWERS

2. All hoppers have one leg.

3. The hopper is the figure at the left.

4. All skeetles have bodies with stars and circles; or All skeetles have stars.

5. The skeetle is the figure at the right.

6. Answers will vary. Some groups and characteristics students may identify: creatures with three arms; creatures with crown-shaped heads; creatures with ponytails; creatures with wings; creatures that have spots; creatures wearing hats.

Name _____

Logic Rules the Jungle

1. Look at the picture at right. What do you think it might be? Why do you think that?

You probably have an idea what the picture shows. That's because you know a rule about zebras. The rule is: All zebras have stripes.

2. All of these are hoppers.

None of these is a hopper.

Finish a rule about hoppers.

All hoppers _____

_____

3. Which of these is a hopper?

Explain your choice.

_____

_____

_____

_____

_____

_____

_____

4. All of these are skeetles.

None of these is a skeetle.

Write a rule about skeetles.

All skeetles _____

_____

5. Which of these is a skeetle?

Explain your choice.

_____
_____
_____
_____

6. Look at the six creatures below. Find a group that has something in common and give it a name. Write a rule for the group.

Show your friends the group of creatures you chose. Then show the creatures that don't fit the rule. Can your friends guess the rule? How many different rules can you write for this set of creatures?

The Great Big Book of Super-Fun Math Activities Scholastic Professional Books

LOGIC AND REASONING

Pack Your Logic Box

 **Using a logic box**

Aim
Students use logic boxes to solve reasoning problems.

Before the Activity
Copy and distribute page 282.

During the Activity
Finish Problem 1 with students to be sure they understand the process of elimination involved in using a logic box. Ask students how, after using Clue A, they know that Jimmy and Timmy don't play horseshoes. (because Zimmy does play horseshoes)

Be sure that students understand that while a YES will automatically mean that some other boxes will get a NO, a NO does not always lead to any YES answers.

After the Activity
Ask students: *What is most difficult about using logic boxes? What strategies did you use to fill in each space in the logic boxes?*

ANSWERS
Here are the completed logic boxes:

1.

	Jimmy	Timmy	Zimmy
Ping-Pong	YES	NO	NO
horseshoes	NO	NO	YES
water polo	NO	YES	NO

2.

	Carla	Chucky	Isabel
Des Moines	YES	NO	NO
Memphis	NO	NO	YES
Scotch Plains	NO	YES	NO

3.

	Ed	C.J.	Sam	Frank
statue	NO	NO	NO	YES
glasses	NO	NO	YES	NO
candle	YES	NO	NO	NO
rabbit	NO	YES	NO	NO

Name _____

Pack Your Logic Box

Hi-ho, gang! I'm Uncle Sal, the new counselor at Camp Confusion. Right now I'm not a happy camper! I'm having trouble keeping track of all these kids. But we can set things straight with some logic boxes. I'll show you how in the first problem.

1. The Brothers Grimmy
Jimmy, Timmy, and Zimmy Grimmy are triplets. They look exactly alike! The only way to tell them apart is by which sport they play. Which triplet is which? I use these clues:

Clue A: Zimmy loves to toss things.

Clue B: Jimmy does not know how to swim.

	Jimmy	Timmy	Zimmy
Ping-Pong			NO
horseshoes	NO	NO	YES
water polo			NO

Clue A says that Zimmy likes to toss things. Horseshoes is the only sport listed where people toss things. I put **YES** in the box where Zimmy and horseshoes meet.

Since Zimmy plays horseshoes, he can't play Ping-Pong or water polo. I put **NO** in those boxes. And now I know that Jimmy and Timmy don't play horseshoes. I put **NO** in those boxes. Now use Clue B to finish the logic box. What sports do Timmy and Jimmy play?

2. Soggy Delivery
Carla, Chucky, and Isabel were happy to hear that they all got packages from home. Too bad I left the boxes out in the rain! The addresses washed off the packages. Only the postmarks are left. Who gets which box? Use the clues and the logic box to find out.

Clue A: The name of Carla's hometown has two words in it.

Clue B: The name of Chucky's home state has two words in it.

	Carla	Chucky	Isabel
Des Moines, Iowa			
Memphis, Tennessee			
Scotch Plains, New Jersey			

3. You Call This Art?
I'm sick and tired of arts and crafts! It's hard enough figuring out what these things are. But now I have to find out who made each one! There's a statue of President Clinton made out of cottage cheese. There's a pair of dog eyeglasses. There's a dirty sneaker candle holder. And there's a rabbit wearing a wig! Use the clues to find out who made what.

Clue A: Ed's shoelaces are covered with wax.

Clue B: C.J. thinks cottage cheese is gross!

Clue C: Sam's dog is always bumping into walls.

	Ed	C.J.	Sam	Frank
president statue				
dog glasses				
sneaker candle				
wig rabbit				

The Great Big Book of Super-Fun Math Activities Scholastic Professional Books

Rah, Rah for Shisima!

Using logical thinking

CULTURAL CONNECTION:
Game from Africa

Aim
Students develop strategies while playing Shisima, a traditional Kenyan game.

Before the Activity
Copy and distribute pages 284–285. Have students form pairs to play Shisima. Each pair of students will need one Shisima game board. Each player will need three counters to use as game pieces. Be sure that each player's game pieces look different from his or her opponent's pieces.

You may want to demonstrate the rules of Shisima before students begin playing. Choose a student to be your partner and play one round of Shisima together as the rest of the class looks on. Encourage the onlookers to read through the rules of Shisima as you're playing so they can "help" you and your partner through the game. They can point out options, mistakes, and strategies.

During the Activity
Visit each pair of students as they play Shisima. Ask: *What strategies do you think it takes to win at Shisima? Have you found that the first player to move usually wins, or do you think both players have an equal chance of winning?*

Extension
If your students enjoyed playing Shisima, check out *The Multicultural Game Book* by Louise Orlando (New York: Scholastic, 1993). The book contains 70 games from around the world, including 10 African games. You can order the book from Scholastic by calling 1-800-724-6527.

ANSWERS
BRAIN POWER: Answers will vary. We found it helpful to avoid the center (the shisima) until absolutely necessary. First, line up two pieces on opposite sides of the board.

Rah, Rah for Shisima!

Does it "bug" you to loose when you play a game? Then use your brain to stay afloat in this game from Africa!

In the game Shisima (shi-SEE-muh), you can really make a splash! It's played by kids in Kenya, which is a country in Africa. (Find Kenya on a world map!) The word *shisima* means "body of water." The game pieces are called *imbalavali* (im-ba-la-VAH-lee). That word means "waterbugs." Want to learn how to play? Then dive right in!

You Need:
3 game pieces for each player (coins, beans, etc.). Your game pieces should look different from the other player's pieces.

Object:
To get three game pieces in a row on the game board.

Number of Players: 2

To Play:

- Both players should place their game pieces on opposite sides of the game board, like this:

- Decide who will go first.

- Player One moves one of his or her game pieces (the imbalavali) along a line to the next empty point on the board. You can move along any line. You can move into the center of the board. That's the shisima.

- Next, Player Two moves a piece.

- Jumping over pieces is not allowed. You can move only one space at a time.

- Players take turns moving pieces. The first player to get three pieces in a straight line (just like tic-tac-toe) is the winner. (If the two players repeat the same moves three times in a row, the game is a tie.)

> ⚡ **BRAIN POWER** ⚡
> Play Shisima a few times. What tips would you give someone who is playing for the first time?

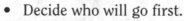

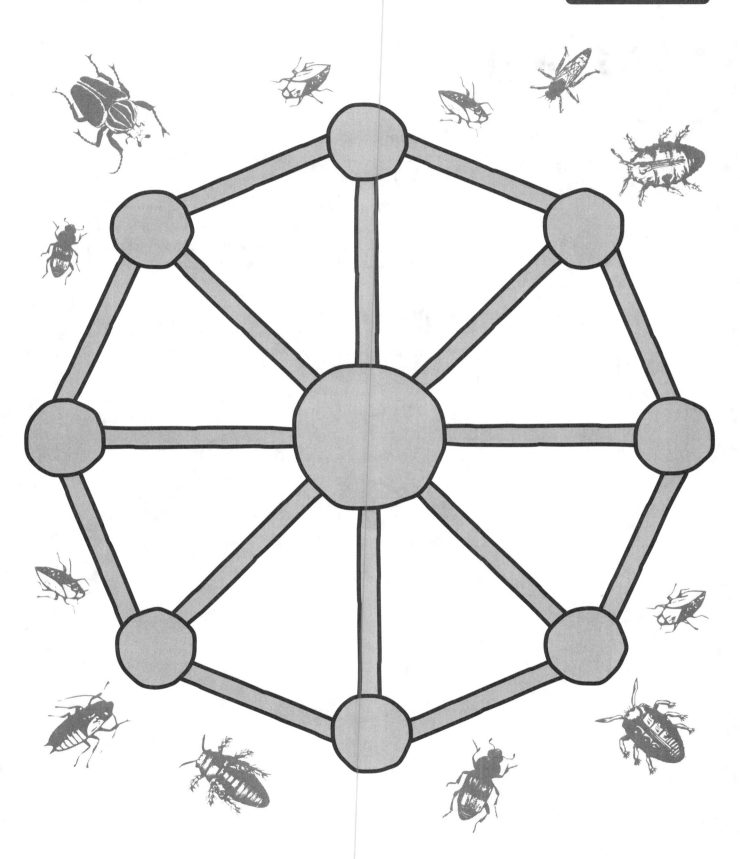

Fishy Logic

 Using logical thinking

 CULTURAL CONNECTION: Game from India

Aim

Students use reasoning and logic to devise a strategy for winning a game.

Before the Activity

Copy and distribute pages 287–288. Point out that this game is based on a game called Bagh-Bandi that has been played in India for thousands of years. Have a student identify India on a world map.

During the Activity

Ask: *Do you think that the fish or the seals had an advantage in winning the game? Why? What strategies did you come up with while playing the game?*

Fishy Logic

It's dinnertime at the zoo, and the seals are hungry. Those tricky fish might just find a strategy to outwit them!

You Need:
20 counters of one color (to be the fish)
2 counters of another color (to be the seals)

Object:
The seals try to eat all of the fish before the fish trap the seals.

Number of Players: 2

To Play:

▶ To set up the board: Decide which player will be the seals and which will be the fish. Put one counter (seal) on each spot marked with a seal. Stack five counters (fish) on each spot marked with a fish.

▶ Players take turns moving one of their counters along any line to an empty spot. The fish player moves first by moving one fish from the top of a stack.

   A seal must jump over a fish (or stack of fish) if there is a free spot on the other side. Each time a fish is jumped, it is "eaten" and removed from the board. Only the top fish in a stack can be eaten.

▶ The fish try to surround a seal so that it cannot move or jump. When a seal is "trapped," remove it from the board.

▶ Fish may not eat seals.

▶ A seal is allowed to jump more than one fish in a move if the spaces are connected.

▶ Winning the game: The fish win if they trap both seals. The seals win if they eat all of the fish.

Fishy Logic is based on a game called Bagh-Bandi. It has been played in India for thousands of years.

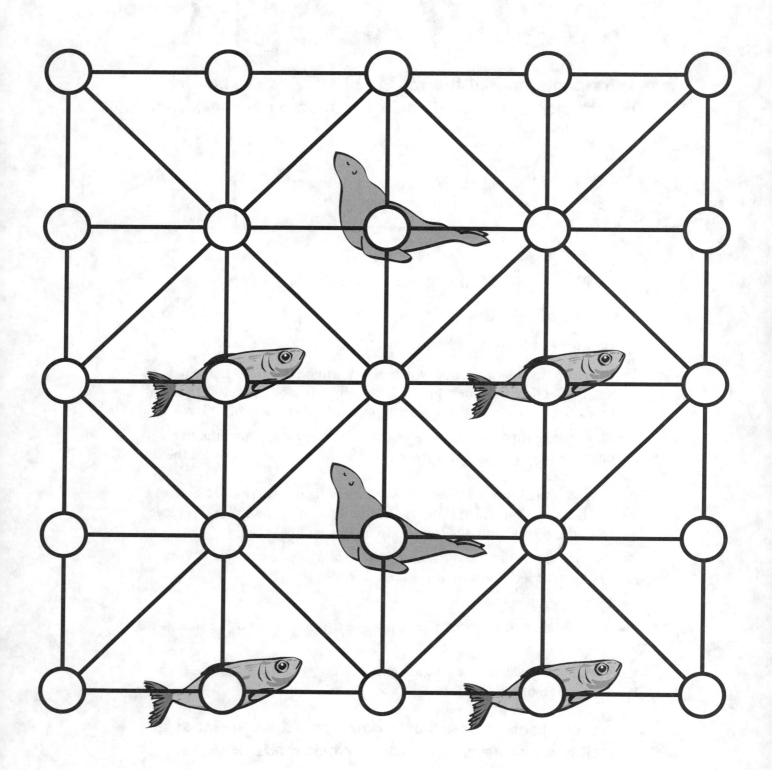

Oware: An African Strategy Game

Using logical thinking

CULTURAL CONNECTION: Game from Africa

Aim

Students use strategy techniques to play an ancient game.

Before the Activity

Initiate a class discussion about the games and toys children in your area enjoy that are not store-bought (hopscotch, tic-tac-toe, tag, building sand castles, etc.). Explain that children all over the world make their own fun using everyday items such as cloth, sticks, rocks, and other objects. Oware, the game in this activity, is just such a game. African children play Oware by dropping pebbles into holes in the ground.

Copy and distribute page 290. Familiarize yourself with the rules of Oware and demonstrate them before students play the game.

Students play in pairs. Each pairs will need an empty egg carton and 48 small counters such as dried beans.

During the Activity

Go over each step to help students set up the game. Putting each student's name on an index card and placing the cards at either end of the egg cartons can denote players' sheds.

After the Activity

Ask: *Did you find any strategies to help you win at Oware? What were they?*

Extension 1

Have class members ask their parents or grandparents to tell them about a game, song, handmade toy, or musical instrument they played with when they were younger. Invite parents and grandparents to visit your class to share their games or have students present what they have learned in class.

Extension 2

For more African games and variations on Oware, look for Jennifer Prior's *The Games of Africa* (New York: HarperCollins, 1994). Highlights *Best Board Games from Around the World* by Robert Dugan (Columbus, OH: Highlights for Children, Inc., 1991) contains 16 board games and playing pieces.

LOGIC AND REASONING

Oware:
An African Strategy Game

Oware (oh-WAH-ray) is a game played in many forms all over Africa. This version is popular among children. Kids drop pebbles into small holes in the ground, pretending they are planting seeds in fields. In the game, they move the "seeds" around the "fields" in a circular motion to imitate the cycle of planting season. Here's your chance to play. Happy planting!

Object:
To have the most seeds in your "shed" at the end of the game.

Number of Players: 2

Setting Up the Game:
- Each player chooses one side of the egg carton to be his or her six fields. Each player also chooses one end of the egg carton to be his or her shed.
- Each player puts four "seeds" in each field on his or her side of the carton.
- Decide which player will go first.

Player 1's shed and fields

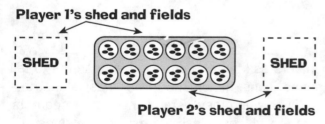

Player 2's shed and fields

To Play:
- Choose one of the six fields on your side of the egg carton. Pick up all of the seeds in that field and move to your right.
- Drop one seed in each field that you pass. If you pass your shed, drop one seed in it. If you pass your opponent's shed, skip over it. Do not drop any seeds in your opponent's shed.

- If your last seed lands in your shed, you may go again.

Player 1 "planting seeds"

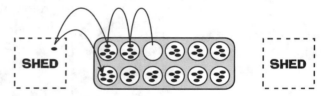

- When all of your seeds have been planted, it's the next player's turn.

Capturing Seeds:
- If your last seed lands in an empty field, you may capture all of the seeds in the field directly across from it.
- Place all of the captured seeds in your shed.

Ending the Game:
- The game ends when all of the fields on one side of the egg carton are empty. The player whose fields are on the opposite side gets to add any remaining seeds to his or her shed.
- Each player counts the number of seeds in his or her shed to see who is the better farmer.

 **LOGIC AND REASONING**

Not-So-Logical Inventions

✍ **Using logic lines**

✍ **CURRICULUM CONNECTION: Social Studies**

🔭 Aim

Students use logic lines to find out when some unusual real-life inventions were created.

Before the Activity

Copy and distribute pages 292–293. Explain that the logic lines in this activity are really like time lines that haven't been filled in yet. Clues help us put the events in order. Walk through the steps in the example with your students to familiarize them with the process.

Extension 1

Have students design their own inventions. They can be practical or silly. Students can try to build their inventions if they like.

Extension 2

Samuel Todd's Book of Great Inventions by E. L. Konigsberg (New York: Scholastic, 1991) is a charming book for younger students about the "world's greatest" inventions, such as french fries and Velcro!

🔑 ANSWERS

1. 1960 high heels
1974 backward shoe
1979 sock Puller-Upper

2. 1903 chicken glasses
1961 fish ads
1968 horse umbrella
1973 electric bone

3. 1840 inflatable hat
1974 self-cleaning house
1987 shower bike
1988 underwater gym

Not-So-Logical Inventions

Use logic lines to sort out some crazy creations!

Ever see a chicken wearing eyeglasses? How about a bike you can ride in the shower? Believe it or not, those were real inventions. We'll tell you about these and other strange-but-true creations. Then you can use logic lines to find out when each one was invented. Logic lines can help you organize information. We'll show you how to use one. Read on!

Delicious Devices

These inventions will give you food for thought: a clock powered by potatoes, square eggs (they look like sugar cubes), and "Meal Markers" that let you write on your food! When were these wacky wonders invented? Read the clues:

Clue A: Square eggs were invented before the other two items.

Clue B: The potato-powered clock was invented before the Meal Marker.

Clue A says the square eggs were invented first. The first year on the logic line is 1981, so we wrote "square eggs" under 1981.

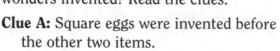

| 1981 | 1984 | 1994 |

square eggs

Clue B says the potato-powered clock came before the Meal Marker. That means the potato-powered clock was invented in 1984 and the Meal Marker was invented in 1994. We filled them in on the logic line. Now you know the year of each invention!

| 1981 | 1984 | 1994 |

square eggs   potato-powered   Meal Marker
                        clock

What to Do:

Read each problem. Use the clues to complete each logic line and put the inventions in order.

1. Amazing Feet! Many people have used their heads to think up inventions for your feet. The "Sock Puller-Upper" lets you put on socks without bending down. Or for flashy feet, try a pair of high heels that light up. Or trick your friends with the "backward shoe"—your footprints will face the wrong direction! When were these invented? Put them in the correct order.

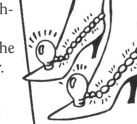

Clue A: The Sock Puller-Upper came after the backward shoe.

Clue B: You could impress your friends with the flashing high heels before you could confuse them with the backward shoe.

1960	1974	1979

2. Wild Inventions Why should humans have all the fun? These kooky inventions are for animals. Chicken eyeglasses were invented to protect the birds' eyes. A horse umbrella stops sunburn. (We're not horsing around!) For dogs, fetching is fantastic with the "electric bone." One inventor wanted to put advertisements on the sides of fish. Some people are hooked on the idea, but it sounds fishy to us! Put these items in order.

Clue A: Chickens could wear glasses before fish could wear ads.

Clue B: Fish could advertise before horses could avoid the sun.

Clue C: You could throw an electric bone to your dog after horses relaxed in the shade.

1903	1961	1968	1973

3. Wet and Wacky! These inventions are all washed up! The "self-cleaning house" has sprinklers inside and waterproof furniture. Or clean yourself—and exercise at the same time—on the "shower bike." Need more wet workouts? Try the "underwater gym." If you can't swim, just put on the "inflatable hat" to help you float. When was each invention made?

Clue A: The self-cleaning house came after the inflatable hat.

Clue B: You could swim in the underwater gym after you could hose down your house.

Clue C: The shower bike came before the underwater gym but after the self-cleaning house.

1840	1974	1987	1988

January Logic

 Completing logic lines

 Aim

Students make logic lines to solve some January holiday problems.

Before the Activity

Copy and distribute pages 295–296.

During the Activity

Tell students that sometimes the information from a clue is useful only after they have read and used some of the other clues. Explain that this is why they should read through an entire problem before beginning to solve it.

For Problem 4, students will need to keep track of names and hobbies that are possible matches and then use the process of elimination to find the correct matches. Suggest that as they work through the clues, they write beneath a picture, in pencil, all the names that could possible match with the hobby. Then they can cross out the names as they narrow their choices.

After the Activity

Ask students what they liked about solving logic problems.

Extension

Challenge students to write the thoughts they had as they used each clue in Problem 2. Encourage them to describe what the clue tells them and why they decided to place names where they did. Students can use the style of description given for Problem 1, or they can use their own styles.

Students can also describe using visual clues, such as Darryl's stickers and a hat with a feather. Ask them to compare this kind of clue with clues about positions such as "between" of "next to."

ANSWERS

2. Sonia, Gil, Rhonda, Ron

3. Gil, Sonia, Ron, Rhonda

4. Rhonda, Gil, Darryl, Ron, Sonia

Name _____

January Logic

Why does Rhonda love January? Because it's filled with so many wacky holidays. But when she and her friends get together to celebrate, things can get confusing. They need **logic lines** to figure out what's going on. Logic lines help put things in order.

What to Do:

Read the first story to find out how to use a logic line. Then use logic lines to solve the problems in the other stories.

1 **PIZZA PIZZAZ**

On the first day of National Pizza Week (January 14), three of the kids ran to Pete's Pizza Shop. "I was first!" shouted Ron. "No, I was!" said Rhonda. Gene's stomach made noises. Pete told them:

Clue A: Ron arrived second.
Clue B: Gene came in after Ron.
Clue C: Rhonda entered before Ron.

Who came in first?

Who was first? Read through the clues again. Clue A says that Ron entered second. Ron's name will go on the line under the second pizza slice.

_____   Ron   _____

Clue B says Gene came in after Ron. Gene's name goes after Ron's on the third line.

_____   Ron   Gene

Clue C says Rhonda entered before Ron. So Rhonda's name goes on the first line. That means that Rhonda was first.

Rhonda   Ron   Gene

2 HATS OFF

The gang celebrated Hat Day (January 18) by wearing silly hats to school. Their teacher, Mr. Pringle, isn't very silly. "Hang those hats up!" he said. Everyone hung a hat in the closet. Who owns each hat?

Clue A: Rhonda's hat has a feather in it.
Clue B: Ron's hat is to the right of Rhonda's.
Clue C: Sonia's hat is next to Gil's, but not next to Rhonda's.

Who owns each hat?

_____   _____   _____   _____

3 SOUP'S ON

When the kids found out that January is National Soup Month, they rushed to the lunchroom. "Soup for everybody!" yelled Cookie the Chef. The kids sat down with their soup mugs. Then . . . **RING!** It was a fire drill. When the kids got back, no one could remember where they had been sitting. But Cookie remembered. She said:

Clue A: Rhonda's and Gil's mugs have stars.
Clue B: Sonia is left-handed.
Clue C: Ron sat between Sonia and Rhonda.

Who owns each mug?

_____   _____   _____   _____

4 HOBBY TIME

Since January is National Hobby Month, the kids wanted to bring their hobbies in for show-and-tell. "Okay," said Mr. Pringle, "but no lizards or frogs!" The next day, the kids made Mr. Pringle guess their hobbies. They told him:

Clue A: Darryl collects stickers.
Clue B: Gil's hobby has lots of pieces.
Clue C: Ron's hobby is done outdoors.

Clue D: Sonia's hobby is at one end.
Clue E: Rhonda's hobby is next to Gil's.

Who has each hobby?

_____   _____   _____   _____   _____

The Great Big Book of Super-Fun Math Activities   Scholastic Professional Books

Wild-Goose Chase

✎ **Using strategic thinking**

✎ **Understanding spatial relations**

➤ Aim
In this game of skill, students learn to use strategies to trap their opponents' pieces.

Before the Activity
Copy and distribute pages 298–299. You may want to laminate the game board for durability. If necessary, practice playing the game with students to be sure they understand the moves that can be made during the game.

 Player 1
Player 2

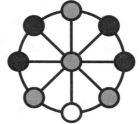

Player 2 cannot move; Player 1 wins.

During the Activity
There is one strategy that will always trap your opponent's pieces—keeping a space between two of your pieces in a line along the outside of the board and moving another piece to the center spot (See diagram).

Some students will discover this pattern after playing a few times. Others will learn the pattern from their opponents, either by losing or by hearing the strategy from the opponent. Encourage students to play with different opponents to continue to learn new strategies.

Extension
After students have played the game several times, have them describe one or two of the strategies they used.

Name _____

Wild-Goose Chase

Can four funny farmers catch four wild and wacky geese?
Or will the geese take a bite out of the farmers first?

You Need:
4 counters of one color (to be the "geese")
4 counters of a different color (to be the "farmers")

Object:
To trap the other player's pieces.

Number of Players: 2

To Play:

- Choose one player to be the "geese." The other player will be the "farmers."

- To begin, place the "geese" on the gray spots on the board. Place the "farmers" on the white spots. The center spot should be empty. Decide who will move first.

- Take turns moving one of your "farmers" or "geese" into the empty spot. (Move wherever the empty spot is on the board. There will always be one, but it will not always be the center spot.) You can move a piece to the empty spot if there is a line connecting your spot to the empty spot. When the empty spot is in the middle, you can move your piece only if it is next to at least one of the other player's pieces.

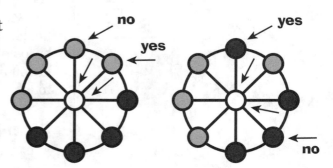

  ✔ Only one piece can be on a spot.

  ✔ Jumping over pieces is not allowed.

  ✔ If you can't move, you're trapped. The other player wins.

HINT: Before you play, try to find a pattern on the board that will trap the other player. Then try to make that pattern as you play.

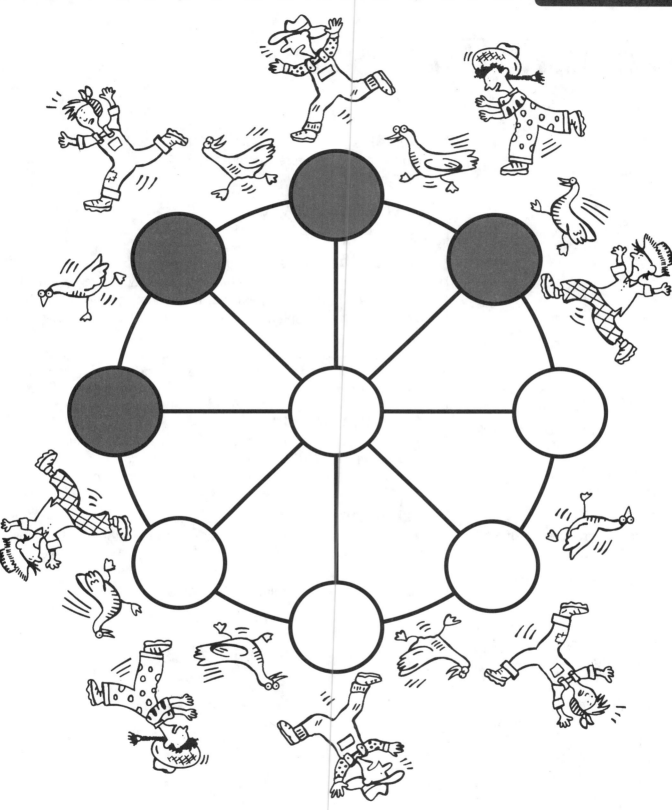

Gobble Up Logic!

 Using a model

 Whole number division

ANSWERS

Plan 1: Six groups of 6 turkeys each

Plan 2: One group of 24 turkeys and one group of 12 turkeys

Plan 3: One group each of 1, 3, 5, 7, 9, and 11 turkeys

Plan 4: A triangle with rows of 1, 2, 3, 4, 5, 6, 7, and 8 turkeys

Plan 5: The square should have 10 turkeys on each side.

Plan 6: Four groups of 6 turkeys and four groups of 3 turkeys; four groups of 7 and four groups of 2; or four groups of 5 and four groups of 4

BRAIN POWER: Answers will vary.

Aim

Students use counters to model the different ways 36 turkeys can be grouped.

Before the Activity

Copy and distribute page 301.

During the Activity

Have students read through the entire activity before they begin to make their plans. Suggest that they count the turkeys in the picture of the given plan to be sure they see that there are 36 of them.

Students can complete this activity individually or in groups. If they work in groups, have them decide together how to make each plan before they begin.

After the Activity

Ask students: *If the number of turkeys changed, do you think every plan would still work? Which plans could work with any number of turkeys? Which plans need a specific amount?*

Extension

Have students make up a new plan and write stories telling how the 36 turkeys used the plan to escape from the farm. Have students illustrate their stories and include a picture of the turkeys grouped according to the plan.

Name _____

Gobble Up Logic!

You Need:
36 counters (to be the turkeys)

The 36 turkeys at Farmer Biddle's farm are fed up. They don't want to end up on a table for dinner! So the turkeys are doing the only logical thing—they're planning to escape!

They know they shouldn't all run out of the barn at the same time. That would attract too much attention. The best way is to split up. But how?

Here's one way: The turkeys could line up in four rows, with nine turkeys in each row. They would look like this:

How else could they escape? That's where you—and logic—come in.

⇒ BRAIN POWER ⇐
Think of other ways the turkeys could split up. Then write a rule that describes your plan.

What to Do:
Here are the turkeys' secret escape plans. Use counters to show how the turkeys will look for each plan. Draw your arrangements on a separate piece of paper. Be sure to use all 36 counters for each plan.

SECRET ESCAPE PLANS
by Farmer Biddle's Turkeys

Plan 1: Six groups. Each group has an equal number in it.

Plan 2: Two groups. One group has half as many turkeys as the other.

Plan 3: Six groups. Each group has two fewer turkeys than the group before it.

Plan 4: One group in the shape of a triangle. Each row in the triangle has one more turkey than the row above it.

Plan 5: One group in the outline of a square. Each side of the square has the same number of turkeys.

Plan 6: Eight groups. Four groups have the same even number. The other four have the same odd number.

The Great Big Book of Super-Fun Math Activities Scholastic Professional Books

SCORING RUBRICS FOR ASSESSMENT

Individual Assessment

Student _____ Activity _____

	Always (4)	Almost Always (3)	Sometimes (2)	Never (1)
Understood the problem/activity				
Planned a solution and completed the activity				
Applied correct mathematics to a solution or conclusion				
Used materials appropriately				
Explained reasoning				
Justified thinking and responses				

Group Assessment

Group Members _____   _____

_____   _____

Activity _____

	Always (4)	Almost Always (3)	Sometimes (2)	Never (1)
Group agreed on a plan				
All group members participated				
Group used time productively to complete the task or activity				
Group members were able to articulate understanding				
Group members collaborated, listened to one another, and showed respect for each other's opinions				

STUDENT SELF-EVALUATION FORM

Name _____

Activity _____

~~~~~~

1. Rate yourself. In the activity, how well did you do these things?
Check the box under **Very Well**, **Well**, or **Not Very Well**.

	Very Well	Well	Not Very Well
I knew what I was supposed to do.			
I followed directions.			
I made a plan and completed the activity.			
I tried different ways to do the activity.			
I shared my ideas.			

2. What mathematics did you use in this activity? _____

_____

_____

_____

3. What did you learn doing this activity? _____

_____

_____

_____

_____

Notes